Obsessional Experience and Compulsive Behaviour
A Cognitive–Structural Approach

This is a volume in

PERSONALITY, PSYCHOPATHOLOGY, AND PSYCHOTHERAPY
A Series of Monographs, Texts, and Treatises

Under the Editorship of David T. Lykken and Philip C. Kendall

A complete list of titles in this series appears at the end of this volume.

Obsessional Experience and Compulsive Behaviour

A Cognitive–Structural Approach

Graham F. Reed

Department of Psychology
Glendon College
York University
Toronto, Ontario, Canada

1985

ACADEMIC PRESS, INC.
(Harcourt Brace Jovanovich, Publishers)
Orlando   San Diego   New York   London
Toronto   Montreal   Sydney   Tokyo

ACADEMIC PRESS, INC.
Orlando, Florida 32887

United Kingdom Edition published by
ACADEMIC PRESS, INC. (LONDON) LTD.
24/28 Oval Road, London NW1 7DX

Library of Congress Cataloging-in-Publication Data

Reed, Graham F.
  Obsessional experience and compulsive behaviour.

  (Personality, psychopathology, and psychotherapy)
  Bibliography: p.
  Includes indexes.
    1. Obsessive–compulsive neurosis.   2. Compulsive
behavior.   3. Cognitive therapy.   I. Title.
II. Series.
RC533.R44 1985   616.85′227   85-13425
ISBN 0-12-584830-7 (alk. paper)

PRINTED IN THE UNITED STATES OF AMERICA

85 86 87 88   9 8 7 6 5 4 3 2 1

To Jean and Lindsey

Contents

Preface

William of Oseney was a devout man, and read two or three Books of Religion and devotion very often, and being pleased with the entertainment of his time, resolved to spend so many hours every day in reading them, as he had read over those books several times; that is, three hours every day. In a short time he had read over the books three times more, and began to think that his resolution might be expounded to signify in a current sense, and that it was to be extended to the future times of his reading, and that now he was to spend six hours every day in reading those books, because he had now read them over six times. He presently considered that in half so long time more by the proportion of this scruple he must be tied to twelve hours every day, and therefore that this scruple was unreasonable, that he intended no such thing when he made this resolution; and therefore that he could not be tied: he knew that a resolution does not binde a mans self in things whose reason does vary, and where our liberty is intire, and where no interest of a third person is concerned. He was sure that this scruple would make that sense of the resolution be impossible at last, and all the way vexatious and intolerable; he had no leisure to actuate this sense of the words, and by higher obligations he was faster tied to other duties; he remembered also that now the profit of those good books was receiv'd already and grew less, and now became chang'd into a trouble and an inconvenience, and he was sure he could imploy his time better, and yet after all this heap of prudent and religious considerations, his thoughts revolv'd in a restless circle, and made him fear he knew not what.

Jeremy Taylor, *Ductor Dubitantium, or the Rule of Conscience,* Vol. 1, 1660.

The study of obsessional–compulsive disorders is one of the most enticing, exciting, and yet frustrating endeavours available to the unwary. Its pursuit has been likened to a journey with faulty maps; in reality, it is more akin to tackling, by night, a fiendishly devised obstacle course which has been wilfully established in the centre of an extensive quagmire. Not, it might be suggested, the sort of activity that can be whole-heartedly recommended to one's friends. Certainly not one to be undertaken voluntarily by any non-masochistic individual who is in full possession of his or her faculties. And yet the field has fascinated distinguished thinkers for over a century, as witness the veritable profusion of articles, monographs, and books in several languages on the subject. This stream of publications has continued unabated ever since the 1880s. Janet's (1903) classical study fills two volumes. Freud wrote more on the topic than any other in psychopathology, devoting fourteen major papers to it.

Why have the problems of obsessional–compulsive disorders continued to intrigue both psychological theorists and practising clinicians? There are at least three related reasons for the fascination those problems have exerted.

First, there is the intellectual challenge presented by any unresolved puzzle, particularly one which has baffled the experts for so long. Especially is this so when the central phenomenon appears at first sight to be a straightforward, precise, and circumscribed piece of psychopathology which should be amenable to the rational application of psychological principles. For, despite the heterogeneity of content, the basic question is simply how certain undesired thoughts (ideas, doubts, fears, impulses, or images) can intrude and persist in the individual's consciousness. How can they dominate the sufferer's awareness for long periods to the exclusion of more immediate, practical issues, more fundamental concerns, more constructive lines of thought, or more gratifying flights of fancy?

The question is much more demanding than it might at first appear. The answer is that at the moment we simply do not know. In fact, we are no nearer to understanding today than our forebears were at the beginning of the century. "Obsessional neurosis," observed Freud (1926), "is unquestionably the most interesting and repaying subject of analytic research. But as a problem it has not yet been mastered. It must be confessed that, if we endeavour to penetrate more deeply into its nature, we still have to rely upon doubtful assumptions and unconfirmed suppositions" (p. 113). This bleak assessment remains basically as true today as it was in 1926.

Second, there usually exists a personal element, because it is only too easy to empathize with obsessionals. They are usually articulate people who, by definition, possess insight; they give clear accounts of their difficulties, their bewilderment, and their agonies of mind. They are impatient with what they perceive to be their own weaknesses, manifesting self-reproach, but seldom self-pity. They are serious-minded and undemonstrative, usually eliciting respect as well as sympathy because of their prolonged struggle to withstand their obsessions, which they recognize to be foolish, although always disturbing and often terrifying.

Third, there are the professional challenges. Obsessional disorders are notoriously intractable, having proved to be surprisingly resistant to conventional therapies. Until recently, the outlook for most sufferers from severe obsessional states was grim. This was an unhappy reflection of the failure to develop new therapeutic approaches, which itself was probably the result of an absence of theoretical advances. During the last fifteen or so years, however, developments have taken place in practice, and, to a lesser extent, in theory. The present situation has been well covered by the outstanding contributions edited by Beech (1974), and a highly readable and thought-provoking account of their work in the behavioural/learning tradition has been given by Rachman and Hodgson (1980).

The problem about the central obsessional *symptom* was outlined above. A much more diffuse set of difficulties awaits us when we turn to the so-called obsessional *traits* which constitute the obsessional (compulsive, anankastic, anal) personality. Taken individually, of course, these traits are unexceptionable; many of them, in fact, are highly valued in our culture. So how can their concatenation constitute a disorder? And why is such a concatenation labelled "obsessional" or "compulsive"? Obsessional symptoms are rare, whereas the obsessional traits are very common. The state or neurosis is fairly readily determined, whereas the criteria of the personality have never been satisfactorily defined. So what have the state and the personality in common? What is the relationship, if any, between them? These questions, it need hardly be pointed out, fall well within the purview of general psychology. But to date psychologists' answers have been far from convincing or have side-stepped the questions, favouring ones which have never been asked.

Allusion was made above to one of the major contributions of clinical psychology—the devising of various techniques for the modification of such classical symptoms as compulsive hand-washing and repeated checking. But it must be pointed out that behaviour therapy's achievements in this area have been for the most part to do with compulsive *behaviour*, rather than with the obsessional *experience* which underlies it. It is this experience which, by definition, characterizes all obsessional states, including the large proportion of them where no unusual behaviour patterns are manifested. Only within the last few years have behavioural psychologists begun to recognize this central problem, the solution to which, it must be added, has so far eluded psychoanalysts, phenomenologists, and eclectic, dynamic psychotherapists. These latter approaches have focused upon the *affective* components of obsessional disorders, and upon the symbolic "meanings" of obsessional experiences and acts. Thus, they have been concerned with the *contents* of obsessions—what they are, and what they signify.

It is the contention of this book that obsessionality, in all its guises, may most productively be regarded as a *cognitive* disorder. It may, therefore, be most usefully remediated through some new version of the currently developing techniques of cognitive therapy. Obsessional difficulties reflect, it is maintained, maladaptive ways of thinking, of reasoning, and of attending to, assessing, processing, and assimilating information. Furthermore, it is maintained throughout this book that the precise *contents* of obsessional people's thinking are too variegated to be of use as a basis for theory formulation or therapeutic endeavour. *What* is thought is not so significant as *how* the thought is reached and maintained. It is the *form*, or structural aspects, of obsessional cognition which is anomalous and which merits investigation.

Some of the apparently insoluble problems of obsessionality have been due to semantic confusions and inconsistent labelling practices. The latter derive primarily from the vagaries of translators, but also reflect idiosyncratic points of view and, let it be admitted, in some cases sheer ignorance of established usages. Clearly, there can be no absolutes here, no "rights" and "wrongs." But at the very least it is convenient if the reader can be clear as to what the writer's labels refer. For the sake of consistency and clarity, the present writer has reluctantly abandoned certain of his own lifetime labelling conventions in an attempt to conform with what appear to be developing contemporary norms. In this book, terms will be used in accordance with the following guidelines:

"*Obsessional*"will be used as a generic term, covering the neurotic state, the personality disorder, the experience in general, the symptoms, the traits, and the individual who manifests any of these.

"*Obsession*"will be used in reference to the central experience, the clinical symptom, which will be defined and discussed in Chapter 1.

"*Compulsion*"will be used in reference to the aberrant *behaviour* which is often manifested in association with the obsessional experience, and will be discussed in Chapter 4.

"*Compulsivity*" or "*the experience of compulsion*" or "*compulsive experience*" will be used in reference to the experience which is at the heart of obsessions. It will be discussed in Chapters 1 and 12.

"*Obsessive–compulsive*" will be used in reference to the clinical state or neurosis, which is characterized by the presence of obsessional symptoms.

"*Compulsive personality disorder*" or "*anankastic personality disorder*" will both be used in reference to the personality or personality disorder, which is characterized by the presence of the personality traits described in Chapter 5.

It is not suggested, of course, that the above scheme will introduce total semantic clarification, nor that it is completely consistent. But the multiplicity of terminological usages in the literature conspire with the very nature of the phenomena in question to preclude this. As a matter of morbid interest, the writer's own preference would be to restrict terms to three adjectives—"obsessional," "compulsive," and "anankastic." But if you can't beat 'em. ...

The structure of this book is simple but, it is hoped, rational and informative. It consists of three sections:

(1) The first section tries to come to grips with both the actual phenomena and the often slippery concepts with which we are concerned. It presents definitions, examples, and relevant data. In short, it attempts to capture the accepted basics of the topic.

(2) The second section is an exercise in exegesis. There is a vast literature of theoretical, descriptive, and speculative accounts of obsessionality. An attempt is made here to summarize and critically evaluate the ideas of a few selected authorities who have made seminal theoretical contributions to the field. There have been, of course, many other distinguished contributors, and their work will be cited elsewhere in the book. But those whose work is summarized in this section are the ones who in some way have established approaches to the topic or have introduced new conceptual lines of attack.

The opportunity is taken in this section to promote the rehabilitation of the reputation of Pierre Janet, the great French medical psychologist. Deplorably, Janet's work has been ignored (or in some cases, explicitly rejected) for many years, despite the facts that his meticulous clinical descriptions have never been bettered and that his conceptual insights were half a century ahead of his time.

The section will conclude with a garnering of various authorities' views of the relationship between obsessional states and personality.

(3) The third section consists of evaluations, syntheses, and discussions, coupled with attempts to indicate the applicability of a cognitive approach to the experience of compulsion itself and to the classical obsessional symptoms of checking, rituals, doubts, and ruminations. The role of affects is considered, and such experimental evidence as exists in regard to the cognitive characteristics of obsessionality is drawn together. The final chapter presents a synthesis of what has gone before, with a summary re-statement of the writer's position.

As it is often the case with a mystery novel, some readers may be tempted (very understandably) to turn to the final chapter directly, in order to find out how the story ends. Unfortunately, unlike the well-crafted fictional tale of suspense, this book cannot promise an ''end''—a neat resolution of the puzzles and a satisfying finale. All that can be offered here is the outline of a new but potentially fruitful approach to the problems which beset any study of obsessional disorders. More importantly, it may lead to more successful alleviation of the distress of sufferers from those disorders. The book represents a plea for further research from a different starting point.

ACKNOWLEDGMENTS

However challenging and satisfying, the writing of this book has been a lonely task. This is doubtless reflected in a certain idiosyncrasy of approach, and I suspect that my arguments will not meet with unmitigated enthusiasm in some quarters. I must shoulder full responsibility for any faults perceived in the work, for no one else has participated directly in its development. However, no man is an island, and in the early stages of this project I was directly stimulated and my thinking influenced by many scholars and clinicians. I should like to acknowledge with gratitude the help of four of these in particular:

The late Dr. John Mackay, my first psychiatric colleague, whose wit, experience and shrewd Scots insights sharpened my fledgling clinical perceptions.

The late Professor E. W. Anderson, who encouraged my developing interest in the study of anankastic disorder.

Professor John Hoenig, who opened my eyes to the subtleties of the phenomenological method and supervised my doctoral work with relentless critical acuity.

Mr. Jack Kenna, my old friend and colleague, who unstintingly shared with me his unparalleled erudition and humane rationality.

1
Obsessions and Compulsions

The purpose of this chapter is to define and discuss the obsessional–compulsive experience. In one sense, this task is relatively clear cut. The symptomatology has been more precisely described than almost any other feature in the literature of psychopathology. Unlike, for instance, the term "the obsessional personality," the definition of "obsessional–compulsive experience" has been agreed to by the vast majority of authorities. Furthermore, during more than a century, that definition has suffered less than any other psychiatric concept from attempts at re-assessment or sub-classification. But there remain, as might be expected, problems and differences of opinion in the areas of semantics and conceptualization. Furthermore, as we shall see, such terms as "obsession" and "compulsion" tend to be misused both by lay people and by some professional clinicians.

OBSESSIONS

The term "obsession" is applied to the experience of an individual who is consciously assailed and preoccupied by ego-dystonic, intrusive, and persistent mental events, which he usually recognizes as being foolish and unacceptable but which, despite all his efforts, he is unable to dispel.

Although he was not the first to discuss the topic, Westphal was the first to provide a formal definition of compulsive ideas in a paper published in 1877. His full definition is now out of favour, but its basis has not been improved upon:

> Thoughts which come to the foreground of consciousness in spite of and contrary to the will of the patient and which he is unable to suppress although he recognizes them as abnormal and not characteristic of himself.

Early French psychiatric authorities concurred with their German colleagues'
view, as witness Magnan's definition of 1895:

> ... a mode of cerebral activity in which a word, a thought or an image imposes itself
> upon the mind, outside of the will, with a grievous anguish which renders it irresistable.

Janet (1903), in his massive contribution to this field, provides no summary
definition, but his meticulous observations include many which agree with the
above. One section of his discussion of the form of obsessions may be translated
as:

> The patient is obsessed, tormented by an idea which imposes itself upon him without
> being justified by the circumstances and without being chosen by the subject him-
> self. ...At least up to a certain point, he feels, as we do, that his idea is absurd, he
> judges and rejects it. ... (p. 67)

Freud's (1917) description stems directly from those of Westphal and Janet:

> Obsessional neurosis is shown in the patient's being occupied with thoughts in which
> he is in fact not interested, in his being aware of impulses in himself which appear
> very strange to him and in his being led to actions the performance of which give him
> no enjoyment, but which it is quite impossible for him to omit. The thoughts (obs-
> essions) may be senseless in themselves, or merely a matter of indifference to the
> subject; often they are completely silly, and invariably they are the starting-point of
> a strenuous mental activity, which exhausts the patient and to which he only surrenders
> himself most unwillingly. (*S.E.*, xvi, p. 258)

In the course of an acute phenomenological analysis Jaspers (1923) explained:

> Now should the self be no longer master of its choice, should it lose all influence over
> the selection of what shall fill its consciousness, should *the immediate content of
> consciousness remain irremovable, unchosen, unwanted*, the self finds itself in conflict
> faced with a content which it wants to suppress but cannot. This content then acquires
> the character of a psychic compulsion. ... (p. 133, original emphasis)

And later on in his discussion:

> In the strict sense of the term, compulsive thoughts, impulses etc., should be confined
> to anxieties or impulses which can be experienced by the individual as an incessant
> preoccupation, though he is convinced of the *groundlessness* of the anxiety, the *sense-
> lessness* of the impulse and the *impossibility* of the notion. Thus, compulsive events,
> strictly speaking, are all such events, the *existence* of which is strongly resisted by

the individual in the first place and the *content* of which appears to him as groundless, meaningless or relatively incomprehensible. (p. 134, original emphasis)

Schneider's (1925) pithy definition has been regularly cited. It was discussed in some detail by Lewis (1936), who translated it as follows:

... contents of consciousness which, when they occur, are accompanied by the experience of subjective compulsion, and which cannot be got rid of, though on quiet reflection they are recognized as senseless.

Lewis's own much-cited definition appears in his contribution to the classical *Price's Textbook of the Practice of Medicine*, first published in 1922, a twelfth edition appearing in 1978:

In this condition the characteristic feature is that, along with some mental happening, there is an experience of subjective compulsion and of resistance to it. Commonly the mental happening—which may be a fear, an impulse, or a preoccupation—is recognized on quiet reflection, as senseless; nevertheless it persists. (p. 1443)

The preceding definitions have all been drawn from the works of the major seminal investigators of our topic. The writers were of German, French, Austrian, and British nationality. But their observations were transported across the Atlantic and have received full acceptance in North America. Thus, Kanner's (1948) authoritative definition runs as follows:

... ideas which keep intruding themselves irresistibly and distressingly upon a person's consciousness, interrupt the orderly sequence of thought, or action, are felt by the person as something foreign to him and unrelated to his usual behaviour, and yet cannot be cast off by him in spite of his realization of their unnaturalness. (p. 638)

Other American authorities on this topic tend to have been avowed Freudians. Adams (1973), Rado (1974), and Nagera (1976) either do not present a formal definition or cite the words of Freud directly. Salzman (1973), a major figure and also of Freudian persuasion, does offer a personal definition:

It refers to thoughts, feelings, ideas and impulses which an individual cannot dispel in spite of an inner desire to do so. The compelling nature of the activity—despite the fact that it may be illogical, undesirable, and unnecessary—is the central issue. Generally such thoughts or feelings are alien to the individual's usual attitudes. ... (p. 9)

Textbooks and instructional manuals usually use one of the classical definitions quoted above, unless the writer happens to have a specific interest in the topic of obsessionality. One example of this, that of Lewis, was cited above. Another authoritative modern textbook formulation is that of Mayer-Gross *et al.* (1954):

> The essential nature of the obsessional or compulsive symptom lies in its appearance as a mental content, an idea, image, affect, impulse or movement, with a *subjective sense of compulsion overriding an internal resistance*. This resistance from the healthy part of the personality, in which the symptom is recognized as strange or morbid, is the essential characteristic by which truly compulsive phenomena can be distinguished from other phenomena of a related or similar kind. (p. 126, original emphasis)

Clearly there have been no radical changes in the definition of obsessions since Westphal's time. The crucial definitional components figure in the official codification of a contemporary committee—the third edition of the American Psychiatric Association's *Diagnostic and Statistical Manual of Mental Disorder* (*DSM* III):

> *Obsessions* are recurrent, persistent ideas, thoughts, images, or impulses that are ego-dystonic, that is, they are not experienced as voluntarily produced, but rather as thoughts that invade consciousness and are experienced as senseless or repugnant. Attempts are made to ignore or suppress them. (p. 234)

DEFINITIONAL CRITERIA

Although not identical in their language or their conceptual emphases, the authoritative definitions quoted above all stress some combination of three features which are generally accepted as criterial in the determination of whether a given experience may validly be termed an obsession:

(1) The experience must have a subjectively *compulsive quality*. That is to say, the subject feels *compelled*, pressed or driven to think or act along certain lines. What he feels to be a "natural" train of thought or activity is disturbed and subdued by th obsessional thought, etc., which is persistent and *preoccupying*. It is *intrusive*, the subject feeling that he is invaded and occupied by it. Nevertheless he accepts that it has an *inner, personal* source. It is *ego-dystonic*, in as much as it does not feel normal or even acceptable to him, and he does not wish to comply.

(2) The thought, etc., must be recognized at some point by the subject as being pointless, irrelevant, *senseless*, or absurd. This is usually taken to indicate that he retains *insight* into the morbidity of his experience.

(3) The experience must be actively *resisted* by the subject. He fights to suppress it or to oust it from his consciousness, but his struggle is unavailing.

Let us examine these three criteria a little more closely. In terms of the first criterion, without doubt, its compulsive quality is the central feature and the definitional core of any obsessional experience. It is the *sine qua non* of such experiences; if it is absent, then, by definition, the experience cannot be validly termed ''obsessional.''

In one sense, furthermore, this criterion may be regarded as subsuming the other two, for the compulsive quality of an experience includes the fact that it is not acceptable to the subject (*cf.* the second criterion), and that he does not wish to comply with it (*cf.* the third). It may be noted that were the experience acceptable to the subject and/or were he to willingly comply with it, then the question of whether he was suffering from an obsession should not arise in the first place.

The military metaphors of ''invasion'' and ''occupation'' were not chosen lightly. The very word ''obsess'' is derived from the Latin for ''sit down upon,'' and to this day its alternative lexical meanings include: ''to sit down before a fortress, to besiege or invest.'' The sufferer is not merely interested in an idea to the point where it preoccupies him; the true obsessional idea is not ego-syntonic, that is, the sufferer feels as though it has been imposed upon him. Despite his own wishes, it occupies and dominates his consciousness.

At the same time, the true compulsive experience involves the realization that the experience originates within the sufferer. To feel invaded by a preoccupying thought, etc., but to attribute its source to some *external* agency is *not* obsessional. This is the hallmark of the *passivity* experiences of schizophrenics.

The reader is referred to Jaspers' (1923) phenomenological analysis of the compulsive experience. There, he emphasizes the individual's subjective limitation of freedom of choice—the inability to select what shall fill his consciousness. He contrasts this with the normal experience of being driven to attend to external stimuli or instinctual drives. He goes on to discuss compulsive beliefs, where the individual finds himself believing something that intellectually he knows to be false, and compulsive urges, where the individual is driven towards some action which is foreign to his nature and seems incomprehensible. The compulsive quality always involves this feeling of conflict within the self.

The second criterion should be viewed as involving two *continua*, a point which has not always been taken into account by various authorities. First of all, the sufferer's recognition that his obsession is senseless, etc., varies over time. Initially, he may be horrified by the apparent oddity of his idea, image, or impulse. It may appear to him not only alien but bizarre, perverted, or ridiculous. But over a long period of time its perceived oddity becomes blunted— in a sense, the subject becomes habituated to its bizarrerie. Second, the recognition of senselessness may cover a wide range, from the feeling that the experience is merely irrelevant or pointless to the feeling that it is shocking, disgusting, or horrifying. We have no way of measuring positions on these *continua*, of standardizing or equating them.

It is possible that the problems involved in determining just how ''senseless''

any given subject regards his obsessions at any given time have contributed to
the fact that this criterion has not received unqualified acceptance. As we have
seen, Magnan did not mention it, and several other authorities have hedged their
bets in the matter. Janet qualified his statement with the words "At least up to
a certain point." Freud's formulation was equally cautious: "may be senseless ...
often they are completely silly. ... " Schneider was equally cautious, but used
a different approach: "though on quiet reflection they are recognized as senseless." Lewis used Schneider's codicil: "Commonly the mental happening ... is
recognized on quiet reflection, as senseless. ... " In his 1936 paper, he stated
flatly: "The recognition that the obsession is senseless is not an essential characteristic. ..." Elsewhere, Schneider (1959) offered an alternative escape clause,
by stating that it is not the content of the obsession that is felt to be senseless,
so much as its "dominant insistence." But this is surely not the way in which
other authorities have used such words as "senseless," "absurd," etc., although
there is no doubt that sufferers *do* regard the persistent, intrusive, and preoccupying quality of their obsessions in this way.

The fact that the subject recognizes the abnormality of his obsession is usually
taken to be evidence that he has retained "insight." The use of the term in this
context is open to debate. But there are other ways in which the victim of an
obsession shows insight; for instance, he identifies the obsession as coming from
within himself, even though he regards it as ego-dystonic. And insight is also
demonstrated by the fact that he realizes that he has a mental problem and solicits
psychiatric help in coping with it.

In terms of the third criterion, for the subject to be preoccupied by a fixed
idea, however senseless, does not in itself constitute an obsession. For the idea
to be classifiable as such, he must be putting up a losing fight against it.

Whereas, as noted above, there is some disagreement regarding the recognition
of senselessness as a criterion in the determination of an obsession, all the major
authorities seem to have agreed as to the central importance of resistance. Lewis
(1936), in criticizing Schneider's (1925) definition, suggested that the recognition
of senselessness should be replaced by emphasis upon resistance. Mayer-Gross
et al. (1954), as we have seen, regarded resistance as the "essential characteristic" of compulsive phenomena. One or two recent writers have in fact raised
objections to the emphasis upon resistance as a criterion of obsessions. These
objections are countered in the following paragraphs. Further discussion of the
phenomenological nature of resistance will be presented in a later chapter.

As with the other criteria, we can encounter problems of interpretation and
conceptualization in discussing resistance. First, like them it is a subjective
experience which cannot be measured or graded in objective terms. Second, for
that reason, it cannot be standardized. It is impossible to say what one individual's
report of the experience means in relation to those of others. Third, resistance
is not an "On—Off" phenomenon. We experience *degrees* of resistance, which
may therefore be viewed as a varying threshold phenomenon. Fourth, there are

two sides to the subjective struggle—the level of resistance is a reciprocal of the strength of what is being resisted. And fifth, resistance varies over time.

Thus, just as there are differing degrees of the perceived senselessness of an obsession, so resistance is experienced as along a continuum of intensity. We are unable to say at what point the level of intensity is sufficient to count as "resistance" in the present context. Even if we could measure the level of experience and determine some acceptable threshold, how could this be conveyed to the subject, upon whose self-examination and verbal report the whole operation is based? To complicate matters, the subject's experience of resistance varies according to his mood state and his perception of the strength of the obsession on different occasions. Certainly, sufferers report that the intensity of their resistance varies from occasion to occasion. They usually describe this in terms of the amount of "willpower" they can summon up at any particular time. "I've been fighting it today, using all my will-power. Last week, I just didn't feel up to it. ... " "I usually struggle with it. Today, I just feel too exhausted. It's a matter of will-power, I suppose. ... " Apart from these day-to-day variations, there seems to be an understandable tendency for resistance to weaken generally as the years of suffering roll by. "It's gone on so long, I can scarcely fight it any more." "After all this time, I'm beginning to give in. I feel as though I've lost any self-control and will-power I once had." The perceived power of the obsession, on the other hand, shows the opposite tendency, being felt to increase in strength the longer the disorder persists. But it also varies from day to day, being affected by the sufferer's morale, by his state of physical health, and by external events.

The pragmatic implications of the above are twofold. First, any estimation of a subject's level of resistance calls for considerable clinical skill and intensive phenomenological investigation. Second, it may well be misleading to rely on the subject's account of his feelings upon a single occasion.

Finally, it may be noted that the fact that the subject resists the obsession implies that it affords him no gratification or good cheer. He is involved in a losing battle with something which is not acceptable to him—a battle, moreover, which seems interminably protracted, exhausting, and, thus, distressing. This may resolve an issue raised by a growing number of contemporary writers (such as Salzman, 1973; Sternberg, 1974; Rachman and Hodgson, 1980; Nemiah, 1980) who have added "suffering" to the three formal criteria of what constitutes an obsessional–compulsive experience. There is, of course, no doubt that obsessions cause distress to the subject (and, in the case of compulsive behaviour, very often to those around him). That is why he presents himself for psychiatric treatment. But unless one is prepared to maintain that fruitless resistance does *not* involve suffering, the proposed addition to the trio of criteria would seem redundant.

COMPULSIONS

As we have observed, the *sine qua non* of an obsession is its *compulsive* quality. And, by any defintiion, compulsions are obsessional. What then is the difference between an obsession and a compulsion? The answer is that there is no substantive difference whatsoever, merely ones of linguistic usage. The semantic confusion arose because of the words used by the classical German writers as opposed to their French contemporaries. German writers use the word *Zwang*, the English translation of which has been "compulsion," while French writers, discussing exactly the same experience, use the word *obsession* which, of course, is translated into English as "obsession." To add to the confusion, there have been inconsistencies in the practice of translaters. As Rado (1974) observes: "by way of different translations, *Zwang* became 'obsession' in London and 'compulsion' in New York" (p. 195).

The outcome of this has been that in English the two words can be used interchangeably or according to any given writer's preference. Just as some English-language writers prefer to use the word "compulsion," so others avoid it, using the word "obsession" consistently. Still others bypass the problem of choice by referring to "obsessional–compulsive symptoms." However, the arbitrary convention has developed among English writers of using the word "obsession" in reference to purely *mental* activity, and the word "compulsion" to apply to associated *physical* activity. Such activity is repetitive and apparently stereotyped, which has led several writers to assume that *any* such behaviour can be regarded as compulsive. This, of course, is entirely erroneous. To determine whether a piece of behaviour may validly be termed a compulsion requires the identical criteria used to identify an obsession.

DIAGNOSTIC DIFFERENTIATION

As we have seen, there are several murky aspects of the formal criteria of an obsessional experience; furthermore, to date there has been no agreement as to possible weightings of the components, beyond the recognition that the compulsive quality is essential. But even as they stand, the three criteria enable clear differentiation to be made between obsessions and other psychopathological phenomena of superficially similar type.

The obsession-like phenomenon most commonly encountered is the *over-valued idea*. In psychiatric terminology, over-valued ideas are beliefs which preoccupy and dominate an individual to an unusual and uncalled-for degree. Such beliefs are often untenable, or at least implausible, though, unlike delusions, they are understandable in terms of the subject's personality and background. And, again unlike delusions, however nonsensical they are, they may be shared by others. They are usually isolated ideas or theories, which do not spring from any philosophical stance or system of religious or political belief. Yet they are held with total conviction and intense affect. The affect leads the holder to devote his energies to the propagation of his idea and to proselytizing activity which bemuses or irritates others. The holders of over-valued ideas range from normal people with "bees in their bonnets," through cranks, pressure-groupers, and street-corner speakers, to the founders of cults and the wildest fanatics.

The dominating and preoccupying nature of over-valued ideas is so similar to that of obsessions that there may well be some relationship between the two. But they are readily differentiated by applying the criteria. The over-valued idea is neither ego-dystonic nor regarded by the subject as senseless or strange. And, far from resisting it, he accepts it whole-heartedly and devotes himself to its dissemination.

Similarly, obsessions can be readily differentiated from the psychotic *delusion*, which may be defined as "a belief which is demonstrably false by the standards of the individual's socio-cultural background, but which is held with complete conviction" (Reed, 1972, p. 141). Such beliefs are also dominating and preoccupying; they are notoriously unshakeable and highly personalized. By objective standards they are invariably erroneous; they are idiosyncratic, often bizarre, and totally incomprehensible to others. They are unlike obsessions, inasmuch as they are ego-syntonic and felt to be acceptable and, indeed, self-evident. Thus, their holders lack insight, finding nothing strange or senseless in their often palpably absurd ideas. And, far from resisting them, they cling to these ideas through thick and thin, in the face of total refutation, and even when the belief in them brings harm or suffering in its wake.

The same comments apply with equal force in the consideration of the *delusion-like ideas*, so well analysed by Jaspers (1923). These are often associated with affective disorders. They are often classified as delusions proper, but they are secondary to other psychic events, such as depersonalization, morbid affects, and hallucinations, and are thus understandable, at least to the clinician. Like delusions proper, they are not felt to be foolish or odd by the sufferer and, despite transient doubts, he does not resist them.

One or two writers have attempted to classify as obsessional the behaviours of sexual perverts and arsonists. These may be regarded as manifesting deviations, fixations, or regressions of instinctual drives. Some of these may indeed possess a compulsive flavour. But although they may be recognized by the subjects as abnormal, they are ego-syntonic and self-gratificatory. The actions are indulged in for enjoyment, whereas compulsive acts are engaged in as attempts to avoid or alleviate overwhelming distress. As we shall see, compulsive behaviour seems never to be anti-social; the suggestion that child-molesting or fire-raising are traceable to irresistible compulsive urges comes better from the mouths of defence lawyers than from those of diagnosticians.

Recurrent thoughts, tics, habits, or stereotyped behaviours are sometimes classified as obsessional. But this classification is only valid if the associated

experience complies with the criteria. As Monroe (1974) points out, repetitiousness alone does not constitute a diagnostic criterion.

POPULAR MISUSES OF THE TERMS "OBSESSION" AND "COMPULSION"

In everyday parlance, "obsession," "obsessional," "compulsion," "compulsive" are consistently used incorrectly, even by people with training in psychiatry
and psychology. The terms are usually employed in a pejorative sense, with
reference to single-mindedness about, preoccupation with, or apparently undue
persistence in some line of thought or action. Thus, a person may be referred
to as "obsessional" or "obsessed" because he evinces concern with social
aspirations, occupational success, or leisure pursuits. The use of the terms in
this way merely reflects the observer's personal judgement of the worthwhileness
of the subject's goals or the amount of energy he allots to them. It may also
reflect envy or fear, as in the case of the hard-working student who is labelled
"compulsive" by his less-committed classmates, or in that of the conscientious
employee whose efforts alarm his colleagues. On the other hand, the observer
may moralistically judge that the subject's energies might be devoted to more
valuable activities than, for example, the game of golf. The observer may sin-
cerely deprecate what appears to him to be anti-social, selfish, or ruthless single-
mindedness in the subject's pursuit of his career or hobby goals. While agreeing
that the ambition to gain promotion, for example, is understandable, the observer
may feel that the subject has lost perspective and is neglecting other duties such
as his family obligations or loyalty to his friends. This may well be a valid
criticism. But to recruit such terms as "obsessed" or "compulsive" to express
the judgement is incorrect, unless our three formal criteria apply. Are the subject's
preoccupations or activities characterized by the compulsive flavour? Does he
regard them as silly? Does he struggle not to think or behave in the manner in
question? Of course not. In the vast majority of cases he regards career ad-
vancement or the lowering of his golf handicap, etc., as perfectly appropriate
goals, feels that he is acting by conscious choice, and finds considerable gratification in devoting time and energy to his pursuits.

   Again, those who engage in such hobbies as stamp- and book-collecting are
often termed "obsessional collectors" (often by exasperated spouses). But, although there is often a very compelling quality about collecting, most collectors
derive great pleasure and satisfaction from their pursuit and make no attempt to
resist the appeal.

   The term "obsessed" is often applied, but in this case benignly, to people
who are in love; they may be described as being "obsessed" by the objects of
their affections. Now, almost by definition, love is not a subject for rational
explanation. Indeed, both the process of falling in love and the state of being

in love often fly in the face of cold, common sense, orderly life-planning, and convenience, and lovers often recognize this. Falling in love certainly has a compelling and dominating quality. But technically it cannot be classified as a "compulsive experience." It is elicited by an external trigger (the person of the loved one) and involves not only compliance but some degree of ecstasy.

In a more general sense, individuals are sometimes castigated for being "obsessed by sex" when they seem unduly preoccupied by sexual fantasies, aspirations of sexual triumphs, or fantasies about sexual objects or activities. But again, such fantasies are indulged in voluntarily, are ego-syntonic, and provide considerable gratification. As Jaspers (1923) put it: "We do not speak of a psychic compulsion when in the course of ordinary instinctual experience our attention is drawn to one thing or another or some desire is awakened" (p. 133).

In everyday speech, the terms "compulsion" and "compulsive" are often used, in a manner parodying the technical convention discussed above, in reference to repetitive behaviour. We apply them also to stereotyped movements, to physical mannerisms, and to habit patterns. For example, unusual body postures and facial twitches may be described as "compulsive," as may be mannerisms such as head-scratching. Entrenched habits, such as nail-biting, coffee-drinking, and smoking, are often termed "compulsions," especially by those who do not share the habits in question. Similarly, regular participation in tennis and jogging, for example, may be described as "compulsive" by those who do not indulge in such athletic pursuits.

Of course, any or all of the above activities *may* be compulsive in a few particular cases. But the point here is that observable behaviour cannot be deemed compulsive unless the formal criteria can be shown to underlie the motor activity. And those criteria are *phenomenological, not behavioural.* Observation alone can contribute nothing whatsoever to the determination of compulsivity, a fact that behavioural psychologists often tend conveniently to ignore. However repetitious a piece of behaviour, however stereotyped, however bizarre, its definition as "compulsive" relies totally upon the form of the associated experience. However often and under whatever conditions an individual trots around the neighbourhood, he cannot be termed a "compulsive jogger" unless he admits that his trotting urge is intrusive and ego-dystonic, that he feels it is absurd, and that he struggles unsuccessfully to resist it.

For exactly the same reason, *no* animal behaviour whatsoever can be correctly classified as "compulsive" or even "compulsive-like." We have no way of determining the phenomenological experience of other members of the animal kingdom. Until we have that capability, the most we can validly state is what we can observe—that the animal is engaged in repetitive, stereotyped behaviour.

At this point, a possible objection should be countered. We have been considering faulty everyday uses of technical terms such as "obsession." But it should be noted that some of the examples cited above, while not correctly classifiable as "obsessions" or "compulsions," may indeed by associated with the obsessional or anankastic personality, which we have not yet discussed. However, just as they cannot be validly termed "obsession," etc., without supportive phenomenological evidence, so they cannot be validly regarded as manifestations of a particular personality structure without consideration of the total pattern of traits displayed by each individual in question.

2
Form, Content, and Modes of Obsessional Experience

A most important point to note is that the definitional criteria for obsession are completely *formal.* They rely upon *generalizable abstractions of the subjective qualities of a given experience*, not upon what the experience is *about*; the former constitutes the *form* of the experience, while the latter is its *content*. For example, the form of something we are reading may be a novel; its content may be the development of a love affair or the complexities of a spy chase. A piece of verse may take the form of a sonnet; its content may be the attributes of the Dark Lady. With regard to the present topic, if we are afflicted with terror that we might be killed during a thunderstorm, the form of our experience is fear, while its content is death attributable to thunderstorms. A subject may be afflicted with a recurrent idea that he was indirectly responsible for the demise of his Aunt Agatha. The form of this experience is the idea; its content is the death of Aunt Agatha. To determine whether the experience may be regarded as an obsession, the subjective qualities of the idea must be examined, not the fact that it is concerned with Aunt Agatha or her departure.

This crucial distinction between the form and content of a mental experience has always been well understood by philosophers. It is less familiar to some psychiatrists and, oddly enough, is relatively unknown among modern psychologists. Now, without decrying for a moment the importance of examining content, it is fair to assert that psychopathology relies upon the establishment and study of form. After all, content is phenotypical. It reflects the up-bringing, the life experiences, and the attitudes of each individual. Form is genotypical: There exist differences across cultures but, within any given culture, general statements may validly be developed. Within psychiatry, theorists have tended to emphasize either content or form at the expense of the other. The Viennese school's interest was primarily in the study of content, the symbolic nature of which lies at the heart of the Freudian approach. Freud himself, although an astute clinical observer, made relatively little analysis of the forms of his patients' experiences. On the other hand, the classical German schools have focused upon form in their search for diagnostic precision. Jaspers concentrated upon the determination of formal characteristics, employing a meticulous phenomenological approach.

In the present instance, as we have seen, there is close agreement between authorities from all "schools"—the criteria for determining what constitutes an obsessional experience are exclusively formal. Theoretically, the content may be of any kind whatsoever, and, therefore, in itself can contribute nothing to the diagnosis. Two simple examples may vivify this point. Let us consider three male patients who complain that their thoughts are dominated by doubts as to their own worthiness and competence. Despite evidence to the contrary, the first may assert wearily that the grounds for his self-reproach are clear—he is useless and unworthy. He does not regard his preoccupying thoughts as irrational, and he makes no attempt to resist them. He may well be suffering from a depressive episode; there is no basis here for classifying his thoughts as obsessions. The second man's self-doubts may well have derived from a life-long history of failure; every day he receives further objective evidence that he is, in fact, one of life's losers. There is no reason for him to regard his poor self-assessment as foolish, so it is understandable that he offers no resistance to its appearance in his consciousness. The third man, however, struggles against his preoccupation, which he recognizes as not being in accord with any objective assessment of his achievements or integrity, and regards it as foolish and unnatural. Only in the case of this last member of the trio is there any justification for regarding his brooding as obsessional, although the content in each case is identical.

Again, let us take the example of three female patients who all report experiences and behaviour manifesting the same content. Each one complains that she is unable to convince herself that she is clean and, thus, finds it necessary to wash her hands repeatedly. In such cases it is not unknown for clinicians to make an elementary diagnostic error of "recognizing" a familiar, classical symptom—the "Lady Macbeth syndrome"—and classifying all three patients as showing grossly compulsive behaviour. From here it is an easy step to the conceptual mistake of assuming that they are all suffering from an "obsessional neurosis." These errors are based upon the hasty presumption that the three patients belong to the same psychiatric category, merely because the *content* of their symptoms is the same. In *form* they may not be the same at all; further investigation might uncover profound phenomenological differences. One woman may report that her belief and behaviour are appropriate, because she has read that the atmosphere in her locality is dangerously polluted. The second may reveal that Jesus Christ is telling her to wash in order to purify herself and all other sinners. The third may complain that she is overwhelmed, despite her best efforts, by ridiculous fears of contamination. It will probably transpire that the first woman is complying with an over-valued idea, while the second is suffering from schizophrenic passivity. Only the third is reporting truly compulsive experiences.

We will discuss the contents of obsessional experience in the next chapter. Meanwhile, let us consider another formal aspect of obsessions—the nature of the mental events to which the criteria are applied and which act as the vehicles of content. For convenience, we will refer to these as the "modes" of obsessional experience.

MODES OF OBSESSIONAL EXPERIENCE

Some authorities have avoided specifying modes by using general, neutral terms such as "mental events," "mental happenings," or "cerebral activity." Others have been more specific, referring to "thoughts," "ideas," "notions," or "preoccupations." Mention has also been made of "images," "urges," "impulses," "anxieties," "fears," "affects," and "feelings." Technically, *any* type of mental experience can carry the hallmarks of compulsion. But in practice, certain modes are reported more frequently than others by obsessional people. It must be borne in mind, of course, that much depends upon the articulateness of the subject and the elicitatory and analytical skill of the clinical interviewer. Clinical case-notes often tell more about the clinician than the patient.

In the writer's experience, the modes of obsessions most commonly described can be grouped under the following headings:

(a) *Fears*. These may be diffuse, such as Mrs. R.'s fears that she herself and everything around her were contaminated. Or they may be quite specific, as in the case of Mrs. P., who suffered from a particular phobic terror of dogs and their excreta. They may bear reference to universal cataclysms, such as Mrs. F.'s fear of an imminent breakdown in world order, due to the spread of drug-taking. Or they may have a specifically personal reference, as in the case of Mr. Z., who went about in state of near-panic, being constantly afraid that he would be attacked by hoodlums. Apart from Mrs. R.'s fears of contamination, which she saw as on-going, the above examples all refer to possible future events. But obsessional fears can also refer to past events or actions or, combined with doubts, to *possible* past actions, misdeeds, or wicked thoughts. Thus, Mr. D. was compulsively afraid that he had killed two elderly strangers; Mr. B. was afraid that he had been involved in the death of his grandmother; while Mr. I.'s fears concerned the condition of the spirit of a work-mate who had died over a year previously.

(b) *Ruminations*. These are persistent and totally preoccupying trains of thought which are circular and non-productive in nature. There have been surprisingly few authoritative attempts to define ruminations and, since Janet, there have not even been any satisfactorily detailed descriptions of the phenomenon.

A few examples may indicate the possible range of types of ruminations. Mr.

E., a sixteen-year-old apprentice, reported a relatively straightforward type: "If I touch the doorhandle, then I pick up other people's germs. But I am already contaminated, so if I touch the doorhandle, then I may leave my own germs upon it, and other people may catch them. The next time they touch the door-handle, they will leave their germs. But they include my germs. If I then touch the doorhandle. ... " Mrs. H.'s ruminations revolved around her own (imagined) wickedness, the nature of God, and the possibility of losing her children: "I am so wicked I am beyond redemption. God will punish me by taking away my children. But God is good; surely He would not do that? Yes, but if He is so good, why did He allow me to be so wicked? That was my fault—I must be punished. ... " Mr. M., a 22-year-old graduate student, had ruminated for several years upon a specific topic, but one which involved ever-extending spiralling. He applied sophisticated argumentation and recruited a wide range of erudition, particularly his theological learning, to the consideration of the question: "What would have happened had God seen fit not to part the Red Sea?"

(c) *Doubts*. These range from apparently simple indecisiveness through to Janet's *l'aboulie*, where the sufferer's doubts are all-pervasive and he complains of a total absence of volitional resources, so that, even if he could resolve a doubt, he would be unable to act upon the resolution of it. There are problems of classification here, because the doubts are often intertwined with fears, and their persistence often renders them inextricable from ruminations. The doubting is commonly concerned with a specific occurrence, memory, or self-assessment, but it may refer to abstract, philosophical questions. In one sense, it is a subjective *condition*, rather than a failure to rationally assess and balance competing facts or arguments. The subject may suffer agonies of doubt in regard to some event or statement where objective evidence exists which renders doubt unnecessary. He may find it impossible to decide between two alternatives, when the logical choice is clear. Or he may eventually arrive at a decision, only to find himself unconvinced that the decision itself is appropriate.

Miss Q., a highly intelligent student, had continual doubts as to whether she would complete her study projects. The doubts preoccupied her to the point where she found it impossible, in fact, to complete the projects in question. Another student, Mr. Y., had doubts as to the quality of his academic work, though he was receiving "A" grades. Mrs. O., a woman of 43, suffered from continual doubts as to whether her most prosaic actions had been right or wrong.

Doubts may be experienced in regard to profound abstractions, such as those of Mrs. H. above, whose doubts included that of whether God was really good, or to bizarre impossibilities such as Mr. B.'s inability to convince himself that he had played no part in the death of his grandmother. But the most common type of doubt is that where the subject is compulsively uncertain as to whether he carried out some routine task, such as locking the front door or posting a letter.

(d) *Mental Rituals.* A less common mode, and one which is difficult to classify with precision, might be termed "mental rituals" (to distinguish them from the "motor rituals" which have often been described). This category would include the obsessional use of particular words or formulaic expressions, superstitious invocations, or protective measures, the counting of objects, and the "numbering off" of segments of thought or action. The reason why such "rituals" (we shall discuss the aptness of this term later) are difficult to classify is that they are secondary to a fear or doubt. The subject engages in them to distract himself from distressing thoughts, to protect himself from feared outcomes, or to quell his doubts. In a general way they may be seen as attempts to ward off evil, like such everyday habits as sub-vocal prayers or the use of idiosyncratic "magic" words. Typical examples would be those of Mrs. R., who, at various stages of her compulsive hand-washing, would find it necessary to say her name sub-vocally, coupled with "a secret word", and Mrs. G., who had to "break up her actions" by numbering them off.

(e) *Discrete Obsessional Thoughts.* Less common than older textbooks suggest are discrete obsessional thoughts. These are encapsulated thoughts or ideas, expressed in unelaborated statements, rebukes, or questions. They ring through the subject's head, disturbing or contradicting his normal train of thought. In earlier times, they were often of a blasphemous or obscene nature, such as "Christ was a degenerate." Nowadays, they are more commonly of a self-denigratory nature, such as the obtrusive comment which plagued Mr. Y.: "You're a dead loss, that's what you are! A dead loss!"

(f) *Urges and Impulses.* These are reported, but, as we shall see, they are often difficult to classify, being not so much urges to action as fears, doubts, and misgivings *about* urges—whether the urge could be, or has been put into effect. On the other hand, *all* compulsive acts are regarded by some workers as subsequent to, caused by, or associated with urges. We shall discuss these points in a later section.

(g) *Visual Images.* Occasionally, encapsulated but recurrent visual images are reported. These are related to some fear, doubt, or misgiving; they may be crystallized "memories" of key events or simply projections of the subject's morbid fantasy. Thus, Mr. D.'s ruminative fears that he had killed two elderly strangers by cutting out their livers were accompanied by a vivid visual image of their disembowelled corpses.

(h) *Affects.* Relatively few writers have mentioned compulsive affects, and fewer still have provided any instructive discussion. There is no doubt that the determination of compulsivity in the experience of affect presents difficulties in diagnosis, as well as conceptual problems. Usually, affect will be found to be secondary to (caused by) the obsessional experience, which is expressed in modes such as fear or doubt, or by the very experience of compulsivity itself. Nevertheless, some patients do report strange feelings which comply with the criteria. Thus, Mrs. G. was overcome intermittently by "a strange feeling, almost like hearing that somebody has just died. ... "

For present purposes a series of fifty obsessional patients was studied by this writer. The patients were of both sexes and were all aged sixteen or over. In all cases, obsessions and compulsions were the predominating symptoms. None was currently suffering from depressive disorder and in no case was there any evidence of schizophrenia, other psychoses, or neurological pathology. In all cases the obsessional symptoms had been present for at least a year; in a few cases they had persisted for a long as ten years.

In only two cases among the fifty were reports of obsessions not elicited (i.e., only compulsions were reported). The remaining forty-eight complained of a total of ninety-seven obsessional experiences. The distribution of these among our categories of modes is presented in Table 2.1.

TABLE 2.1
The Distribution of Obsessions Across Modal Categories

Modes of Obsessions	Numbers Reported	Percentage of Total Modes (Rounded)	Percentage of Individuals (Rounded)
Fears	31	31	65
Ruminations	19	20	40
Doubts	18	19	38
Mental Rituals	7	7	15
Discrete Thoughts	2	2	4
Impulses [a]	17	18	35
Affects	2	2	4
Images	1	1	2
Totals	97	100	203

[a] It can be argued that all compulsions are responses to compulsive impulses. This has not been assumed here; what have been reported are cases where impulses were recognized by patients, and distinguished from fears, doubts, etc.

To the best of the present writer's knowledge, only Akhtar *et al.* (1975) have published an objective survey of the prevalence of the various modes of obsessional experience. They reported that of eighty-two Hindu patients in northern India, the obsessions of 75% were in the mode of doubts, 34% thoughts, 25% fears, 17% impulses, 7% images, and 2% "miscellaneous."

Unfortunately, the classifications used by these workers are defined somewhat idiosyncratically. Thus, "obsessive doubt" is defined as: "An inclination not to believe that a completed task has been accomplished satisfactorily." This definition is surprisingly restrictive for, as we have seen, obsessional doubts may be entertained in regard to almost any topic or fact, ranging from abstruse philosophical issues to such mundane and trivial questions as whether the individual's recollection that he took a bath on a particular Wednesday is correct. Again, the definition comprises one example of what Janet termed the *sentiment d'incomplétude*. But as Janet made clear, this is not limited to such narrow areas as the completion of tasks: It is a generalized *failure of conviction* which may focus upon any mental or physical function or any situation, event, account, memory, or belief.

Akhtar *et al.* define "obsessive fear" as: "A fear of losing self-control and thus inadvertently committing a socially embarrassing act." But obsessional fears may be of almost any conceivable event, object, situation, or action. As we have seen, they range from diffuse fears, such as the spread of nuclear radiation, to specific ones, such as the fear of dogs, from the fear of unlikely events, such as an imminent interplanetary collision, to that of realistic contingencies, such as possible bankruptcy. The definition provided by Akhtar *et al.* refers to a specific, future possibility. But many obsessional fears relate to the past and link up, on the one hand, with doubts and, on the other, with obsessional ruminations. "I may have inadvertently caused another motorist to swerve at a given intersection. If he did, he may have fatally struck an innocent pedestrian. If that happened, then I fear that I have been responsible for somebody's death. ..." Meanwhile, it need hardly be pointed out that the above definition, while avowedly identifying a *form* of obsession, veers dangerously towards the specification of *content*.

Clearly, the Akhtar *et al.* study, while most worthy in intention, and presenting some very interesting findings, suffers from serious definitional shortcomings. But three major difficulties face *any* investigator attempting to establish frequencies of modes in obsessional experience:

(1) Any system of classification will encounter difficulties in establishing valid and acceptable classificatory definitions.
(2) The various modes, however carefully defined, tend to *overlap*. "I keep wondering whether I am really as bad as I think I am. It's terrifying. ..."

This report can surely not be classified as specifically an idea, a doubt, or a fear. It is a combination of all three.

(3) While one obsession may predominate in any given case history, the majority of obsessional people suffer from *multiple* obsessions. (This is clearly indicated by the totals in the frequency studies reported above.) Obsessionals tend to be secretive about their problems. Initially, they can scarcely avoid outlining their predominant difficulties, because these are why they have solicited help. But they may not reveal associated obsessional problems for some time, and then only if an appropriate relationship has been established with the clinician. Thus, the longer the obsessional sufferer is studied, the more complicated the picture becomes. There will usually be many more obsessions than the one(s) contained in the initial complaint (the "presenting symptom"). And these will probably be interrelated, so that instead of one discrete obsession, the clinician may find that there exists a densely textured obsessional tapestry. Thus, Mrs. G. was originally diagnosed simply as a "compulsive hand-washer" and was referred for treatment to alleviate her crippling washing rituals. It was these she had originally complained of in presenting herself for psychiatric attention. But it transpired that she was the victim of an intricate web of interconnected obsessional fears, doubts, and misgivings, and that compulsive mental and physical rituals permeated almost every aspect of her life. Mr. D. was regarded as suffering from "an obsessional fear that he had killed two strangers." In fact, it turned out after several interviews that this particular fear was associated with several others, with a related obsessional image, with a plethora of obsessional doubts, with obsessional ruminations, with a variety of compulsive urges, and with acts and rituals of a protective nature.

Thus, it seems unlikely that a full picture of any obsessional patient's experiences can be derived from a short interview conducted on a single occasion. Yet this has been the method employed in most modern studies of the nature of obsessional experience.

3
The Content of Obsessions

As we have seen, the criterial attributes of obsessional experience are entirely *formal*. For the determination of whether a particular experience should rightly be regarded as an obsession, therefore, its *content* is irrelevant. The formal criteria can be applied to any experience, whatever its content. For instance, some obsessional patients worry about the possibility of contamination. But worrying about contamination, however distressing this may be, does not in itself constitute an obsession. To determine *that*, we must ascertain that the worry has a compulsive quality, that the individual regards it as irrational, and that he struggles unsuccessfully to rid himself of it. The content of the experience—"contamination"—is beside the point. Many people fear or worry about contamination, without this constituting an obsession. Similarly, it is not unknown for obsessional people to be preoccupied by fears that they might have been involved in causing traffic fatalities or might in the future kill their babies. But an individual may brood upon those contents—motor accidents and infanticide—without the broodings having the hallmarks of obsessional experience.

However, form can only be identified by the examination of verbal reports, which usually focus upon content. In reporting the nature of their problems, informants seldom say: "I am engaged in a continual, fruitless struggle with an irrational, but overwhelming fear." They are much more likely to say: "I am terrified of cats." The clinician must then proceed to determine the phenomenological quality of this experience. This may not be simple, because the patient's pre-eminent concern is with content—the cats.

In any case, the nature of the content of any given experience possesses its own intrinsic interest. Indeed, psychoanalytic and most other "dynamic" approaches focus almost exclusively upon content, what it symbolizes, and its developmental implications. Even those theorists who are opposed to psychoanalytical formulations cannot entirely dispense with the consideration of content and what it may imply. And it is an interesting fact that, just as with modes, while, technically, an obsession can have any content whatsoever, there is a tendency for the contents of obsessional experiences to revolve around particular topics. Study of published case reports and clinical illustrations will show that during more than a century certain content themes recur with a regularity which is well beyond chance. As might be expected, there have been shifts of emphasis, reflecting changes in social knowledge, values, and concerns. Our attitudes, beliefs, and concepts are largely culturally determined: All of us are the products of our up-bringings, which themselves reflect our culture and the times in which we live. Clearly, it is most unlikely that radiation hazards will figure among the contents of an individual's thinking if the concept of nuclear energy has not yet been introduced in the society of which he is a member. And equally, in a given culture which has long abandoned any belief in the supernatural powers of inanimate objects, it will be quite rare to find an individual the contents of whose thoughts include rock-worship. But despite such shifts of emphasis, the contents of obsessions have tended to conform to recognizable themes or topics. The aim of this chapter is to indicate the wide range of possible contents, while attempting to classify these common themes.

In the first section of the first chapter of Janet's (1903) classical work, he devotes sixty pages to descriptions of the various contents of obsessional ideas. He groups them under five main headings: (a) Sacrilege; (b) Crime; (c) Self shame; (d) Shame of one's body; and (e) Hypochondria. For each category, Janet offers a variety of clinical examples, described in meticulous detail. A few of these examples will be summarized here, to give some flavour of the content material reported.

(a) *Sacrilege (l'obsession du sacrilège)*. Case 2L8, a 55-year-old woman, felt that the Devil intervened in everything she did. She could not engage in such everyday activities as eating her soup or changing her vest without thinking that at that moment she was doing something agreeable to the demon.

"Claire," a demure virgin of 28, eventually admitted that she would suddenly envision the genitalia of a naked man engaged in polluting the eucharistic host.

(b) *Crime (l'obsession du crime)*. "Za ... ," a 32-year-old man, had entered a seminary at the age of 20 to indulge his taste for theological disputation. His preoccupation became such that his superior referred him for medical treatment and expelled him, after persuading him to change his line of study. "Za ... " now took up the study of ethical problems and questions of crime and punishment. He became obsessed by urges not only to commit all the theological sins but the secular one of ravishing and murdering a female.

"Ger ... " was obsessed by the thought of cutting off her little girl's head and immersing her in boiling water.

(c) *Self shame (l'obsession de la honte de soi)*. "Claire" is given as an example of a group feeling *moral shame* about all their actions and thoughts. Her scrupulosity and concern with religious actions was paralleled by her distress regarding her defects in the very areas where she wished to behave best. Her belief that her confessions and communions were badly carried out led to interminable prayers and to written confessions, the preparation of each of which took 15 days. Her anguished remorse was non-specific and all-encompassing: "It is as if I have committed all possible crimes. ... "

"Dev ... " showed compulsive remorse of an unusual kind. A skilful musician, he was constantly assailed by the idea that he played badly and that it was wicked to play so badly.

(d) *Shame of one's body (l'obsession de la honte du corps)*. "Wye," a man of 27, had been obsessed for about ten years by the belief that the movements of his arms and legs were odd. "I feel that I lack spontaneity, that my movements are unnatural. I am all stiff. ... "

"Pol," a woman of 24, was horribly tormented by the thought that she had a little mark on her left nostril.

Following ruminations about adultery, "Vg" became constantly obsessed by the thought that his genitals did not really belong to him.

(e) *Hypochondria (les obsessions hypocondriaques)*. "Jean," a man of 30, was as extreme in his hypochondriacal concerns as he was in his scrupulosity, being continually preoccupied by thoughts of death. He could not attend a funeral without becoming ill with terror, and trembled at the very sight of a funeral attendant. He could not pass the local town hall between nine and five, because between these hours the office of the registrar of deaths was open.

The thought of death also preoccupied "Bal," but in her case it took the indirect form of obsessional brooding about her age and those of people around her.

"Qei" examined all her food carefully, for fear that pieces of needles were embedded therein, and washed her hands continually in case they had been infected by unclean contacts.

"Obs" was obsessed by the idea that there was something stuck up her nose which could only be released by a major nose-bleed.

"K1" complained of a burning sensation in her thigh, which she attributed to the passage of a pin she must have swallowed.

Thus, as Janet indicates, obsessional contents range from the dramatic to the banal. He points out, however, that unlike the equally diverse but unconnected *idées fixes* of hysterics, the contents of obsessions are interrelated. His group headings, he says, are presented merely for expository convenience, because in practice there is considerable overlapping between the categories. Thus, members of the "Sacrilege" group are simply exaggerated examples of those in the

"Crime" group, while those in the "Self shame" group are naturally related to thoughts of "crime."

Janet argues convincingly that certain generalizations can be made about the contents of obsessions. These include:

(a) Obsessions have reference to the individual, rather than to objects in the outside world. They refer above all to the correctness of one's own acts and one's will.

(b) In contrast with the ideas of hysterics, obsessional people are overcome by thoughts deriving from the clash between what they believe to be their own wickedness and their personal moral beliefs and wishes: "*la malade est obsédé par la pensée d'un acte qu'il voudrait ne pas faire.*" (p. 61)

Related to the interconnectedness of obsessional contents is the significant fact that severe obsessionals seldom suffer from a single, discrete obsession. The longer a patient is studied the more obsessions will be discovered over and above the original "presenting symptoms." Obsessional people are often embarrassed about their experiences, and when forced to seek help they typically report only the most incapacitating of their problems. But after a trusting relationship has been established with the clinician, they will reveal more and more examples of their obsessional–compulsive difficulties. The contents may be quite diverse, although they can often be traced back to one "primary" source. The clinician will discover a veritable network of obsessional ideas, doubts, and fears, each further revelation representing another node in the net. Or, to change the metaphor, the obsessional–compulsive experience may be seen as a cancer which can extend in all directions. For example, Mrs. R. was initially referred for psychiatric treatment simply because she suffered from compulsive hand-washing. It slowly transpired that although the hand-washing was the most handicapping of her problems, she was also beset by obsessional ideas about contamination (which directly precipitated the compulsive behaviour), pollution, illness, death, time, and sex. Perhaps springing from these were covert kitchen, bathroom, and general household cleaning rituals, counting rituals, and a compulsive need for prescribed order and arrangement of her possessions. Similarly, she suffered from obsessional thoughts and fears in regard to semen, vaginal secretions, and menstrual flow. Despite herself she was plagued, on the one hand, by aggressive and destructive urges and, on the other, by urges towards sexual relationships and lascivious activity. Above all, she was obsessed by self-reproach and denigration—she was wicked and unworthy, and she lacked the will-power either to improve herself or to control her thoughts and actions. In fact, apart from the "Sacrilege" group, Mrs. R. reported *all* Janet's types of content. Janet's case illustrations include many examples of this sort, as do those of Freud which are reported in detail.

This multiplicity of contents in individual cases is to be expected in view of the findings reported in the previous chapter. If a given individual experiences a number of modes, it would seem unlikely that the content of the experiences should be restricted to a single type of content. So it is puzzling to find that Rachman and Hodgson (1980) report exactly that. Of a sample of eighty-three patients, we are told, 73% had single, predominating obsessions. The authors claim that a similar finding was reported in the Akhtar *et al.* (1975) study, where 75% of the patients had single obsessions. However, this claim does not appear to coincide with the findings of the Akhtar *et al.* study itself, where 51% of the subjects are reported to have suffered from *multiple* obsessions. The suspicion that some misunderstanding has occurred here is reinforced by the fact that the percentage distributions across content categories attributed to the Akhtar *et al.* study by Rachman and Hodgson differ in every category from those actually reported in the original article.

The determination of appropriate categories for the grouping of content themes involves another sort of problem, one which inevitably leads to some arbitrary decisions. An individual may be compulsively preoccupied by thoughts about his own moral defects, with particular reference to an episode of marital infidelity; he broods upon the unlikelihood of divine forgiveness for this transgression and fears that his will-power is too weak to prevent further sinning. Should this compound experience be classified as "self-reproach," "sin," "morality," "sex," "disloyalty," "God," or "will-power"? Or should it appear under all seven headings or some selection of them? Another subject may suffer from compulsive fears of social interaction, based upon her belief that her nose is malformed because of bone disease contracted during her work as a hospital technician. Should this be categorized as "social inadequacy," "self-denigration," "physical deformity," "hypochondria," "disease," "contamination," or "occupation"? The difficulties, in fact, are those encountered in our determination of modes—the overlapping of categories and the multiplicity of obsessional experience.

The task of deciding the categories themselves is rendered difficult because of the different levels of analysis which are possible. Clearly, various hierarchies of content can be derived, with some categories subsuming others. And it would be a most inelegant classificatory system which mixed categories of grossly different specificity, for instance "Society," "Sin," and "Noses." This problem, coupled with the subsequent one of allocating actual experiences to whatever categories are eventually decided upon, gives some insight into the difficulties of decision-making suffered by the very people under discussion. And, as with them, the temptation is to introduce as many categories as there are experiences, which would make the whole exercise pointless. At the other extreme, attempts to achieve parsimony and elegance in classification invite the possibility of under-inclusion, which is equally unenlightening. For instance, the obsessional experiences of no fewer than eighteen of the eighty-two patients studied by Akhtar *et al.* (1975) were unclassifiable under the system employed.

An essential prerequisite of any classificatory endeavour is that the phenomena to be classified are, in fact, of the same kind. The Akhtar *et al.* study used five categories—(a) "Dirt and Contamination," (b) "Aggression," (c) "Inanimate–Impersonal," (d) "Sex," and (e) "Religion." Four of these will be familiar to any clinician with experience in this area. Indeed, they figure among the classes used by Janet (with whose work Akhtar *et al.* do not appear to be familiar). But the third category—"Inanimate–Impersonal"—does not coincide with clinical experience and runs directly counter to Janet's observation that the contents of obsessional experiences have personal reference and do *not* refer to external objects. Examination of the description of this suspect category provided by Akhtar *et al.* reveals that they are referring to counting and totalling, checking (of locks, bolts, etc.), and arranging (of books on shelves, etc.)—i.e., to compulsions. In other words, the category in question, unlike the others, covers *behaviours*, not *experiences*. The researchers describe their content categories as "thought contents," but to this third category they attribute acts, not thoughts. The inclusion of this category significantly affects their reported distribution of contents, since to it are allocated the "experiences" of twenty-two of the eighty-two subjects, accounting for 27% of the contents surveyed.

Thus, despite the approval given to the Akhtar *et al.* classificatory system by Rachman and Hodgson (1980), the system is unsatisfactory on two grounds. First, it is unable to account for the experiences of almost a quarter of the cases studied. And second, it allocates the experiences of more than a quarter of the cases to a category which belongs to a different realm of discourse.

In studying the fifty cases in the present series, a revised and expanded version of Janet's list of categories has been employed for classifying the content themes of obsessions. His first category, that of "Sacrilege," was abandoned. As might be expected, religious concerns are much less frequent nowadays than they were at the turn of the century, and in only one case in the present series did thoughts of God assume significance. In that case, doubts and fears about divine judgement were secondary to generalized feelings of shame and self-reproach. (It need scarcely be mentioned, of course, that this finding is probably culturally determined. It presumably would not apply to patients from more devout populations, such as those where the influence of an established religion was more powerful.) Janet's second category, that of "Crime," was abandoned also, but for different reasons. What he describes under this heading might equally well be termed "Sin," on the one hand, or "Harm to Others," "Violence," or "Aggression," on the other. His third category, "Self Shame," was broken down to discriminate between moral shame/guilt and general self-denigration. His other two categories were retained, and four new ones were added—"Death," "Contamination," "Possible Harm to Self," and "Possible Harm to Others." Initially, the present writer had assumed that a substantial number of reported contents would be of a sexual nature. But in the present series this proved not to be the case, and the category was abandoned. This does not, of course, mean that sexual thoughts, desires, fears, doubts, and fantasies did not figure among the contents of these patients' mentation. The point is that they did not, in this sample at least, figure *as obsessions*. They were not characterized by the three formal criteria. This should surely not surprise those who accept the psychoanalytic viewpoint. For, according to Freud, the function of obsessions is to *prevent* the emergence of unacceptably libidinous material into consciousness.

There is nothing sacrosanct about the final list, of course; the overlapping of categories is still possible and, like any other classificatory system, it cannot in itself resolve the problem of multiplicity. But it offers the pragmatic advantages of being sufficiently precise within categories to facilitate allocation and sufficiently wide across categories to encompass the vast majority of instances.

As in our discussion of modes, each category will now be briefly described and examples presented.

(a) *Shame of Self (Social Adequacy and Abilities)*. This category includes contents which express the feelings of self-depreciation and self-denigration which are very common among obsessional people. They reflect the insecurity under which Schneider (1925) subsumed his "anankastic" group, which is characterized by compulsivity, and are central also to Janet's "psychasthenia" and Freud's "obsessional neurosis." The self-denigration ranges from generalized feelings of social inadequacy to concerns about deficiencies in particular areas of competence. One individual may be compulsively worried that he is unacceptable to other people, a figure of fun, pity, or contempt because of his lack of social skills, his boring personality, or his general stupidity. Another may be compulsively preoccupied by his intellectual inability to succeed in the study of geography. In a few cases there may be some basis for these poor self-judgements, but in the majority they do not coincide with objective evidence. Ironically, however, the individual's worries, doubts, and preoccupations may impair his actual performance, so that his negative judgements become confirmed in fact.

Examples of compulsive shame of a generalized kind would include that of Mr. A., aged 21, who had shown a profound lack of social confidence since he was 13. His timidity, shyness, and solitariness reflected a compulsive belief that he was socially inadequate in a general sense, and that for this reason people laughed at him. Mrs. B., aged 27, also believed that people laughed at her and had always been shy and self conscious. She developed compulsive doubts about her social acceptability, with consequent fears of social groups.

Compulsive shame about specific deficiencies was experienced by Miss Q., in regard to her imagined lack of intelligence and unsuitability for academic work. She was sociable and popular, was highly regarded by her teachers, had an IQ of 127 and an excellent academic record. Similarly, Mr. Y., a successful student with an IQ of 137, developed compulsive doubts and ruminations about his intellectual capacity. These seriously impeded his university studies.

(b) *Shame of Self (Moral and Characterological)*. The self-shame of the first group in (a) above springs from perceived judgements of capacities and performance in the context of social expectations. Sufferers see themselves as defective by comparison with others. In the present group, the perceived defect is by comparison with the individual's own standards—of virtue, responsibility, or propriety. He reproaches himself for his immorality, sinfulness, weakness of character, or lack of integrity. The question of whether other people detect these defects is of less significance. The compulsive self-recriminations may have reference to the individual's general immorality or character-weaknesses, whether or not these have been manifested in behaviour, or to specific wicked acts of commission or omission, bouts of temptation, or evil thoughts. The specific acts may have occurred in fact (e.g., an extra-marital love affair or the denigration of a colleague) or may be imaginary (e.g., doubts about whether one was indirectly responsible for an accident).

Examples of generalized shame and self-reproach would include that of Mrs. H., aged 39, who suffered from compulsive ruminations about her wickedness and the judgements of God. Mr. P. experienced compulsive self-recrimination regarding his weakness of character, his "complexes," and his sinfulness.

An example of shame for an actual specific piece of behaviour is that of Mr. W., an intelligent wages clerk of 45, who compulsively reproached himself for his former drinking habit. Mrs. O., a 43-year-old housewife, suffered from compulsive self-reproach for her masturbation. Mrs. X., aged 55, was compulsively preoccupied by guilt about an episode of marital infidelity which had occurred ten years previously. Imaginary acts inducing preoccupying guilt include Mr. D.'s "murder" of two elderly strangers and Mr. B.'s involvement in the death of his grandmother.

(c) *Shame of One's Physique*. In accordance with Janet's group, this category is restricted to contents concerned with some physical defect of the individual. There is obviously a danger here of confusion with the next category (hypochondria), but the shame aspect makes discrimination possible in the majority of cases. People with hypochondriacal concerns are wont to suffer more from self-pity than from self-reproach. Furthermore, members of this "Shame" group are preoccupied by anatomical characteristics rather than functions. The characteristics are judged to be defective relative to the rest of the population, but usually there is little if any objective evidence to support the judgement. Usually, the shame is felt in regard to some particular physical feature, but in some cases the individual is worried about his or her appearance in general.

For example, Miss A. reproached herself for being the possessor of an "ugly" face, which she felt "looked too young." Miss D., on the other hand, was ashamed of her appearance in general, regarding it as being "unsatisfactory." Both these young ladies were actually of normal appearance, and facially were judged by observers to be quite attractive. Mr. U. was compulsively ashamed of his height. In fact, he was a tall man, of over six feet, but normally proportioned; most men would probably be proud to possess his build. Mr. C. was beset by shame that his penis was malformed, an assertion which was denied by medical examiners.

(d) *Hypochondriacal.* This category includes compulsive preoccupations with health and worries about bodily functions. It may overlap with the preceding group, as noted above, but lacks the element of self-reproach. In a few cases it may also overlap with the next category, that of "Death." In a logical sense it could also be said to subsume the "Dirt and Contamination" category, but the experiences of patients contributing to that group have their own phenomenological flavour, as we shall see. Compulsive hypochondriacal experiences are often associated with reports of pain with no organic basis and with a variety of psychogenic somatic complaints. Commonly reported also are feelings of lassitude and mental "woolliness"; less frequent are the extremes of full-blown cases of depersonalization and derealization. In themselves, experiences of pain, somatic disturbance, lassitude, and depersonalization are, of course, contentless, which is why they are not allocated a category of their own here.

Mr. Q., aged 35, complained of pains in his neck, coupled with associated anxieties. He accepted that there was no physical basis for the pains but had compulsively suffered from them for four years, eventually having to give up his job as an accountant because of them. Mr. P. and Mr. U. were both concerned with their general health, lacked energy, and suffered from panic attacks. Mrs. S. suffered from depersonalization and had difficulty in swallowing food for fear of a lump in her throat. Mrs. E. also had difficulty in swallowing food, complaining that her throat "felt stiff." Mrs. X. suffered from tinnitus and Miss K. from torticollis; in neither case was any organic basis for these compulsive feelings ever discovered. Several patients suffered from migraine-like headaches, several others from attacks of panic, and still others from bouts of faintness or dizziness.

(e) *Death.* The death of a friend, relative, or workmate seems to have precipitated or exacerbated the obsessional problems of several patients in the present series and become the topic of obsessional ruminations in at least two cases. In another two cases, ruminations, fears, doubts, and self-reproach centred upon the patients' possible responsibility for, in one case two imagined murders, in another the death of the individual's grandmother. In one case, death by suicide was obsessionally brooded upon, as a release from the patient's suffering. In two other cases, compulsive fears of death were experienced in the context of hypochondriacal anxieties, and in one case as possible divine retribution for evildoing. Thus, the category overlaps with those of "Possible Harm to Self," "Possible Harm to Others," "Hypochondriasis," and moral "Self-Shame." Surprisingly, the metaphysical implications of death as a subject for rumination did not figure in this series, although it has in several other cases in the writer's experience.

Examples include those of Mr. I., whose problems were initiated by, and revolved around, the death of a workmate, and Mr. W., who had ruminated for fourteen months about the death of his only friend. As mentioned earlier, Mr. B.'s compulsive doubts were in regard to the possibility of his involvement in the death of his grandmother, while Mr. D.'s ruminations, doubts, fears, and rituals all sprang from the imagined murders of two strangers. Mrs. H. suffered from compulsive fears of death as a result of her wickedness.

(f) *Dirt and Contamination.* Under this heading figure compulsive fears, doubts, and preoccupations about dirt and the spread of disease. Sometimes specific disorders such as tuberculosis, cancer, and radiation sickness are mentioned, but more often the expressed concern is to do with the general dangers of germs, infection, contagion, and contamination. The individual is almost always fearful that he will be the victim of the contamination, but in some cases this is intermixed with fears that he himself will contaminate others. Thus the category overlaps not only with "Hypochondria" but also with both "Possible Harm to Self" and "Possible Harm to Others." It has been kept separate here partly because it has always been regarded as one of the classical features of obsessional disorder, partly because it is readily identifiable, and partly because it is reported in association with, or as the cause of, such classical compulsive activities as cleaning and hand-washing, as well as many cases of checking. Fears of dirt, germs, and contamination also tend to become increasingly pervasive and to dominate the clinical picture in those cases where they occur.

Related to the generality and pervasiveness mentioned above are two phenomenological features which give this category its own subjective flavour. First, the fears are so non-specific that they are difficult to describe or discuss. Sufferers use terms like "contamination" for want of more precise identifying words for an experience of horrified awareness of a nameless, creeping process. In other words, the experience verges upon being content-less. Second, a terrifying feature of this "process" is that it is felt to be insidiously but continuously encroaching upon the individual's life-space. Every day more and more features of the environment are affected, so that fewer and fewer "safe" objects and areas are left. To make matters worse, the individual's calendar is increasingly filled with dates and times which are felt to be particularly dangerous. On those days and at those times, the unknown horrors are more threatening, while the rate of encroachment accelerates and more objects and places are vulnerable. The writer has known extreme cases where only a few days in the year remained relatively "safe" and where so many environmental features had been "contaminated" that the patient had perforce to exist in one circumscribed area of one room. And even this limited safety zone could only be maintained by increased vigilance and the constant introduction of protective rituals, both motor and mental.

In the present series, Mrs. R., Mrs. G., Mr. E., and Mr. F. had all been initially referred for treatment of their incapacitating hand-washing. In each case, the washing and associated rituals were found to spring from pathological fears of dirt and contamination. The same applied to Mrs. O.'s compulsive checking, which was bound up with her fears of dirt and germs.

(g) *Possible Harm to Self,* and (h) *Possible Harm to Others.* Our examination of obsessional modes revealed the prevalence of fears, so it is not surprising that obsessional contents should include concerns with possible harm. (In fact, the "Fear" mode also included contents to do with shame, death, dirt, and hypochondriasis.)

For the sake of convenience, we may consider "Harm" under five headings: (1) the general *nature* of the harm envisaged (e.g., physical assault or attacks upon one's integrity); (2) the actual *outcome* envisaged (e.g., a broken jaw or social disgrace); (3) the *instrument* of harm (e.g., a fist or the dissemination of lying accusations); (4) the *agent* or source of harm (e.g., the neighbourhood bully or a jealous colleague); (5) the *victim* of harm (e.g., oneself or members of one's family).

We may now consider each of these aspects of "Harm" as it applies to obsessional experience, based upon, and using examples from the present series.

(1) In many cases the general nature of possible harm is clear; complaints include disease and violence. Other sorts of harm, such as those to do with the victim's career, reputation, emotional state, or financial situation, were noticeably absent. But in other cases, the envisaged harm is non-specific, being undescribable or expressed in terms of cataclysm or supernatural intervention. Thus, Mr. E. was afraid of germs, Mr. Z. of violence; but Miss D.'s fears were concerned with being looked at, which in itself is not harmful, while Mrs. H. was smitten with terror of disasters she could not describe.

(2) The actual outcomes of envisaged harm were scarcely ever specified, even in those cases where the general nature of the harm could be identified. For example, the fears of germs expressed by Mr. E. and Mrs. G. were not related to the contraction of a specific disease, or the effects thereof. The social fears of Mr. P. and Miss D. could not be rationalized or expressed in terms of untoward results. Death as an outcome was occasionally mentioned, but in a very generalized way. In such cases, the precise nature of the death or what led up to or caused it were not specified; in fact, the word "Doom" would seem to convey the subjects' experiences better than the word "Death."

(3) In several cases the instrument of the envisaged harm was what was brooded upon, rather than the nature or result of the harm. Thus, Mrs. N. was afraid of thunder, Mrs. P. of dogs, Mrs. O. of electrical switches, and Mrs. S. of snakes. But, as with most phobic people, what made these sources of fear dangerous was not specified. They did not think in terms of injury due to dog-bites, electric shocks, or snake venom. Mr. Z. was exceptional in being able to describe the nature, instruments, and results of the possible harm which preoccupied him. He was compulsively afraid of being attacked in the street or at a dance by hoodlums, who would leave him severely injured.

(4) Unlike paranoiacs, the members of the present series did not attribute the possible harm to particular individuals or groups. Reference was never made to wicked relatives, hostile neighbours, or jealous colleagues; nor were suspicions voiced about the evil policies and practices of organizations such as the Roman Catholic Church, Freemasonry, the government, or political parties. The source of harm was apparently not considered, except in terms of malignant fate. Where it was specified, the source agent was the individual himself. Thus, Mr. T.'s fears were to do with the possibility of dreadful traffic accidents. He himself would be responsible for these; by swerving into the opposite lane of traffic he would cause not only a major head-on collision but a subsequent chain of pile-ups among approaching vehicles.

(5) In the majority of cases, the potential harm threatens the individual himself; but in about a quarter of the "Possible Harm" cases in the present series, other people were seen to be threatened. In all but the last of the examples cited above, the victim of possible harm is the individual in question. Mr. T., on the other hand, while presuming that he would receive serious injuries in the forthcoming crash or crashes, was more concerned with the harm to be suffered by other road-users. Mr. S. felt that his mother would suffer some terrible fate should he fail to carry out his rituals correctly, while Mr. D. was terrified that he might engage in a spate of sadistic murders.

Eighty-eight contents appeared in the complaints of the forty-eight members of the present series who reported obsessional mental experiences. These contents were distributed as in Table 3.1.

TABLE 3.1
The Distribution of Obsessional Contents Across Categories

Content Categories	Numbers Reported	Percentage of Total Contents (Rounded)	Percentage of Individuals (Rounded)
Shame of Self (Social Adequacy and Abilities)	17	19	35
Shame of Self (Moral/Character)	11	12	23
Shame of One's Physique	6	7	12
Hypochondriacal	13	15	27
Death	8	9	17
Dirt and Contamination	8	9	17
Possible Harm to Self	19	22	39
Possible Harm to Others	6	7	12
Totals	88	100	182

4
Types of Compulsive Behaviour

Clearly, there are problems of logic involved in attempting to describe compulsive acts in terms of either modes or contents. Instead, the aim of this chapter will simply be to categorize compulsions in terms of the types of behaviour manifested. Some attention will also be paid to the inferred psychological purposes of these acts and their antecedents.

Theoretically, as noted earlier, any mental event may be characterized by obsessionality; in the same way, any sort of physical activity may be compulsive. But in practice, as with obsessional modes, compulsive modes tend to fall into certain categories.

No generally acceptable system of categorizing compulsions has yet been developed. Lewis (1957) proposed that a differentiation should be made between compulsions which control obsessional urges and those which yield to them. A "controlling compulsion" diverts or suppresses the underlying urge and, thus, shows no direct relationship with it. For example, Mr. S. found it necessary to go down on one knee five times whenever he experienced the obsessional fear that some harm was about to strike his mother. A "yielding compulsion," however, is one which is a direct expression of the urge. For example, Mr. E. engaged in compulsive hand-washing and refused to touch door handles or anything which might have been on the floor because of his obsessional fears about germs, disease, and corruption. Nemiah (1980) and others have followed Lewis's suggestion, while Akhtar *et al.* (1975) used the dichotomy as their only basis of classification of compulsions. But this procedure would not appear to be particularly useful for classification purposes, since it is not based upon the direct observation of compulsions at all. It does not classify compulsions themselves but *inferences* drawn by the observer about their psychological functions, which is quite a different question. To classify compulsive behaviour, the first prerequisite is to describe the various behaviours. The crucial question is: "What is done?" The controlling/yielding approach tells us nothing about *what* is done.

It represents one possible answer to a very important, but quite different question: "*Why* is it done?"

The systematic classification of compulsions requires, it is suggested, at least two steps, subsequent to the determination of what behaviours are in question (i.e., the application of the criteria). The first step is to describe what is being done in each case—to produce an account of the actual physical behaviour manifested by each individual in a sample of compulsive people. The second step is to attempt to find communalities among the array of descriptions. Obviously, the most satisfactory system of classification would be one which employed clear, operational definitions, and achieved maximal economy in the number of classes derived, but which was capable of encompassing all individual cases. But its most important feature would be that it grouped the descriptions in a plausible, logically consistent, and clinically useful manner.

Like other workers, the present writer has failed to develop a fully satisfactory system of classification. But in my experience, the compulsive behaviours most commonly described can be grouped under the following headings:

(a) *Checking*. One of the several dictionary definitions of the word "check" is "test, examine accuracy of." In the present context it is used in reference to re-examinations and re-doings avowedly for the purpose of ensuring that some action has in fact been carried out correctly or that some desired state of affairs exists. We shall devote a later chapter to a discussion of compulsive checking, but for now let us note that it is usually applied to the execution and completion of routine activities, generally ones related to security, orderliness, and accuracy. The most well-known examples are those of checking that locks and bolts have been secured, that gas taps, electric switches, and water faucets have been turned off, and that appliances have been correctly adjusted or switched off. Subjects aver that such checking is in the interests of the security and safety of the home or premises. The search for orderliness is represented by checking that such possessions as clothes, toilet items, household effects, tools, and equipment are "appropriately" arranged or housed. The need for accuracy is reflected in the checking of columns of figures, tables, and totals, and the re-examination of accounts, bills, cheques, and vouchers. Similarly, the subject may anxiously re-examine his own statements and repeatedly check his recollections, as though unsure of their accuracy. Unfortunately, a single check seldom satisfies the obsessional person and may initiate a weary round of checking and re-checking.

Examples of the types of compulsive checking which are most commonly reported would include that of Mr. N., who was unable to go to bed until he had repeatedly checked all the household locks, bolts, and switches, a task which took him at least an hour. Mrs. E. found it necessary to check the results of her domestic chores exactly seven times. The daily work of Mr. U., a local government officer, was increasingly impeded by his need to check and re-check ledger entries and schedules of routine visits. Mrs. R. kept a detailed diary, which she would consult after every clinical interview "to check that what I told you was accurate."

Such examples of compulsive checking as those cited above are by far the most usual. They appear on the surface to be gross exaggerations of the sensible precautions of many normal people and could be taken to be simply reflections of unduly heightened conscientiousness. They are prosaic in their content and are seldom reported as "presenting symptoms." They can be readily rationalized by subjects, although their compulsive quality can cause inconvenience, irritation, and occupational handicap. But checking can also occur in more bizarre contexts, in association with compulsive rituals and obsessional doubts and fears. Mr. D. had to check at regular intervals each day that his imagined "victims" were alive and well. Mrs. P. continually checked her doorsteps, paths, and lawn for any signs of animal excrement. Mrs. F. checked with local hospitals, police, and newspapers that no drug-connected catastrophe had occurred in the region.

(b) *Motor Rituals*. The present writer has some reservations about the loose use of this term in the literature, but it has become conventional and so will be employed here. It is used in reference to repetitive, patterned acts of a stereotyped kind, especially where the repetitions comply with some formulaic or numbering system. The latter are taken to be selected on the basis of "magical" or superstitious beliefs, which is why the word "ritual" was introduced. The compulsive acts involved may be trivial, prosaic, and unobtrusive, such as Mr. L.'s compulsion to flick doorjambs with his fingers. This he had to do four times as he walked through any doorway. Mr. U. had been compelled since his schooldays to "round off" the full stops in anything he wrote, by lightly drawing three circles around each stop. Miss I. had to cross and uncross her fingers three times after completing such tasks as posting a letter or clearing her desk.

The acts may be bizarre, as in the case of Mr. I., whose compulsive rituals included turning round in the street three times, while intoning: "I am myself!" It may be noted in passing that such public display is unusual, since obsessionals tend to be reserved and secretive about their problems. Those afflicted by compulsions try to conduct them in private or disguise their activities to prevent them from attracting attention. Thus, Mrs. R., who was crippled by fears, ruminations, and hand-washing and a variety of motor rituals, appeared to the casual observer to be a poised, cheerful, and well-integrated person. She maintained this appearance by skilfully masking her rituals when in public. For instance, she was compelled to touch a locket three times with each finger and thumb on certain occasions. She would prevent this activity from being noticed by keeping the locket at the bottom of her handbag, in which she would rummage on the pretext of searching for her cigarette lighter.

As with what we termed earlier "mental rituals," motor rituals seem to be employed as distractive, defensive, or aversive measures of the kind described above as "controlling compulsions." Subjects report that they engage in them

to distract their attention from disturbing thoughts or situations, to defend themselves from feared eventualities, or to avert the occurrence of such eventualities.
Everyday parallels in normal people include such superstitious habits as throwing
a pinch of spilled salt over one's left shoulder or crossing one's fingers when
walking beneath a ladder.

(c) *Avoidance Behaviour.* These are activities engaged in to avoid feared objects, places, or situations. The fears are usually phobic, and so are preoccupying
in the absence of the anxiety-provoking stimulus or even when the appearance
of the latter is impossible. The psychological function of avoidance behaviour
is thus the same as that of motor rituals but its manifestations are different,
inasmuch as the behaviour does not show ritualistic features. It includes geographical avoidance, achieved by the selection of "safe" routes or locations.
Thus, Mr. B. could move about his neighbourhood only by prescribed routes,
to avoid crowds and the spirit of his grandmother. Sometimes geographical
avoidance cuts out all possible routes, and the subject is unable to leave home
at all. For example, Mrs. P.'s fear of dogs prevented her going far from home
except by car or public transport, while Mrs. K.'s similar fear of dogs was so
intense that she would not venture out of the house. Mrs. S. was also unable to
leave her home, but in her case the problem she was avoiding was a phobic fear
of travel itself.

In some cases, the avoidance behaviour is not geographical *per se*, but responds
to the probabilities of the feared stimulus, e.g., in certain occupations. Thus,
Mrs. G. found herself compelled to leave various jobs as a result of her fears
of contamination. In other cases, simple avoidance is involved: The subject
refuses to touch or approach certain objects. Mrs. O.'s phobic fears prevented
her from touching electrical appliances and switches.

In a few cases the avoidance behaviour is not so clearly motoric. Subjects
may hide, panic, or faint at the mere possibility of the dreaded occurrence. Mrs.
S. was often compulsively unable to swallow food for fear of developing a lump
in her throat.

(d) *Arranging Objects.* Obsessional people often experience a compulsive need
to arrange or order objects in the environment. The ordering may derive originally
from rational judgements as to the most efficient or convenient layout of tools,
spare parts, or domestic utensils. Or it may have some apparent aesthetic origin,
related to symmetry and balance in the positioning of crockery, books, or pictures. Alternatively, it may be quite idiosyncratic and may involve enforcing
some arbitrary regulation which has no conceivable basis in pragmatic convenience or aesthetic preference, even for the subject himself. As noted above, this
compulsive arrangement may be subsequently compulsively checked. To the
observer, compulsive arranging appears identical with the activities of normal,
tidy-minded people. The major difference is the accompanying experience of

compulsivity; but the subjective prescriptions to which the compulsive arranger adheres are usually more precise, stringent, and rigid than those of the most house-proud of normal persons. At the same time, the distress and frustration experienced by the obsessional person as the result of non-compliance is of a different order from the irritation felt by the normal, tidy person. The obsessional person feels profoundly disturbed by any deviation from his prescribed order and feels compelled to re-impose the *status quo*. For example, Mrs. H. arranged the contents of her front room in a precise manner; any deviation was regarded by her as confirmatory evidence of her wickedness in the eyes of God. Mrs. E. arranged her household objects with meticulous precision and according to a fixed routine, checking the completion of her chores seven times.

(e) *Washing and Cleaning*. A majority of cases under this heading are ones of hand-washing. But instances do arise of the compulsive washing of clothes, teeth-cleaning, or the cleaning of possessions or parts of the home, such as the lavatory, wash-basins, or doorsteps.

Hand-washing is a well-known, indeed classical, example of compulsive behaviour. It is easily identifiable and is referred to in most psychiatric textbooks. But it has not been well described, presumably because few psychiatrists have personally observed the activity itself. It is a much more complex phenomenon than is generally realized, and some of its components rightfully figure under other headings, particularly that of "motor rituals." It has been made a category here, it must be admitted, simply because of its fame and conventional usage. We shall discuss hand-washing in more detail in a later chapter.

Unlike washing and cleaning in normal life, the compulsive versions are not carried out simply because of the presumed degree of dirtiness of the object in question or the length of time since it was last washed. If there is a criterion of "washing need," it is subjective, rather than objective; indeed, far from being objectively perceived to be soiled, the object in question may never be allowed an opportunity to get dirty. For example, both Mrs. R. and Mrs. G. spent most of their waking hours in washing their hands. Mrs. G. spent only about fifteen minutes on each occasion, but would return to the washbasin forty to fifty times each day. Mrs. R. washed her hands only five times each day, but each washing took between three and four hours. Each lady not only scrubbed her hands until they were raw but insisted upon immersing them in undiluted disinfectant. At certain times, each wore protective gloves; the gloves themselves had to be washed compulsively. In each case, the washing was subject to complex rituals, numbering, and checking. Any deviation from the "correct" procedural order was penalized or compensated for by prescribed numbers of repetitions of the segment of activity in question. Thus, compulsive washers differ from normal washers not only in their criteria for determining when to wash, but also in their criteria for determining how the washing should be done and when the task has been satisfactorily completed.

(f) *Counting and Numbering.* Although considered here under a separate heading, these behaviours might equally well be classed as sub-categories of "motor rituals." But the behaviour involved—the vocal enunciation of sequences of numbers—is consistent and readily identifiable, and its appearance in at least a small number of cases seems to justify the allocation of a discrete category. The category subsumes at least three uses of counting, presumably reflecting different psychological functions. The first involves the counting aloud of objects, of steps in some activity, or of words in a sentence. A normal parallel might be the ticking off of one's fingers to prevent the forgetting of any steps in an argument. The second is the counting aloud which precedes the initiation of a sequence of actions. A normal parallel is the saying of "One ... two ... three—Go!" to signal the commencement of a race or other timed task or competition. Another example is the use of the same phrase to summon up fortitude prior to an activity, e.g., plunging into cold water. The third usage does not seem to have been described or even identified in the literature, except by the present writer (Reed, 1968). It involves what might be called the "numbering off" of segments of behaviour or thought. It appears to represent attempts to structure the on-going flow of experience by introducing punctuation or emphases. For example, Mr. C. found it necessary to "do things by numbers" when engaging in such toilet activities as brushing his hair or teeth. Mrs. G. differentiated quite clearly between her "counting" and her "numbering." She used the word "numbering" in reference to the first two usages above: "I say, ONE I've eaten the meal, TWO I've put my knife down, THREE I've put my fork next to it, FOUR I've pushed my chair back. ... My numbering helps me to be *decisive.* ... " Her "counting" she described as: "when numbers run through my head like tunes in other people's heads. ... "

(g) *Tics and Stammers.* These are often mentioned in the literature, although, of course, it must not be assumed that compulsivity marks all such cases.

(h) *Miscellaneous.* This heading is an admission of the limitations of the present classificatory system, because it covers those compulsive acts which are not readily classifiable under the main headings. These are often morbid exaggerations of habits and mannerisms which are quite common in normal life, where they do not bear the hallmarks of compulsivity. Examples would include compulsive finger-clicking and jerky speech. But some compulsive actions can be bizarre or grotesque, though not ritualized or avoidant and unrelated to checking. For example, Mr. J. found himself compelled to pick up such detritus as discarded bottle-tops and slivers of broken glass.

As with modes of obsessions, there exists considerable *overlapping* among the above categories. The "checking" and "motor rituals" categories overlap, because, as we have seen, checking itself is often ritualized. To achieve some resolution of his doubts, the obsessional may feel driven to conduct a given number of re-checks after the initial check. Or he may find it necessary to check in a certain order, perhaps followed by various permutations of the sequence. For example, Mr. N. would spend at least an hour before retiring in checking the refrigerator door, the oven gastaps, the heating appliances, locks and catches on three doors and numerous windows, and all electric light switches, in that order. If the order was disturbed or his attention was distracted, he would find it necessary to start all over again. But this time he would have to complete the whole sequence three times. If any doubts arose during the re-check, he would do everything again five times but in reverse order. As this involved turning the lights on again to see the locks and switches, he would be assailed by agonies of doubt and indecision, often finding it necessary to get up in the middle of the night to check upon his re-checking. But this involved switching on the lights again. ...

Again, there is an overlap between ritualization and compulsive washing, because the latter almost invariably involves intricate patterning and predetermined sequences of movements. For example, Mrs. R.'s hand-washing was a highly patterned complex of refined behaviours, involving particular movements made various times in a specified order and according to different rhythms. As with Mr. N., any deviation led to compensatory repetitions a prescribed number of times, these differing according to the stage which had been reached in the sequence.

As will have been noted in the examples cited above, there are also overlaps between the ''arrangement'' category and both ritualization and checking, while there are obvious relationships between the ''counting'' category and ritualization, checking, and washing.

Again, just as with modes of obsessions, the problem arises of *multiple* compulsions. Two-thirds of the patients in the present series suffered from more than one compulsion, as indicated by the fact that eighty-four types of compulsion were shared by only thirty-six individuals. The extreme examples were those of Mrs. R. and Mrs. G. The latter's presenting symptom was compulsive hand-washing. But, as in the case of Mrs. R., each washing session was preceded by the compulsive arranging of the soap, disinfectant, nail-brush, and towel. The arrangement was then submitted to compulsive checking. Her washing was highly ritualized and involved counting and numbering. At all times, including the washing sessions, she compulsively avoided contact with any of a variety of objects which she classified as dirty or contaminating. To complete the picture, she suffered when tense from compulsive facial twitches and a slight stutter.

An interesting fact which should be noted is that compulsive acts are almost never anti-social. Indeed, the writer is not aware of a single report of truly compulsive behaviour involving serious misconduct. Occasionally, such a report does appear; but on close examination it transpires that the behaviour in question does not show the hallmarks of compulsion. Compulsive behaviour is often bizarre or grotesque, but it is not violent, threatening, or criminal. This has been confirmed by the majority of authoritative writers. Thus, Freud (1896) observed that compulsive acts never involve aggression. Jaspers (1963) was equally definite: "Often individuals who are experiencing such phenomena will comply with these urges, when they are harmless (e.g. move chairs, swear, etc.), but they will successfully resist criminal urges or those with distressful consequences, e.g. murder of a child, suicide ... " (p. 136).

Schneider (1958), after commenting upon the misuse of the word "compulsion" in criminal court proceedings, states: "True compulsive behaviour is practically never punishable behaviour" (p. 96). Similarly, Anderson (1964) concludes: "If urges are relatively harmless like checking, washing or similar rituals the patients normally give in. If they are dangerous like murderous impulses, urges to attack people, set fire to things, etc., the patients oppose them successfully" (p. 27).

In summary, while obsessional thoughts may include content of an aggressive, hostile, or perverted nature, they appear to be never acted upon or put into effect by compulsive behaviour. But a note of caution must be sounded here. All the above observations apply to compulsive behaviour in obsessional neuroses (where obsessions and compulsions are the predominant features) or in obsessional personality disorders. But, as we have seen, obsessions and compulsions appear as subordinate features in other disorders or conditions. In the context of a severe depression, a compulsion to commit suicide and/or murder one's spouse or children may well be put into effect in the absence of appropriate treatment and care.

Of the fifty patients in the present series, thirty-six complained of compulsions. Only two of these suffered from compulsions alone; the remainder suffered from combinations of obsessions and compulsions. Those showing compulsive behaviour complained of 84 compulsions. The distribution of these compulsions among the various categories is presented in Table 4.1.

As observed earlier, the Akhtar et al. (1975) study used a simple dichotomous grouping of compulsive modes according to function. The only other objective examination of compulsion frequency known to the writer is that of Stern and Cobb (1978) This is a most interesting study, which gives the frequencies of types of compulsions among a sample of forty-five patients diagnosed as suffering from obsessional neurosis. (It is to be presumed that all members of the sample displayed compulsions although, oddly enough, this is not mentioned in the study.) Eight "sub-divisions" were derived from the literature and clinical experience: (a) Repeating; (b) Checking; (c) Cleaning; (d) Avoiding; (e) Slowing; (f) Striving for Completeness; (g) Being Meticulous; and (h) Other. Unfortunately, the authors do not define these class headings, offering instead an illustrative example of each. Using these examples it would appear that the "Checking,"

Table 4.1
The Distribution of Compulsions Across Categories

Types of Compulsions	Numbers Reported	Percentage of Total Types (Rounded)	Percentage of Individuals (Rounded)
Checking	20	24	56
Motor Rituals	15	18	41
Avoidance Behaviour	17	20	47
Arranging Objects	11	13	31
Washing	8	10	22
Counting	6	7	17
Tics and Stammers	5	6	14
Other	2	2	6
Totals	84	100	234

"Cleaning," "Avoiding," and "Other" categories are exactly the same as those used here. The "Repeating" category appears to refer to what we have termed "Counting and Numbering" (a more precise title, it might be suggested, because the behaviours in question are certainly not simply of a repetitive nature.) The "Being Meticulous" category seems to be exactly the same as what we have termed "Arranging Objects." This leaves two categories which are not represented among our headings—"Slowing" and "Striving for Completeness." The first derives from Rachman (1974) who has emphasized what he terms "primary obsessional slowness." This category has not been used here, because it does not seem to be specific, being simply a feature of much obsessional thinking and behaviour. Nor would it appear to be primary; it is an understandable result of the ruminative thinking and indecisiveness which are characteristic of obsessional disorder. In the same way, Stern and Cobb's "Striving for Completeness" refers to the *sentiment d'incomplétude*, which characterizes much obsessional experience and which underlies in particular our "Checking," "Motor Rituals," and "Counting" behaviours.

Stern and Cobb report the frequencies of the various modes in the form of percentages of patients: (a) Repeating, 40%; (b) Checking, 38%; (c) Cleaning, 51%; (d) Avoiding, 51%; (e) Slowing, 4%; (f) Completeness, 11%; (g) Meticulous, 9%; (h) Other, 4%

As with the present findings, Stern and Cobb found multiple compulsions to be quite prevalent. They also acknowledge overlapping among categories, observing that: "It is important to note that each behavioural form was not exclusive."

Reference to Table 4.1 will show that pronounced discrepancies exist between the findings of Stern and Cobb and those of the present study in all categories except "Avoidance Behaviour." These discrepancies doubtless reflect differences in definition, coupled with the fact that Stern and Cobb did not differentiate a "Motor Rituals" category. This was the third most highly frequented category in the present study.

What does seem somewhat surprising about Stern's and Cobb's findings is that just over a half of their sample engaged in compulsive washing, a finding which can hardly be attributed to differences in definition or identification. What is more likely is that this high proportion of washers was a result of referral practices and the fact that their patients were highly selected. The sample was drawn from patients especially referred by other psychiatrists and general practitioners for participation in a Medical Research Council investigation, whereas the present series was composed of patients routinely referred for treatment.

5
Compulsive Personality Disorder

So far in this book we have been examining obsessions and compulsive actions. These are regarded as *symptoms*—manifestations of some underlying pathology or dysfunction. The phenomena have remained perplexing and intractable and so continue to intrigue both practising clinicians and theorists. But the problems involved in studying compulsive experience are as nothing compared with those to be met in approaching compulsive personality disorder, to which we must now turn.

Typical of the confusion surrounding this topic is the question of what the disorder in question should be called. It has been variously designated as: "The Obsessional Personality," "The Obsessive Personality," "Obsessional Style," "Obsessional Personality Disorder," "Compulsive Personality Disorder," "The Anal Character," "The Anal–Erotic Character," and "Anankastic Personality Disorder," as well as variants and combinations of these. The origins of some of these terms will be traced later in this book. Meanwhile, it may be noted that there seem to be no significant differences between their referents. In other words, these are merely different labels for the same thing—a personality structure characterized by certain *traits*. We shall employ the label "Compulsive Personality Disorder," simply because that is the one used in the third edition of the A.P.A. *Diagnostic and Statistical Manual* (*DSM*III). And purely for convenience we shall employ Schneider's (1958) term "anankast" to refer to an individual with a compulsive personality disorder.

Of much more crucial importance than the question of terminological preference is the depressing fact that no clear operational definition of the personality disorder has yet evolved. As we have seen, obsessions and compulsions can be fairly readily identified by applying three formal criteria. No such precise criteria exist for defining the compulsive (or any other) personality disorder. Many descriptions have been published, of course, but these consist merely of lists of adjectives referring to personality traits and typical behaviours. Sometimes these

44

attributes are incorporated in a thumb-nail sketch of a composite, fictitious individual of the type in question. There are all sorts of conceptual, semantic, mensurational, statistical, and methodological problems inherent in attempting to apply this approach with any consistency in the examination of individuals. We shall defer discussion of some of these problems to the next chapter. Meanwhile, as Ingram (1961a) has suggested, we can provisionally define the compulsive personality simply in terms of what psychiatrists say it is. Unfortunately, not all psychiatrists say the same thing. The variations are largely a matter of emphasis, reflecting different theoretical assumptions. There are also semantic and connotative problems which will be discussed in some detail in a later chapter. But there remains a common core of agreement. And concatenations of the traits in question are in fact regularly reported by practising clinicians.

The main purpose of this chapter is to collate and briefly discuss the traits (attributes, characteristics) most commonly accepted as being among the constituents of the compulsive personality disorder. The list has been drawn from a wide variety of sources, including psychiatric textbooks, medical reference books, and clinical reports. But in each case at least one "primary source" authority is cited, and no attribute has been included which has not been mentioned by more than one authority. A few attributes have been excluded because it is impossible to say whether they are *traits* or *symptoms*. These are of interest in themselves, and will be discussed later in the book.

Accuracy

One of the components of the anankast's fussiness is his insistence upon accuracy—in the completion of tasks, in descriptive accounts and recollections, in plans and instructions. Typically, he goes to great trouble to ensure that any task he undertakes is carried out with meticulous care even when this may not be justified. Thus, in filling out a form or questionnaire he will comply with agonizing precision, requesting elaboration of the instructions, raising semantic quibbles, and refusing to be rushed. Jones (1918) points out that this tendency commonly leads to "undue pedantry," with a fondness for very precise definitions and exactitude.

In the same way, obsessional patients who are asked to give their personal history will often reply at inordinate length and in quite unnecessary detail, feeling a need to provide exact locations, dates, and often times of apparently insignificant events. Accuracy, of course, is very valuable in appropriate contexts, as Monroe (1974) points out.

Intolerance of Ambiguity

The term "intolerance of ambiguity" has been used by psychologists in descriptions of the anankast and thus stands as a characteristic in its own right.

Logically, however, it is merely the opposite way of expressing the need for precision, a trait which appears later in this list. If there are differences, they appear to be merely ones of emphasis or application.

The anankast is irritated or disturbed by tasks, information situations, or social relations which do not lend themselves to order and distinct parameters. Instructions must prescribe for every situation with legalistic nicety. Plans must be detailed and cover every exigency. The leaving of loopholes or provision for improvisation causes anankasts frustration and impatience. They strive for clarity, definition, and clear-cut boundaries. Mental problems or arguments which are not amenable to "either-or" answers are intolerable. This characteristic is discussed by Salzman (1973).

High Level of Aspiration

This is another of the crucial characteristics of the anankast. To the discrepancy between his aspirations and his abilities Schneider (1958) ascribes the feeling of inner inadequacy which is the hallmark, and in a sense the basis, of his "insecure psychopath" group. The discrepancy in any given situation promotes tension and self-annoyance which act as a continual drive to further activity. The anankast is reluctant to "give up" until he has mastered even a relatively unimportant task. In cognitive tasks nothing less than complete success or "A" grades will satisfy him. This is one aspect of what is normally described as his perfectionism (q.v.).

Concentration

The anankast usually has high powers of concentration; his singlemindedness is reflected in his application to tasks of all kinds. He is far less open to distraction than most people and more capable of rivetting his attention on the job in hand. In certain circumstances this may, of course, be inappropriate, depending upon the nature of the task. Some tasks may be carried out automatically, and their performance does not justify total conscious attention; others may require vigilance for a variety of possible environmental changes or feedback. Gutheil (1949) observes that the obsessional patient's intention is to achieve complete concentration on a particular thought, to the exclusion of all other ideas. The impossibility of this implies that a constant struggle accompanies the process of thinking. The anakast will claim that he or she "likes to do things one at a time and do them thoroughly." This focussing of energy can be maintained for what seems to the observer surprisingly long periods. Clearly, this characteristic is closely associated with conscientiousness (q.v.) and persistence (q.v.).

Conscientiousness

"Conscientious" is defined (S.O.E.D.) as "1. Obedient to conscience; habitually governed by a sense of duty; scrupulous. ..." In one sense, conscientiousness is the positive form of scrupulosity (*q.v.*). The latter involves doubts about the morality or propriety of thoughts or deeds. The former simply refers to thinking or doing in conformity with moral precepts and sense of duty. And this conformity with ethical and social codes is reported to be typical of anankasts. They are marked by a sense of duty, undertaking tasks seriously and with a somewhat exaggerated sense of responsibility. They are strict taskmasters, both with themselves and with others. Their moral standards are strict and they may be prudish and unforgiving in their judgements of others. (Ironically, however, their personal behaviour may not be so marked by rectitude, especially where sexual mores are concerned. The clinical literature is replete with accounts of the turbulent and often perverted sexual behaviour of obsessional patients.)

Control

A well-documented characteristic of the anankast is his control, the restraint he exerts upon his feelings, his behaviour and, where possible, his fellows and the environment. Indeed, Salzman (1973) conceptualizes a variety of anankastic traits as the products of control exerted in several spheres. This approach would apply to a number of the attributes listed here, including discipline, rules, order, inflexibility, and thoroughness.

Stress on Trivial Details

Clinicians often notice that anankasts tend to "dot every i and cross every t," a tendency associated with the search for precision (*q.v.*), scrupulosity (*q.v.*), and perfectionism (*q.v.*). The characteristic results in what to the observer seems to be an absurd emphasis on trivial detail or on considerations which are not of central relevance to the issue in question. The anankast seems driven to take into account every factor which might have some bearing, however indirect or peripheral, on a current task or problem. This proliferation of factors blinds him to the main issue. Typically, he "fails to see the wood for the trees," while his uncertainty leads to yet further extension of the web of detail. Fenichel (1945) refers to this tendency as "displacement onto a small detail"; in psychoanalysis, he claims, these small and insignificant things turn out to be substitutes for important ones. Rado (1974) provides several good examples of the "specializing ... in trifles."

Discipline

Several authorities, including Mayer-Gross *et al.* (1954), have stressed the anankast's predilection for control (*q.v.*), acknowledgment of societal hierarchies, and abidance by regulations. He attempts to exert the same control over subordinates as he does over himself, often being regarded as tyrannical by his subordinates and subservient by his supervisors. His loyalty to any institution for which he works and his adherence to its precepts is unquestioning. Obviously, such traits are closely related to his liking for order (*q.v.*), rules (*q.v.*), his conscientiousness (*q.v.*) and reliability (*q.v.*), and to a lesser extent his inflexibility (*q.v.*) and thoroughness (*q.v.*).

There seem to be at least two components of this trait: a preference for hierarchical structures and clear "chains of command" and a liking for and response to orders and regulations. Both of these may be seen as facets of orderliness (*q.v.*).

Doubts

Doubt or uncertainty is stressed as a predominant characteristic of anankasts by practically all writers on the subject, including Lange (1927) and Stekel (1927).

Janet (1903) describes beautifully the agonies of doubt—*la manie du doute*—which he regarded as the central feature of obsessionality. Anderson (1964) describes compulsive ideas as being characterized by oscillation between belief in some psychic content and the knowledge that it is not true. The patient ruminates: "What if ... ?"

Inconclusiveness

Inconclusiveness can be defined as the failure to experience a sense of completion. It involves uncertainty and a lack of satisfaction that a question has been answered appropriately, that events have run their course, that a job has been done or a dilemma resolved. Matters are not felt to be rounded-off or concluded. This experience of dissatisfaction has not been studied closely by English-language authorities, but it is mentioned by most writers as a central experience in both obsessional states and compulsive personalities. Ingram (1961b) cited the word "inconclusive" as appearing twelve times in his sample of textbook descriptions, being the fourth most commonly cited characteristic of the obsessional personality.

For Janet (1903), what he termed *"les sentiments d'incomplétude"* was a central feature of obsessionality. It is described as one of the three groups of *"les stigmates psychasthenique."* There he discusses it in detail, identifying its existence in four areas—action, intellectual operations, emotions, and personal perception. Frequent references to the concept are made throughout his study.

Indecisiveness

The indecisiveness of anankasts is notorious, both in lay parlance and in the professional literature. Prior to making a decision or choice, they are wont not only to painstakingly marshal the relevant evidence but also to be over-meticulous in their consideration of it. Furthermore, they tend to make the situation unnecessarily elaborate by taking into account matters which are trivial or of only tenuous relevance to the task in hand. This tortuous process, which disregards the significance of the problem in question, makes them reluctant to arrive at a firm decision. They are painfully slow in so doing and clearly suffer agonizingly in opting for one alternative among several.

The problem is worse, of course, in fluid situations where variables are changing or unpredictable, or in ones upon which the obsessional is unable to impose order. And vicious circles develop, because indecisiveness itself breeds further indecisiveness. Affectively loaded situations—such as those which involve split loyalties, personal interests, and moral conflicts—will elicit extreme indecisiveness, with concomitant frustration and self-reproach leading to preoccupation, rumination, and distress.

All these features have been amply documented, ever since Janet's classical study (1903). And long before Janet's time, of course, accounts had been given of cases of gross indecisiveness which sound as though they would have been attributed nowadays to obsessional disorder. Janet (1903) discusses *le sentiment d'indécision* as a component of *les sentiments d'incomplétude*. Straus (1948) sees indecision as related to perfectionism (*q.v.*), the obsessional's actions being dependent upon "unrealizable expectations."

Meticulousness

"Meticulous" is defined as "timidly precise about details, slavishly accurate or correct or proper" (*P.O.D.*). Meticulousness is one of the attributes ascribed by Fenichel (1945) and by Rado (1974) to the obsessional. Clearly it is congruent with, or overlaps with, other anankastic attributes such as accuracy (*q.v.*), detail (*q.v.*), order (*q.v.*), precision (*q.v.*), and propriety (*q.v.*).

Obstinacy

Obstinacy or stubbornness means intractability and is generally taken to refer to an unwillingness or inability to change; it may range from mute pig-headedness through to aggressive defiance. Obstinacy was included by Freud (1908) in his well-known triad of anal traits. It has been discussed by many subsequent writers, including Jones (1918), Fenichel (1945), Monroe (1974), and Nemiah (1980). Most psychoanalytic writers have followed suit, but the trait is seldom mentioned by authorities of other persuasions. However, there is a clear overlap with rigidity (*q.v.*), inflexibility (*q.v.*), and persistence (*q.v.*), terms which are regularly employed by non-Freudians. The difference in adjectival usage presumably reflects either levels of analytic approach or connotative assumptions. "Obstinacy" emphasizes social behaviour, whereas "rigidity" has primary reference to cognitive or neural functioning. Connotatively, "obstinacy" has a pejorative flavour, whereas "rigidity" is relatively neutral.

Orderliness and Method

One of the most noticeable characteristics of the anankast's behaviour is the way in which he attempts to impose order and systematization on his life. In observable behaviour, this may be seen in his proclivity for working by rules (*q.v.*), his preference for routine (*q.v.*), formal arrangements and regularity, his social conformity, and his dislike of untidiness, mess, and laissez-faire approaches. His workday life tends to be carefully programmed, and his possessions must be arranged in a prescribed manner. This style of behaviour reflects attempts at orderliness and systematization in his thinking. The anankast seems to set himself rules by which he abides inflexibly for the most part. He likes to "have his ideas straight," he tackles mental tasks with a methodical approach, and he checks answers doggedly. He devises series of rigidly established touchstones for application to problems and moral issues. In all of this there figures his predilection for watertight categorization (*q.v.*) and a striving for classificatory boundaries, criteria, rules, and generalizations of a specificity and clarity to which everyday problems are seldom amenable.

Orderliness was postulated by Freud (1908) as one of the great triad of traits characterizing the anal–sadistic character. To the psychoanalyst it represents a displacement of the early obedience to parental demands relative to toilet training. In obsessionals, as Fenichel (1945) points out, it is a reaction formation, so that opposite modes of behaviour can break through in a paradoxical manner. At the same time, the obsessional's liking for orderliness subsumes an appreciation of *discipline* (*q.v.*), both for himself and for others. Thus, he usually adapts well to service in disciplined, hierarchical organizations, particularly the armed forces and the police.

There are two other aspects of orderliness which also lend themselves to certain occupational demands. Abraham (1923) alludes to the anal character's liking for "indexing and registering, in making up tabular summaries, and in all kinds of statistics." But the limitations of such proclivities must be borne in mind. They are of more advantage in the lower and middle ranks of bureaucracy than at higher, policy-making levels. As Straus (1948) and Rado (1974) observe, obsessional order is not only inflexible but seems to serve no purpose. To this should be added, however, that it *can* serve a purpose if it happens to make a good fit with occupational requirements (Monroe, 1974; Nemiah, 1980).

Over-categorization

Overlapping at the conceptual level with several of the other characteristics is the anankast's tendency to establish discrete and over-precise categories and concepts. Janet (1903) discusses false dichotomizing, which he terms "*la manie du tout ou rien*." Freud (1936) refers to compulsive systematizing as "a caricature of science" because it falsifies reality. Both authorities, of course, are making the point that in real life categories and concepts are seldom totally finite and discrete. The term "neurotic typing" has been applied to the tendency to classify ideas into virtually exclusive categories.

Patterning

Clinicians observe that just as anankasts attempt to categorize items of experience, so they attempt to enforce regularity and pattern upon them. In strictly cognitive spheres, this may be manifested in a striving to smooth or regularize items of information, ideas, or precepts. But the best-known and most often reported examples are in perceptual–motor activities involved in the arrangement and tidying (*q.v.*) of rooms and possessions. Items on desk-tops and the contents of wardrobes must be laid out in particular ways. The positions of pictures and mirrors are continually adjusted to ensure that they hang exactly in accordance with horizontal/verticality (Janet, 1903; Jones, 1918; Abraham, 1923). Thus, it may be argued that it is not patterning *per se* which has been observed, but the abidance by rules (*q.v.*) and precepts. Patterning may then be seen as one facet of the obsessional's search for order (*q.v.*) and regularity.

Pedantry

A "pedant" is defined (*P.O.D.*) as: "One who overrates or parades book-learning or technicalities or insists on strict adherence to formal rules, dry-as-dust, doctrinaire, red-tapist." This clearly overlaps with several other of our characteristics and certainly catches the flavour of a major aspect of obsessionality. It has been mentioned as typical of the anankast by Jones (1918), Schneider (1958), and Monroe (1974), among others.

Perfectionism

At all levels, from the performance of trivial tasks to his philosophical ruminations, the anankast may be regarded as striving for perfection. Many anankasts, in fact, complain that their besetting problem is their "perfectionism." As Anderson (1964) points out: "In particular perfectionism has its roots in this type of personality. It springs from the rigidity of such people, their lack of adaptability etc." Rado (1974) describes the obsessive as "the ultimate perfectionist." Jones (1918) and other psychoanalysts postulate that perfectionism is central to the anal character, as it symbolizes the act of defecation. Straus (1948) avers that it "serves to overcome the paralysis of action. ... perfectability alone permits action."

Perseveration

"Perseveration" is a technical term which should not be confused with "perseverance" or "persistence" (*q.v.*); it is defined by Warren (1935) as: "1. the tendency of a feeling, idea, act, or disposition to recur with or without the aid of associative tendencies; 2. the tendency of any mental formation, once initiated, to remain and run a temporal course; 3. (*path.*) the persistent repetition or continuation of a word, sentence, or action after it has been once begun or recently completed."

Thus, it bears reference to behaviour, without any etiological assumptions and certainly without any recourse to questions of will-power, determination, strength of character, etc. It is simply a term which describes objectively any mental or behavioural activity which runs on or recurs. It may be seen as rigidity (*q.v.*) expressed in on-going activity. Clinicians often apply the term "rigidity" to the patient's outlook, moral standpoint, or general attitudes; they use the term "perseveration" in reference to the patient's inability to modify methods in carrying out a task or to alter lines of approach in tackling a problem. (A more extreme version of perseveration is the passive repetition associated with brain damage.)

Persistence

This trait is described by most writers as characteristic of obsessional, anal, and anankastic style. Jones (1918) and Abraham (1923), among others, point out that intense persistence is manifested by the anal character, but often after prolonged procrastination. Abraham further comments that the anal character's perseverance is "largely used up in unproductive ways, dissipated in the pedantic observance of fixed forms. ... " The characteristic is related to high aspiration (*q.v.*), control (*q.v.*), discipline (*q.v.*), and reliability (*q.v.*). It is usually defined as "continuing to do something despite obstacles," which suggests the exertion of will-power and determination, unlike perseveration (*q.v.*).

Precision

The anankast prefers tasks, instructions, and situations which are well defined and clear cut. He is happiest in a regulated and determined situation where actions are prescribed by rules (*q.v.*) and precedents, as opposed to ones which may demand improvisation or intuitive responses. The characteristic then overlaps with meticulousness (*q.v.*), accuracy (*q.v.*), detail (*q.v.*), orderliness (*q.v.*), and rules (*q.v.*). It has been stressed as a trait by many writers, from Janet (1903) to Rado (1974).

Propriety

Propriety refers to the correctness of conduct. It includes, first, an awareness of what is socially prescribed and the details of decorum (the "proprieties"). Second, it implies the acceptance of these standards and adherence thereto. The anankast is usually described as being formal, conventional, and decorous in his bearing and as striving to conform with social prescriptions for "'proper'' conduct and attitudes. The characteristic thus accords well with his liking for rules (*q.v.*) and order (*q.v.*), his punctiliousness (*q.v.*), and his rectitude (*q.v.*). Janet (1903) stressed this aspect, as did Schneider (1925), while Fenichel (1945) has discussed it from the psychoanalytic viewpoint.

Punctiliousness

Punctiliousness refers to an emphasis on the minute observance of forms (of address, courtesy, honour, and ceremony). It subsumes conformity with, and obedience to, the nicer points of social behaviour, the emphasis being upon formal details. It is thus closely associated with propriety (*q.v.*), discipline (*q.v.*), rules (*q.v.*), detail (*q.v.*), order (*q.v.*), and rectitude (*q.v.*). Its association with the latter was noted by Schneider (1925) in his description of the insecure psychopath.

Punctuality

Punctuality is the observance of appointed time. It is mentioned specifically as one of the characteristics of the obsessional/compulsive personality by Fenichel (1945), Mayer-Gross *et al.* (1954), and Nemiah (1980). Several psychoanalytic writers have discussed the anankast's concern with time, and punctuality may be seen as the temporal dimension of order (*q.v.*), precision (*q.v.*), adherence to rules (*q.v.*), precision, (*q.v.*), and discipline (*q.v.*). It may be noted, however, that there has been some disagreement among authorities as to whether punctuality is in general a valued concept for the anankast, or whether his insistence that appointed times be strictly observed is restricted to the behaviour of others rather than to himself.

Rectitude

"Rectitude" may be defined as moral uprightness. Schneider (1925) emphasized high moral standards as being centrally characteristic of individuals of insecure personality. They judge themselves harshly by comparison with these standards, although they constantly attempt to behave with the utmost punctiliousness (*q.v.*). On the other hand, of course, it is possible to interpret correct behaviour as reflecting a sensitivity to the proprieties (*q.v.*) rather than expressing true rectitude. Thus, Fish (1964) describes, not anankasts' righteousness but their "self-righteous attitudes,'' a skeptical view which is shared by Salzman (1973)

Reliability

Freud (1908) referred to persons of "anal character" as "trustworthy." This is one way of describing an attribute characterized by consistency, steadiness, and predictability. In this sense of the word, anankasts have been described as reliable by Jones (1918), Mayer-Gross *et al.* (1954), and Nemiah (1980).

Rigidity, or the Inability to Shift

Closely related to the striving for order (*q.v.*) and routine (*q.v.*) is the regularly reported clinical finding that the anankast lacks flexibility—in thought, as in conduct. Having undertaken a task, he will see it through, becoming disturbed if forced to change his method or objectives or to leave anything undone. This in itself can be a most worthy and socially desirable attribute. But in the case of the anankast it must be stressed that this drive to completion may be counterproductive, because it does not allow for changing situational demands, where cessation or re-direction would be appropriate. Similarly, the anankast's manner of handling a task or approaching a problem is relatively unshifting, as is his general systematization and his ordering (*q.v.*) of the activity and the environment. Thus, at a number of levels the anankast may be reliable (*q.v.*) and effective; but he functions less efficiently, and with disturbance and indecisiveness (*q.v.*), if faced with change and the need for flexibility. His approach may thus be singularly maladaptive. Rigidity has been stressed particularly by Janet (1903), Anderson (1964), and Salzman (1973).

Routine

Closely related to his striving for order (*q.v.*) is the anankast's preference for tasks, situations, and programs of a structured and familiar type. Wherever possible he will himself impose regularity and definition upon his daily activities. Routine is referred to by Fenichel (1945) in the context of obsessional system construction, which he discusses at length.

Rules

The anankast's preference for order (*q.v.*) and discipline (*q.v.*) is reflected in his liking of, and subservience to, rules. He prefers rules and regulations to be precise (*q.v.*), detailed (*q.v.*), and inflexible. Janet (1903) mentions this characteristic on several occasions, and it has been highlighted by modern writers such as Rado (1974) and Monroe (1974).

Scrupulosity

"Scrupulous" is defined (*S.O.E.D.*) as: "1. Troubled with doubts or scruples of conscience; over-nice or meticulous in matters of right or wrong. 2. Prone to hesitate or doubt; cautious or meticulous in acting, deciding, etc. ... 3. Careful to follow the dictates of conscience; strict in matters of right and wrong ... 4. Of actions, etc.: Characterized by a strict and minute regard for what is right. ...''

The references to conscience serve to remind us that the adjective is derived from ''scruples,'' which were originally to do with ethical quibbles springing from questions of theological interpretation. And, indeed, until relatively recent times the content of anankasts' scrupulosity was commonly of a religious nature. The patients of both Janet and Freud were often concerned with whether their moral views and behaviour were strictly in accord with their religious dogmas. In modern times, the religious aspect has diminished, reflecting changes in social attitudes and preoccupations. But anankasts are still concerned with moral issues and with questions of rectitude (*q.v.*) and propriety (*q.v.*). The formal characteristic of scupulosity is the sense of unsurety which lies at the heart of Schneider's (1925) approach. This acts as an inhibitor of action, despite minute attention to precepts, which was beautifully described by Jeremy Taylor more than three hundred years ago.

Symmetry

Closely related to patterning (*q.v.*) is the anankast's need for balance and symmetry. He is disturbed by asymmetry and dissonance in perceptual input and will arrange objects in attempts to enforce balance. Ferenczi (1926) and Schilder (1935) discuss symmetry compulsion in terms of attempts to preserve mental equilibrium between instinctual eroticism and punitive control. Stekel (1927) notes that many compulsives try to do everything in a ''balanced'' way. For instance, the individual may feel that both legs must come out of bed at the same time. Stekel sees this as an expression of the ''bipolarity'' which he postulates as the basis of obsessional disorder.

Thoroughness

''Thoroughness'' here refers to the care taken in completing a task or engaging in a line of thought or action. It was regarded by Jones (1918) as an important aspect of the ''anal character,'' associated with efficiency and the desire for perfection (*q.v*). Monroe (1974) lists it as one of the anankastic traits having adaptive value. It may be seen as reflecting conscientiousness (*q.v.*), precision (*q.v.*), and adherence to rules (*q.v.*).

Tidiness and Neatness

Fenichel (1945) and Nemiah (1980) have stressed tidiness and neatness as being characteristic of the obsessional–compulsive personality. Several other psychoanalytic writers have mentioned these traits as components of one of Freud's triad—orderliness (*q.v.*). They may be taken to be behavioural expressions of the anankast's need for order (*q.v.*), his liking for rules (*q.v.*), and his preference for routine (*q.v.*) and are clear reflections of patterning (*q.v.*). It should be observed, however, that ever since Jones's (1918) study of the "anal character," clinicians have noted that anankastic tidiness is restricted to surface appearances. The top of the anankast's dressing table may be exceedingly clean and neat, objects upon it being arranged with fussy precision, but the interiors of the drawers may tell a different story, underwear and socks being crammed in quite haphazardly.

6
Compulsive Personality Disorder: Psychometric Studies

All we have done so far in regard to the compulsive personality is to list and describe a number of traits or characteristics which have been authoritatively judged to contribute to it. But clearly these judgements are quite subjective, being derived from the experiences of individual clinicians. Surely, it may be suggested, there must have been attempts to examine the topic in a more objective and scientific manner? There certainly have. In fact, although there have been relatively few psychological experiments carried out in relation to obsessionality, there have been an inordinate number of psychometric studies (usually employing some version of factor analysis) of the compulsive personality. Indeed, the sheer quantity of reports, combined with their frustrating inconclusiveness and the tedious nature of the material, have succeeded in blocking the present writer's virtuous intention of producing a critical review for well over a decade. Fortunately, there are others who do not share the same obsessional hang-ups, and the reader is referred to the painstaking review by Pollak (1979), who cites 114 references without nearly exhausting the relevant literature. However, the present writer reluctantly concluded that any attempt to survey the literature in the conventional manner would of necessity be so hedged about by qualifications as to make its conclusions scarcely worth the energy required of the reader to struggle through it.

Instead of a conventional overview, therefore, this chapter will be restricted for the most part to summary answers to a few central questions, and pointers to some of the more influential studies. This somewhat idiosyncratic format, it is hoped, will provide some orientation for the intrepid explorer who desires to gain access to the literature jungle. At the same time, it will offer some clarificatory reminders, indicate the methodological red herrings, and provide pointers to the conceptual snares and delusions, contradictions and confusions with which the field bristles. The chapter will conclude with a closer examination of one important paper, selected as a casebook microcosm of what the present writer sees as the sorts of problems which characterize the great majority of psychometric studies in this area.

MEASUREMENT OF THE PERSONALITY

QUESTION 1:   Have questionnaire items indicating the presence of the traits listed in the previous chapter been presented to subjects and the results subjected to statistical analysis?

ANSWER: No. No factor-analytic or other study has been reported which used items reflecting *all* the traits listed earlier.

QUESTION 2:   Have there been any such studies using *some* of the listed traits?

ANSWER: Yes—many (see, e.g., Cooper and Kelleher, 1972; Foulds, 1965; Kline, 1967; Lazare *et al.*, 1966; Paykel and Prusoff, 1973; Stone and Gottheil, 1975). Researchers have selected different combinations of the traits mentioned by different clinical authorities and produced for each trait a questionnaire item(s) presumed to elicit its presence or absence in the respondent.

QUESTION 3:   Have these proven the existence of a compulsive personality?

ANSWER: It all depends on what you mean. ... Factor-analytic techniques do not "prove" anything. They simply summarize data by indicating clusters of correlations. These clusters are the "factors" referred to in the titles of several associated techniques. In the same way, factor analysis cannot reveal some hidden truth. It can examine only such data as are submitted to it and examines them only in the sense of showing what goes with what.

QUESTION 4:   Have compulsive personality traits been shown to cluster together?

ANSWER: Yes. All studies have derived a relevant factor, and many of them two, three, four, or five varieties thereof.

[The reader will forgive being reminded once more that the results of factor analysis and associated techniques are entirely dependent upon the original data. If you put nothing but various types of tomatoes into your food processor, it may reasonably be assumed that some sort of tomato purée will emerge. When many of the items used in a factor-analytic study are to do with obsessionality, the factors which emerge will probably include at least one to which obsessional items have contributed. When *all* the items used are to do with obsessionality, then all the factors must also be to do with obsessionality. Conversely, if *no* obsessional items are included, then no emergent factor can be identified as obsessional.]

QUESTION 5: Does the fact that several factors have been derived in some studies mean that there are several types of compulsive personality?

ANSWER: Not really. It usually means that when all the items included are obsessional there is nothing else for a response to one given item to be correlated with except other obsessional items. However, the fact that certain patterns can emerge is of interest. For example, Comrey's (1965) "compulsion" factor was contributed to by several sub-groups: need for other (loading 0.72), liking for routine (0.62), drive to completion (0.61), meticulousness (0.55), cautiousness (0.53), personal grooming (0.35), and impulsiveness (-0.37). Orderliness has appeared as a factor in its own right in many other studies where non-obsessional items were included (e.g., Lazare et al., 1970). In their study of responses to their obsessionality inventory, Cooper and Kelleher (1970) derived three separate components: (a) concern with being clean and tidy; (b) a feeling of incompleteness; and (c) checking and repetition.

[One difficulty arises in considering such distinct factors or components. Do they represent sub-categories or variants of one personality type, or simply individual component traits? Much depends on the selection of the original items.]

QUESTION 6: Has the validity of any of these factors ever been established?

ANSWER: No, never. But there is a problem here. Validity studies would presumably require that the items were answered by respondents of known personality types. But those of compulsive personality could only be identified by the very subjective judgements that the psychometric exercise is intended to circumvent. Furthermore, the subjective judgements would be based upon the self-same items that are under study.

QUESTION 7: Is a measurement of obsessional–compulsive personality included in any of the major, established personality tests?

ANSWER: No.

QUESTION 8: Has the groundwork been done—have suitable sets of items been completed by large random or representative samples of the normal population?

ANSWER: No. This is an important question because, as we are dealing here with a hypothesized personality type, we are concerned with normal traits, not abnormal symptoms. Thus, findings drawn from large samples of normal individuals are indicated, and those samples should either be drawn at random or selected as representative cross-sections of the general population. Findings from psychiatric populations are necessary to answer other questions (e.g., those to do with symptomatology). But for this basic question, the inclusion of psychiatrically disturbed respondents may cloud the issue. Such a procedure introduces many intervening variables and invites such questions as: "To what extent do these responses reflect the respondents' underlying personality, as opposed to their current psychological disorders?"

In fact, the majority of subjects used in the studies under consideration here have been psychiatric patients. Some studies have recruited normal respondents, but these have been from quite non-representative groups such as university students (e.g., Kline, 1967) or soldiers (e.g., Gottheil and Stone, 1968). A notable exception has been the work of Cooper and Kelleher (e.g., 1972) but even their large groups of normal subjects have belonged to neither random nor representative samples.

QUESTION 9:   Are any tests or scales available which were designed specifically to measure the presence of compulsive personality traits?

ANSWER: Yes. The best-known and most reputable are: (a) The Hysteroid–Obsessoid Questionnaire or HOQ (Foulds, 1965); (b) The Lazare–Klerman Trait Scales (Lazare *et al.*, 1966); and (c) The Leyton Obsessional Inventory or LOI (Cooper, 1970).

THE ANAL CHARACTER

QUESTION 10: Has there been any empirical evidence for the existence of Freud's "anal character" as a separate entity?

ANSWER: Oddly enough, many, if not the majority, of factor-analytic studies in this area have been examinations of personality patterns derived from Freudian theory. Outcomes have been mixed and very difficult to interpret, largely because of the problems involved in determining the implications of specific items. Much depends on the criteria in use and what is to be regarded as acceptable evidence. Many studies have shown, for example, a relationship between orderliness and cleanliness. But this alone can scarcely be taken as evidence for the validity of the concept of anality.

[Presumably, each reader must decide for himself. As a matter of interest, Fisher and Greenberg (1977) have summarized the "Pro" view and Rachman and Hodgson (1980) the "Con."]

PERSONALITY AND PERSONALITY DISORDER

QUESTION 11:   Do any tests enable a distinction to be made between the "personality" and the "personality disorder"?

ANSWER: No. The tests (scales, questionnaires, inventories) are simply "scored" additively. Presumably the person suffering from a personality disorder possesses more traits or holds those he does possess with more intensity. But no evidence exists to validate this, so no score-criteria lévels have been developed.

QUESTION 12:   People display certain traits in an extreme degree but other traits only mildly. Is this allowed for in the studies and reflected in test "scores"?

ANSWER: No. Neither item-lists nor tests have allowed for the differential weighting of responses. In fact, almost all of them have required only binary answers—Yes or No, True or False. The possession of a trait has generally not been regarded as lying on a continuum, but only as being present or absent. This raises problems in the use of self-appraisal questionnaires, which have been discussed by Reed (1969a). As I pointed out, a severely anankastic patient with gross obsessional symptoms including protracted hand-washing would "score" 1 on the item: "I am 'fussy' about keeping my hands clean." But so would every normal, self-respecting physician or baker, for example.

COMPULSIVE PERSONALITY AND OBSESSIONAL NEUROSIS

QUESTION 13:   Is there any psychometric evidence that obsessional neurosis is more likely to appear in individuals of compulsive personality?

ANSWER: As we have seen, clinical observations and surveys (e.g., Ingram, 1961b; Rosenberg, 1967) have reported this, but two reviewers of the psychometric literature, Slade (1974) and Pollak (1979), claim that factor-analytic studies have demonstrated separate and independent trait and symptom factors. This assertion is largely based on a paper by Sandler and Hazari (1960), which is discussed by both Slade and Pollak with great respect and at considerable length. Both the Foulds group (Foulds, 1965) and Cooper and his associates (e.g., Cooper and Kelleher, 1972)

have made sterling contributions to the measurement of obsessional traits and symptoms, but neither group seems to have
studied this particular question. Rachman and Hodgson (1980)
have criticized the LOI because several of its "symptoms" items
could equally well be classified as "traits" (e.g., "Do you hate
dirt and dirty things?"). If you put onions and tomatoes into
your food processor, but insist on calling onions "tomatoes." ...

The present writer intends to finish this chapter in a way quite unlike what has
gone before, by considering the Sandler and Hazari (1960) article in some detail.
It is an appropriate subject for such attention for two reasons:(a) It is a minor
classic, the most influential and oft-cited report of its kind in this particular area;
and (b) It is a textbook example of what raises doubts in the writer's mind about
many psychometric studies—that sophisticated techniques are being employed
to study dubious basic data.

Let it be acknowledged immediately that the paper is impressive—a simple
yet elegant study, conceptually engaging, employing immaculate methodology
and reported with lucidity and grace. It may be summarized as follows: Sandler
and Hazari examined the responses of 100 neurotic patients to a personality
questionnaire. The latter was in fact the Tavistock Self-Assessment Inventory,
which consists of 867 statements, each of which the subject is required to mark
as "True" or "False" in regard to himself. Sandler and Hazari extracted 40 of
these statements which were regarded as having reference to compulsive character
traits and obsessional symptoms and subjected the data to factor analysis. Two
factors were identified, and the original items were then classified according to
their projection on two reference vectors, A and B, obtained through rotation of
the Centroid factor axes through 45°. The two groups of items represented "two
tendencies which, in their appearance in this group of patients, appear to be
more or less unrelated."

The A-type items (16 in all) include such statements as: "I take great care in
hanging or folding my clothes at night"; "I hate dirt or dirty things"; "I try to
be perfect in my work." Taken together they "present a picture of an exceedingly
systematic, methodical and thorough person, who likes a well-ordered mode of
life, is consistent, punctual and meticulous in his use of words. He dislikes half-
done tasks, and finds interruptions irksome. He pays much attention to detail
and has a strong aversion to dirt." As the authors point out this is very similar
to descriptions of the obsessional or anal-reactive character. The descriptive
statements are ego-syntonic, representing "traits of character which conform to
the possessor's ideal standards for himself."

The B-type items, on the other hand, all resemble the symptoms of obsessional
neurosis: "I am often inwardly compelled to do certain things even though my
reason tells me it is not necessary"; "I often have to check up to see whether

I have closed a door or switched off a light"; "I am troubled by bad and dirty thoughts." Taken together they suggest "a person whose daily life is disturbed through the intrusion of unwanted thoughts and impulses into his conscious experience. Thus, he is compelled to do things which his reason tells him are unnecessary, to perform certain rituals as part of his everyday behaviour, to memorize trivia, and to struggle with persistent 'bad' thoughts."

So far, Sandler and Hazari have neatly demonstrated: (a) a difference between a type of character bearing the hallmarks of what has been called "compulsive personality," "anal-reactive," or "anankastic"; (b) a constellation of symptoms which are obsessive-compulsive in type; and (c) that furthermore, the relative independence of the items on the two vectors suggests that obsessional/compulsive symptomatology has no direct association with compulsive personality structure.

However, the authors now proceed to speculations which lead to a *non sequitur*. After discussing the B-type items they conclude: "In spite of the obvious description of the items in this group as 'symptoms', one may wonder whether, in mild form, the pattern found here exists in patients who do not break down with an obsessional neurosis. ... If the picture presented here represents a personality type, which in exaggerated form might appear as obsessional neurosis, then it would seem legitimate to apply the description *obsessional personality* to this type of person."

Thus, having nicely established a distinction between "personality" and "symptoms" in the field of obsessional disorder, Sandler and Hazari proceed to label the symptom constellation as a personality type also, thus producing a trichotomy: (i) An anankastic or obsessional personality (A-type) which they term the *"reactive–narcissistic character"*; and (ii) "The true *obsessional* picture" (B-type), representing a continuum from obsessional personality or "chronic worrier" to (iii) "obsessional neurosis" or "obsessional state."

This classification may well fit the clinical facts and have nosological validity; as it happens, the present writer finds much to commend it. But the point here is that the step from a personality/symptom dichotomy to a personality 1/personality 2/neurosis classification is a doubtful extension from the empirical findings, which is nevertheless treated with the same certainty as the findings themselves. The validity of this speculative extension might readily have been demonstrated by examining the results of careful classified diagnostic groups. But—and here is the soft centre of the whole study—*the experimental group was not differentiated at all*. The material was collected from patients admitted to the Tavistock Clinic over a period of two years. Differential diagnoses were not taken into consideration: "The population studies consisted of the first 50 men and the first 50 women to complete the Inventory." The authors might defend their procedure by claiming that they were not primarily concerned with cross-validating clinical diagnoses, so that the identification of criterion sub-groups was irrelevant. But this argument can scarcely be maintained. If the population happened to be

composed of hysterics or attention-gaining psychopaths, for instance, the conclusions of the study could not be taken seriously. The results themselves would
still be interesting, but only in so far as they demonstrated self-deception or
simulation in the assumption of compulsive traits and symptoms by non-com-
pulsive patients.

The other way of stating the above criticism is that without classification of
the experimental group there can be no evidence that the Sandler–Hazari items
are valid in the first place. It has not been shown that they can, in fact, identify
patients suffering from obsessional disorder or differentiate those with compulsive personality structure from those displaying obsessional symptoms.

Sandler and Hazari were not attempting to construct a "test," but their item-
list was rapidly put to that use, which made its validity a question of immediate
importance. Orme (1965) reported that the mean scores of fifteen obsessional
patients and fifteen phobic patients on thirteen Sandler-Hazari B-type items were
almost identical. As for the items' ability to discriminate between obsessional
symptoms and traits, the present writer (Reed, 1969a) administered the scale to
sixty patients—twenty suffering from severe obsessional symptoms, twenty with
pre-morbid obsessional traits, and twenty non-obsessional controls. No significant differences were found between the groups on A-type items, B-type items,
or total sums. Similar negative findings have been reported by Snaith et al.
(1971) in a study of fifty depressives. Thus, however plausible and sophisticated
the Sandler–Hazari study, it is very doubtful whether it tells us much about
compulsive traits or obsessional symptoms.

7

The Natural History of Obsessional Disorder

In a prize-winning paper, Pollitt (1960) discussed the value of natural-history studies in the examination of mental disorders, using his own data regarding a series of obsessional patients for illustration. Briefly, a natural history of a mental disorder is an assembly of quantitative material describing the incidence of the disorder, its onset, characteristics of individuals suffering from it, its development and outcome, and other relevant factors. Special problems are encountered in applying this sort of approach to obsessionality. Not only are there the common methodological problems of sampling and control, but obsessional disorders are rare, tend to be confounded with other conditions, and lend themselves to misdiagnosis. To make matters worse, it is often difficult to make valid comparisons between studies, because different researchers have tended to apply different criteria and to use different categories in, for example, the assessment of therapeutic success rates. For many years only one follow-up study of a group of patients of reasonable size was published, this being Lewis's (1936) account of a series of fifty patients. Since the 1950s, however, a number of very competent English-language studies have appeared, including follow-up information—notably Pollitt (1960), Ingram (1961a, 1961b), Grimshaw (1965), Kringlen (1965), Skoog (1965), and Lo (1967). There have been some good reviews of this material, including Templer (1972), Black (1974), and Rachman and Hodgson (1980). The present chapter, then, will present only the most schematic of outlines of what is now a very substantial literature.

Ideally, it would have been desirable to offer parallel natural histories—one of obsessional–compulsive disorder (obsessional neurosis, state, etc.) and one of compulsive personality disorder. But this is impossible in practice because, while there is a plethora of data revelant to the first disorder, there have been literally no objective studies of the second. The compulsive (anankastic) personality has not been ignored; but unfortunately, its study has largely been limited to consideration of it as a concomitant or precedent of the neurosis or state.

INCIDENCE AND PREVALENCE

The findings of eleven studies published up to 1967 have been summarized in tabular form by Black (1974, p.21). About 3% of all neurotic patients are diagnosed as obsessional. Between 0.3% and 0.6% of psychiatric out-patients and between 3.5% and 4.5% of in-patients are so diagnosed. A major post-1967 demographic study by Hare *et al.* (1972) covering 846 in-patients from English and Welsh national statistics and 464 who had attended the Bethlem–Maudsley Hospital reported figures of the same order. The prevalence of obsessional disorders in the population at large is not really known, but Woodruff and Pitts (1964) and others have offered an estimate of 0.05%. Discrepancies probably reflect the fact that some hospitals and clinics specialize in particular disorders. Diagnostic conventions also vary, particularly between countries. This may explain why obsessional disorders seem to be more prevalent in Scandinavia (cf. Skoog, 1959; Kringlen, 1965), although admittedly real national differences may exist.

SEX RATIO

Several writers have suggested that more women than men suffer from obsessional disorders. But this may have reflected not only diagnostic referral practices but special factors such as hospital-bed availability, as in Ingram's (1961b) series, where 62% were female. Ingram (1961a) observed that the larger the group studied, the nearer the sex ratio approaches unity, which was supported by Black's (1974) summary of eleven studies. Of an overall total of 1336 cases, 651 were men and 685 were women, a ratio of 49 to 51, which suggests that women are not significantly more predisposed to obsessional disorder than men. However, there may well be sex differences in the *types* of obsessional disorder suffered. Rachman and Hodgson (1980) reported that in their series no less than 86% of the compulsive cleaners were women. This difference existed in the present series also, but not to the same dramatic extent; of 8 washer/cleaners, 5 were women, 3 were men. On the other hand, of the 19 cases in the present series which involved ruminations, 13 were men. Both these differences, of course, may be culturally determined.

SOCIAL CLASS

Reports that obsessional disorders are more prevalent among people from the middle and upper classes have received some slight support (e.g., Hollingshead and Redlich, 1958; Ingram, 1961b), but the major study by Kringlen (1965) reported no significant difference between obsessionals and controls where class was concerned. It is probable, in any case, that the question of class is confounded with those of intelligence, educational levels and verbal articulation.

FAMILY SIZE AND BIRTH ORDER

Snowdon (1979) studied the case histories of 156 obsessional neurotics, comparing them with 1000 matched controls. The mean family size of the obsessionals was smaller than that of the controls. Among the male obsessionals, significantly more were first-borns.

INTELLIGENCE

The intellectual characteristics of obsessionals will be considered in detail in Chapter 18. For the present, it may be noted that the majority of authorities have asserted that obsessionals are of superior intelligence. This judgement has been based, of course, upon clinical impressions; but there has been some objective, psychometric evidence which supports it. Most often cited are the findings of Slater (1945), who reported that the scores of twenty-five obsessional neurotics on Raven's Progressive Matrices were significantly higher than those of anxiety neurotics, hysterics, and mixed neurotics. The same results were found, using Cattell's 2A and 2B intelligence tests and the Shipley vocabulary test. Ingram (1961b) compared the performance of seventy-six obsessionals with those of anxiety neurotics and hysterics on Raven's test and the Mill Hill vocabulary test, with substantially the same result. But in the present writer's opinion, such findings of the superior intelligence of obsessionals may simply reflect biased sampling due to referral practices. My own survey (Reed, 1966) indicated that the WAIS IQs of obsessionals were not significantly different either from those of matched psychiatric controls or the published standardization norms.

MARITAL STATUS AND FERTILITY

Ingram (1961b), in his survey of 89 obsessional in-patients compared with 100 hysterics and 100 anxiety neurotics, found that 68% of the men and 40% of the women were single, giving an overall celibacy rate of 51%. This is significantly higher than that for the anxiety neurotics (27%) but not than that for the hysterics (48%). These figures, in particular the high celibacy rate for men, have been confirmed in several other studies. An exception is that of Kringlen (1965), which reported quite low celibacy rates (40% for men and 39% for women). However, as Black (1974) has pointed out, Kringlen's study covered a follow-up period averaging thirty years. Hare et al.'s (1972) major survey found celibacy rates of almost 50% for men and 27% for women. The male celibacy rate was higher than those for other neuroses, for affective psychoses, and the national census, being exceeded only by that for schizophrenia. Hare et al. found that the fertility of married obsessional neurotics is lower than that of any other group, even including schizophrenia; this applied to both men and women. It was not attributable only to the high proportion of childless marriages, nor did the researchers feel that it could be explained in terms of social class.

Socio-cultural factors may well operate in this area. Akhtar (1978) found that obsessional patients in India did *not* show high rates of celibacy and low fertility. He suggested that this might be due, for example, to the strong pressures against intended bachelorhood within Indian families.

GENETIC PREDISPOSITION

Many authorities have believed that inheritance plays a major role in the acquiring of both obsessional traits and obsessional symptoms. Such evidence as exists seems to support this view, but it is as yet not conclusive.

The conventional ways of assessing genetic contribution to mental disorders have included twin studies, pedigree studies, and studies of adoptive parents and children. As yet, there seems to be no evidence of the third kind of assessment relative to obsessional disorders. We will consider evidence using the first two tactics separately.

Twin Studies. Given that both obsessional neurosis and monozygoticity are rare, the chances of both twins in a MZ pair suffering from obsessional disorder is extremely improbable. Assuming that 0.05% of the general population have obsessive–compulsive symptoms and that the frequency of MZ twins is about 1 in 132 live births, Woodruff and Pitts (1964) pointed out that the expected incidence of a MZ twin with obsessional disorder is about 1 in every 300,000 persons. If concordance were random, then the occurrence of an obsessional co-twin would be *1 in 600 million*. Marks *et al.* (1969), using slightly different prevalence figures, raised the estimated odds against such an occurrence to *1 in 800 million*. Even one pair of MZ twins, both suffering from obsessional disorder, would be statistically extremely improbable and would of itself constitute sugges-tive evidence of a genetic factor in obsessional disorder.

In fact, there have been reports of more than twenty such concordant twins in Europe and North America, and eighteen in Japan. The case is weakened by the absence of zygosity evidence in some reports and by dubious diagnoses. But these criticisms cannot be levelled against at least two cases—those reported by Woodruff and Pitts (1964) and Marks *et al.*(1969)—plus three cases recorded by the Medical Research Council Psychiatric Genetics Unit (Shields, 1973).

As Rachman and Hodgson (1980) have argued, obsessional ideas and com-pulsive habits shared by twins may be simply the result of inter-twin influence (social transmission) rather than indicative of genetic contribution. However, this argument surely applies with more force to the content of such experiences, rather than to their form.

Pedigree Studies. As is true of twin studies, the results of those studies which have examined the relatives of obsessional patients tend to have been clouded by the use of loose diagnostic criteria as well as by sampling weaknesses and the absence of control data.

In a well-known early study of the 100 parents and 206 siblings of 50 obsessional neurotics, Lewis (1936) reported that 37% of the parents and 21% of the siblings manifested obsessional personality traits. No other study has reported such percentages, but a similar tendency is discernible in more recent surveys, such as those of Brown (1942), Kringlen (1965), and Rosenberg (1967).

Lewis found that while psychiatric problems of various kinds were relatively common among his patients' relatives, none of them had suffered from explicit obsessional disorders. Again, subsequent findings, though not so extreme, have been in the same direction. Rosenberg (1967) found only 2 cases of obsessional neurosis among 547 first-degree relatives of the 144 obsessional patients in his series. Even the reported higher level of other mental disorders among relatives means little without control figures for other categories of target groups such as those provided by Brown (1942) and Greer and Cawley (1966). These showed that the incidence of mental disorder among the relatives of obsessionals was higher than that among relatives of anxiety-state and hysterical patients, but the differences are not statistically significant (see Black, 1974).

PRE-MORBID PERSONALITY

Despite the spirited and protracted debate that has gone on since the beginning of the century as to the degree and nature of the relationship between obsessional–compulsive symptoms and personality traits, the quantitative data are scarcely conclusive. Natural historians have been mainly interested in assessing the extent of obsessional traits possessed by patients prior to the onset of clinical disorder. Black (1974) has done his usual admirable job of tabulating and summarizing the findings of the major studies, despite their differing criteria and methods. The main point to emerge is that an average of 71% of the obsessional patients surveyed had been regarded as having pre-morbid obsessional personalities.

A major problem besetting researchers in the area, of course, has been the absence of any objective personality measure. The researcher's assessment is often biased by his theoretical assumptions, which determine the questions he asks. Furthermore, he must rely to a large extent upon the patient's self-assessment, which is biased by his current travail, and upon the selective memories of the patient and his family.

Finally, there is a woeful shortage of control data. The exception is Kringlen's (1965) study: 70% of his obsessional patients had moderate to marked pre-morbid obsessional traits. But so did 47% of his control group of anxiety states and hysterical and depressive neurotics. The difference is statistically significant, but nevertheless some qualms can be forgiven.

AGE OF ONSET

The mean age at which obsessional symptoms first appear is in the early twenties. However, Black (1974), using data from eight studies, observed that the age distribution is skewed; the highest incidence of first appearance is between the ages of 10 and 15. More than 50% of obsessional patients develop symptoms by the age of 25, and 85% by the age of 35. Only 5% report symptom onset after the age of 40.

PRECIPITANTS

Several researchers have attempted to determine whether particular events or features seemed to precipitate their patients' disorders. However, different definitions of such events have been used, and different time limits prior to the onset of symptomatology have been specified. Thus, Ingram (1961b) claimed to have identified significant events in 69% of 89 cases, but included features which had occurred up to a year prior to onset. At the other extreme, Lo (1967) used a period of six months prior to onset and identified precipitants in 56% of 88 cases. Other reports have varied between these limits. There seem to have been no reports of significant factors or changes immediately preceding onset, and it cannot be shown, of course, that the factors reported here were actually precipitants. At the same time, no authority has suggested that significant events or changes have *caused* the disorder, as opposed to precipitating it.

Types of presumed precipitants have varied widely. Pollitt (1957) reported that sexual and marital problems were most common in his series, constituting 30% of all precipitants, as opposed to 3% among non-obsessional controls. Ingram (1961b), on the other hand, found such problems in only 19% of his series, as compared with 23% of the controls. Pollitt (1957) found that death or illness of a near relative accounted for 15% of his cases, as opposed to 2% of the controls. Ingram's (1961b) equivalent figures were 18% and 25%. In short, there is little consistency among reports, which probably reflects the difficulty of deciding which factors are to be regarded as "significant" and which significant factors are to be regarded as precipitants.

TYPE OF ONSET

At first sight it would appear straightforward to describe the beginnings of a clinical disorder. Is it gradual or sudden? Are there warning signs before the development of the disorder? Whether sudden or not, are its beginnings full-blown, fragmentary, attenuated, or embryonic? But a variety of definitional problems immediately arise, of which the central one is how to determine what constitutes the "beginning." Eventually, investigators' criteria must be arbitrary, which probably accounts for some variations between reports.

Most authorities seem to state or imply that severe obsessional disorders are characterized by an acute onset. Skoog (1965) reported that this occurred in 47% of his 251 anankastic patients, as did Rachman and Hodgson (1980) in regard to 51% of their 83 patients. However, other studies have reported a majority of gradual onsets, or of serial episodic onsets. Here may be one key to the divergences. The main disorder, on account of which the patient is driven to seek help, may have an acute onset. But there can have been different types of precedent, often overlapping.

Precursory Non-specific Symptoms. Many investigators have reported that their patients had displayed *non*-obsessional symptoms prior to the onset of their obsessional disorder. Both Skoog (1965) and Kringlen (1965) reported the prevalence of psychosomatic, hypochondriacal, and depressive symptoms and anxiety in the pre-morbid pictures.

Precursory Obsessional Symptoms. The acute symptoms of 62% of Skoog's (1965) "acute onset" patients had been preceded by others. These were not of themselves disturbing enough to constitute an episode or state.

Previous Episodes. The main disorder may appear after one or more other episodes which have cleared up in some cases with a total loss of symptoms and usually within a relative short time. Of Pollitt's (1960) 150 patients, 100 had suffered such earlier episodes; 82 of these 100 had required treatment. On average, each such patient had experienced two previous attacks. In general, these earlier episodes had taken place in childhood, adolescence, or early adulthood; 79% of them had lasted less than a year.

THE COURSE OF OBSESSIONAL DISORDER

Although obsessional disorders are chronic, their courses typically show fluctuations, and patterns of development may be traced. Ingram (1961b) found four such patterns of disorder prior to treatment, in his natural history based on a review of 89 in-patients:

(1) *Constant, worsening.* An unremitting course, with definite deterioration— 35 cases (39%).
(2) *Constant, static.* An unremitting course with no changes for some time prior to admission—13 cases (15%).
(3) *Fluctuating.* Periods of worsening and relative improvement without freedom from symptoms—29 cases (33%).
(4) *Phasic.* A period or periods of remission of symptoms since their first onset—12 cases (13%)

·Kringlen's (1965) patients cannot be directly compared with those of Ingram; Kringlen's study was a follow-up, conducted many years after their discharge from hospital and thirteen to twenty years after their first admission. However, several of the patterns of development identified by Kringlen are strikingly reminiscent of Ingram's. Only 5% had shown constant worsening, but 30% had been constant and static, remaining the same without remittance; 20% had fluctuated, and 5% had experienced a phasic course with symptom-free intervals.

No support has been found for the suggestion that improvement is time-related and thus associated with the duration of study or follow-up.

PHYSICAL TREATMENTS

Perhaps because of the early recognition that conventional psychotherapy tended to be ineffective with severe cases of obsessive-compulsive disorder, a wide variety of physical treatments have been tried. The evidence up to 1970 has been succinctly summarized by Sternberg (1974), who laments the small-sample studies and the lack of controls. But, in any case, it is fair to say that the results reported after an extensive range of physical procedures—ECT, brain surgery, and chemotherapy—have not been unduly promising. In many instances, a treatment has proved to be effective in countering some associated state or condition, but has not modified the obsessive-compulsive problem itself. For example, anxiety associated with obsessional symptoms has been demonstrably relieved by several tranquillizers, narcotherapy, modified insulin, and leucotomy. Tension has been reduced by monoamine oxidase inhibitors, chlorpromazine, stilbestrol, and leucotomy. Depression has been lifted by ECT, MAOIs, tricyclic antidepressants, and leucotomy.

At least with severe cases of obsessive-compulsive disorder, pre-frontal leucotomy was the favoured procedure during the 1940s, 1950s, and 1960s. In many cases, this surgical intervention (in one of its several forms) has been shown to lift depression and relieve tension and anxiety. But it is a non-specific procedure, producing different results in different patients. It is a serious operation, with a 3% to 4% chance of fatal outcome. It is, of course, irreversible. It produces profound personality changes, with a marked blunting of sensibilities and meticulousness. But of even more central relevance for our present discussion, the evidence is mixed in regard to its remediation of obsessive–compulsive symptoms, For instance, Freeman and Watts (1950) reported satisfactory results after operating on 85 obsessional patients. However, neither obsessional thoughts nor compulsions were removed. The leucotomized patients simply felt less disturbed by them. Again, in a very detailed and extensive study, Sykes and Tredgold (1964) found that their patients' obsessive–compulsive symptoms persisted post-operationally. Their improved states reflected only decreased tension and reduction in their personal standards.

It is at least possible that a similar effect occurs as a result of treatment with clomipramine, a drug which is currently very much in favour, and which seems to have replaced other physical treatments as the one of choice. Clomipramine is a tricyclic antidepressant drug, and there is ample evidence of its efficacy in the treatment of depression, despite its wide range of distressing side-effects. However, whether it can be validly regarded also as a specifically anti-obsessional drug (as suggested by, e.g., Capstick, 1975) is a different question. It has long been recognized, of course, that there is some sort of connection between obsessionality and depression, and we shall be discussing the intricacies of the relationship in Chapter 13. An elevation of mood enables the obsessional person to cope more effectively with his or her problems. But whether the mood-altering agent can therefore be regarded as directly responsible for the diminution of obsessive–compulsive symptoms is surely open to doubt. In arriving at a decision, the reader will be aided by a number of good, modern surveys of the findings to date, such as Insel and Murphy (1981), Ananth (1983), Marks (1983), Mavissakalian (1983), and Jenike (1983). Most recently, the logical weaknesses and professional biases manifested in much of the literature have been elegantly and convincingly analysed by Emslie (1984).

OUTCOME

The assessment and comparisons of outcome studies is beset with difficulties— probably even more so in the case of obsessional disorder than in that of disorders which are more prevalent and more readily determinable. Investigators vary in their application of diagnostic criteria, in the samples they use, in the length of follow-up, and in the classifications they employ to describe patients' conditions at follow-up. The original data considered vary enormously: Factors involved include type of therapy employed, number and duration of treatment sessions, and length of treatment, as well as such undeterminable but significant variables as individual differences between therapists. In particular, as would be expected, the outcome on follow-up is directly associated with the original degree of severity of the disorder. And this, in turn, is usually reflected in the type of treatment prescribed, so that studies of in- and out-patient populations cannot be directly compared.

The major large-scale follow-up studies were published between 1953 and 1966 and were concerned with patients who had been treated with conventional psychotherapy and adjunctive physical treatments. Black (1974) presents a tabular summary of no less than sixteen such studies, published before 1971. Follow-up times ranged from one to thirty-five years. On the average, 60% of out-patients had remained improved at follow-up but only 46% of erstwhile in-patients. Studies of mixed out- and in-patient groups found improvement rates averaging 57%.

In more recent times, behaviour therapy has enjoyed widespread use. If its adherents' enthusiastic claims can withstand the test of time, the outcome picture should radically change. But, so far, the position is far from clear. As might be expected, the early studies were usually of individual cases and were poorly controlled. Meyer *et al.* (1974) surveyed 62 behaviour-therapy cases reported before 1971; only about 55% had been judged to be improved. However, during the 1970s, BT methods changed, and exposure, response prevention, and *in vivo* modelling became the favoured techniques. Referring to Meyer *et al.*'s "somewhat gloomy epitaph" as a summary of the first phase of BT applied to obsessional disorders, Rachman and Hodgson (1980) go on to state: "The altogether happier present outlook is a measure of the extent of recent advances" (p. 355). Such confidence is, of course, admirable. But it should be pointed out that hard, supportive evidence is not yet readily available. Despite the detailed exposition of their work, Rachman and Hodgson do not provide a succinct account of its results with follow-up data, perhaps because at that time their major research program had not been completed. They do state, however, that the gross failure rate in their series was between 20% and 28%. Marshall (1981) points out that these results are slightly worse than those of either Foa and Goldstein (1978) or Meyer *et al.* (1974), but suggests that the differences are due to the fact that the Rachman studies were somewhat better controlled and more complete.

SOCIAL AND OCCUPATIONAL ADJUSTMENTS

A few follow-up studies have examined later social adjustment and work capabilities as well as relief from symptoms. In general, social interactions seem to diminish significantly, although the evidence is mixed. Again, the severity of the disorder, as indicated by whether in-patient treatment had been deemed necessary, is reflected in subsequent social adjustment. Thus, 77% of Grimshaw's (1965) series of out-patients showed satisfactory social relationships at follow-up, whereas fewer than 20% of Kringlen's (1965) erstwhile in-patients showed this. There is, perhaps, another factor operating here, which is not specific to obsessional disorders. Admission to hospital for any period over about a month can represent a dramatic shift in the patient's social relationships. Normal contacts, interests, and experiences shared with friends and neighbours are of necessity curtailed or cease altogether. And meanwhile, patients tend to embrace institutionalization, in the sense that they begin to share the interests and pursuits of fellow-patients, accept staff members as role models and confidants, and submerge themselves in the micro-neighbourhood of the ward.

On the other hand, a significant point about obsessionals, observed by Lewis (1936), is that the majority of them continue to work. Indeed, they prefer to be busy, while welcoming the patterned structures and routines offered by many types of occupation. To a large extent, of course, the ability to carry on working is a function of the severity of the disorder and, subsequently, whether improvement is attained. Of the thirty patients in Noreik's (1970) series whose improvement had been maintained at follow-up, twenty-two had demonstrated stable working ability. Of the twenty-four who were graded "unchanged," only three had such working ability; none of the ten whose condition had deteriorated demonstrated this ability.

COMPLICATIONS

Complications are usually defined as new symptoms or events associated with a disorder but not part of the original clinical picture. The complications most often associated with obsessional disorder have always been depression and schizophrenia. And a fundamental (and still unresolved) problem is whether in some cases the psychotic symptoms should be taken to be complications of the obsessional disorder or the obsessional symptoms taken to be complications or portents of the psychosis. There is a vast literature, and the debates have been too complex to be even touched upon here; the reader is referred to such authorities as Lewis (1936) and Stengel (1945, 1948). We shall be discussing the relationship between obsessions and depressions later in this book. Meanwhile, attention will be drawn merely to one or two of the more important survey reports.

Schizophrenia. The argument made by many writers subsequent to Bleuler (e.g., Birnie and Littmann, 1978) that obsessional disorder is a variant, attenuation, or precursor of schizophrenia accords with clinical experiences. But it is not supported by the findings of Pollitt (1957), Ingram (1961b), Ray (1964), Kringlen (1965), Lo (1967), Rosenberg (1968), and Bratfos (1970). These workers have reported that very few (0.0% to 3.3%) of their obsessional neurotics were subsequently diagnosed as schizophrenics.

Roughly the same proportion of schizophrenics are reported to have suffered from obsessional symptoms. Rosen's (1957) survey of 848 schizophrenics found that 3.5% had shown obsessional symptoms. All of these appeared prior to or concurrent with the onset of the schizophrenia.

Depression. Rosenberg (1968) found that 34% of his obsessional neurotics subsequently developed depressions. However, so did 25.7% of his anxiety neurotics; the difference is not statistically significant.

Where the proportion of depressives with obsessional symptoms is concerned, Gittleson (1966), whose work will be examined later, reported that 31.2% of a large sample of depressives showed obsessional symptoms. The incidence of pre-morbid obsessional personalities was twice as great among them as among the depressives without obsessional symptoms.

In short, the data are suggestive, but not conclusive. It is difficult to say whether the concomitance of symptoms is more pronounced than among other clinical groupings, and whether it refects some subtle underlying relationship or is simply coincidental overlapping. A skeptical but parsimonious explanation might be that it demonstrates nothing more than deficiencies in nosological conceptualization and the exactitude of diagnostic procedures.

8

The Seminal Psychiatric Theorists

THE PSYCHIC ENERGY APPROACH: PIERRE JANET

In Britain and America Janet is respected as one of the founders of French academic psychology and as a contributor to psychiatric studies of hysteria. But remarkably little is generally known of his ideas; none of the current standard English textbooks in experimental or clinical psychology makes more than a passing reference to his work. Even the standard histories of psychology and psychiatry refer to him only as a pupil of Charcot who made a systematic study of hypnotism in relation to hysterical phenomena, introducing, for instance, the concept of "dissociation." Such an account fails to recognize Janet's work in many other fields, his encyclopaedic scholarship, his meticulous clinical observations over forty years, and his outstanding psychological theorizing. Most important of all it fails to give credit to Janet's study of the compulsive personality which, for phenomenological detail and brilliance of conceptualization, overshadows any similar study before or since. This limited appreciation of Janet's achievements among British and American psychopathologists is presumably due in part to the fact that most of his major works have never been translated into English. (His best-known book was *Etat mental des hysteriques* (1892); the translation (1901) is difficult to obtain. His Harvard lectures, published in 1907 as *The Major Symptoms of Hysteria*, and his *Les Médications Psychologiques*, translated in 1925 and published under the title *Psychological Healing*, are the only other of his works to have ever been available in English.) A secondary reason is that several of his major propositions seem to have been ignored or misunderstood. The third, and most generally recognized, reason is that his work was overshadowed by Freud's more dramatic and controversial postulations. Finally, Janet was directly in line with and subsequently unfairly associated with the now discredited school of thought which regarded all mental illness as being the outcome of "degeneracy" or morbid, deteriorating genetic strains.

Janet's major study of obsessional symptomatology and personality was *Les Obsessions et la Psychasthénie* (1903), a monumental work in two volumes, the second of which was written in collaboration with a colleague, Dr. F. Raymond. It would be impossible to pay full tribute here to Janet's breadth of vision; suffice it to say that for profundity of thought, clarity of expression, and clinical acuity he stands second to none.

Janet conducts a meticulous phenomenological examination of a variety of compulsive patients. In summarizing these he detects a characteristic running through them all—"*l'incapacité d'éprouver un sentiment exact en rapport avec la situation presente.*" For this inability to respond directly and appropriately to objective reality he introduces the term "*la perte de la fonction du réel.*" He argues that there is a vast difference between the psychological mechanisms concerned in handling, on the one side, memories and imaginary and abstract situations, and, on the other, real objects and situations. All normal people possess the faculty of apprehending and integrating present reality. They are capable of interpreting cues received through perception or performance and of utilizing this input of information for the direction of subsequent operations. Janet points out that this is in fact a highly complex procedure, and he postulates that there is a special psychological mechanism which performs this integrative activity—"*la fonction du réel.*" The *psychasthene* is a person who lacks this reality co-ordinator. Janet makes the interesting observation that such patients do *not* suffer from disturbance in purely mental activities, but only in their application to real, concrete situations. He points out that disturbances of reasoning, attention, and the appreciation of situations do not occur in the patient's ruminations and reveries and that he can order his thoughts logically and coherently. It is only when he has to interact with the environment that he experiences difficulties in attention and comprehension. Janet ascribes phobic behaviour, feelings of indecision, and "*les sentiments d'incomplétude*" to the same basic cause: "*ils ont perdu le sentiment que nous avons toujours, à tort ou à raison, de faire partie de la réalité actuelle, du monde présent*" (Janet, 1909, p. 355).

According to Janet, the patient is not only relatively incapable of appropriate response to reality but is aware of his incapacity. His emotional disturbance is the result, not the cause, of this subjective inadequacy. For, whereas the sensation of "not being in complete touch with things" is experienced by the normal person during illness or fatigue, it is in such cases only transient. In the case of the obsessional it is a continual experience and one which is more evident the more important the situation. The inadequacy of his responses is recognizable by the observer, and Janet claims that patients' relatives will report their social incompetence, clumsiness, and inability to perform practical tasks. Given the choice they will be happier in occupations far removed from material realities. Above all, they enjoy philosophic discourse; they can become terrifying metaphysicians, and, says Janet blandly, they are sometimes psychologists.

To this loss of the "*fonction réel*" Janet traces depersonalization and derealization. He also attributes to it the experience of *"déjà vu."* The essential of this, he says, is not so much an affirmation of the past as a denial of the present.

"La perte de la fonction du réel" is an explanatory construct derived from the careful application of phenomenological method to a wealth of case material. Janet goes on to re-conceptualize it in terms of academic psychology. But first he considers various interpretative approaches to the subject and makes a reasoned case for a view which he terms *"psychasthenia."* In contradistinction from both the "intellectual" and the "emotional" aetiological standpoints, the psychasthenic explanation conceives the problem to be due to the lowering of "psychological tension." The choice of the word "tension" in this context was unfortunate. The term is now generally used with reference to feelings of strain or suspense or to contracted musculature. In this sense the obsessional patient is certainly not characterized by any *"abaissement de la tension psychologique,"* a fact which practising clinicians are quick to seize upon in objection to Janet's theory. But Janet was using the term in its other technical sense, as meaning a "disturbance of equilibrium." His views would certainly elicit far more current attention were the term translated as "input integration," "schematization," "plan mechanism," or "cortical programmer." The concepts evoked by these terms are among several theoretical models which have aroused excitement among psychologists in recent years. Janet's equilibrium hypothesis preceded some of them by more than half a century. Janet showed that the integrity of normal responses is dependent upon an intricate complex of interrelating factors, rather than a simple act of will or attention. Our awareness at any moment of time may be expressed in a particular focus of attention, but this is merely the dominant expression of a dynamic balance of mental activities. These include the active inhibition of perceptual and cognitive responses as well as excitatory processes. This balance or equilibrium is seen by Janet to be based on a hierarchy of psychological phenomena. The components of this hierarchy range from physiological mechanisms up through reflex activity and simple learning to the automatic co-ordinated processes involved in habits and skills. Only when all these dynamic processes are working in an appropriately integrated manner can any given set of stimuli elicit optimal responses. By "lowered psychological tension" Janet means a dynamic deficiency in this schematic equilibrium, which results in the incapacity for effective response. He sees neurotic reactions as examples of the "inferior and exaggerated operations" which typify such incapacity. Those primitive reactions slowly replace biologically effective functioning such as the perception of reality, decisiveness, and joy in living: *"C'est pourquoi je suis disposé à considérer cette agitation comme 'une substitution, une derivation qui remplace les phénomènes supérieurs supprimés' "* (Janet, 1909, p. 364).

Janet applies this theory with great acumen to the problems of obsessive thought. He points out the futility of intellectual activity which does not culminate in interaction with reality. If intellectual elaborations are not related to real outcomes or experience they do not facilitate the individual's healthy development, however high the level at which they take place. They may, in fact, hinder development by themselves becoming substitutes for reality behaviours so that the sufferer increasingly postpones activity in favour of internal debate.

Janet's theory is purely psychological. It is elegant, closely argued, and supported by a wealth of case material and by suggestive findings in other fields. But several objections must be raised.

Janet seems throughout to be discussing obsessional *personality* (though to him this is a form of *illness*). In contradistinction to many other workers, he takes this basic "sick" personality as his central subject and discusses symptoms only as manifestations or traits thereof. The reader is never quite sure whether he realizes that the symptoms can appear in association with a number of other illnesses. However, he stresses throughout that they are to be seen in hysterics and in normal individuals suffering from fatigue, shock, etc.

Partly because of the above, some doubts may be entertained as to the level of diagnostic precision employed in categorizing his case material, especially as the diagnosing seems to have been carried out by a variety of psychiatric colleagues at La Salpetrière.

Of more central importance in examining his theoretical constructs, it would seem that he regarded the "lowering of psychological tension" as being responsible for almost all neurotic and personality disorders. It is *not* specific to obsessionality, although such cases are used to exemplify the theory.

The theory is not immediately amenable to experimental disproof or support any more than is Freud's. Janet suggests that the proof lies in the hands of the neuro-physiologists. His aetiological presumption is in the "degenerative" line. He presumes that psychasthenia is constitutionally determined and that, once "triggered off," some form of degenerative neurological process takes place. There is nothing unscientific about this sort of theoretical model-making. But the fact is that in almost eighty years the neuro-physiologists have *not* provided any supporting evidence. And, perhaps more significantly, his theory does not seem to have generated any disprovable hypotheses, much less any psychological experimentation aimed directly at its verification. Of course, this may be attributable to the prevailing ignorance regarding his theories which was referred to at the beginning of this section.

The patients Janet describes are predominantly characterized by diffuse anxiety, timidity, indecisiveness, social insecurity, and fatigue. The majority belong, in fact, more to Schneider's "sensitive" group than to the anankastic.

Janet stresses that psychasthenes are only disturbed in their contact with reality, and not in their mental activity. This seems questionable—the very compulsivity of ideas and doubts is itself abnormal, as are such phenomena as hypermnesia.

Janet also claims that "important" situations are more "real." But he does not explain how degrees of "importance" are to be gauged. Some obsessionals report compulsive difficulties and indecisiveness only in relation to what they themselves regard as routine, unimportant situations.

THE PSYCHOANALYTIC APPROACH: SIGMUND FREUD

Like his contemporary, Janet, Freud's first interest as a psychiatrist was in hysteria, which was the "hot topic" during the final decades of the nineteenth century. But, again, like Janet, he soon became interested in the problems of obsessional disorder, which he came to regard as the most perplexing and provocative area of psycho-pathology. Unlike Janet, he did not make a concentrated, intensive attack on the topic and did not devote a book to it. But, as Strachey points out: "Freud probably discussed obsessional neurosis more often than any other disorder—from the beginning of his career almost to the end of it" (*S.E.* XVI, p. 261*n*). In an appendix to Volume X of the Standard Edition, Strachey lists fourteen of Freud's papers which contain major discussions of obsessional neurosis. But scattered references abound, the last one being in *Moses and Monotheism*, which was published in 1939. The major references listed by Strachey were published between 1894 and 1926, but no less than seven appeared in the period 1901 to 1918. (Janet's *magnum opus*, it will be recalled, was first published in 1903, being the result of many years of study and clinical investigations. Unlike Freud, who published a little at a time over a long period, Janet presented, in one massive work, a fully developed application of his psychological theories to obsessional disorders.)

Freud's first theoretical contribution to the study of obsessionality appeared in 1894 in his paper "The Neuro-Psychoses of Defence" (*S.E.* III, pp. 45-61). There, he begins by criticizing Janet's view that the primary feature of hysteria is the splitting of consciousness based in an innate weakness of the capacity for psychic synthesis. Instead, Freud asserts that the splitting of consciousness, at least in one extreme form of hysteria (termed by him "defence hysteria"), is the result of an act of will. The patient's intention is to defend himself against a distressingly conflictual experience:

. ... in them there was no question either of a grave hereditary taint or of an individual degenerative atrophy.

For these patients whom I analyzed had enjoyed good mental health up to the moment at which *an occurrence of incompatibility took place in their ideational life*—that is to say, until their ego was faced with an experience, an idea or a feeling which aroused such a distressing affect that the subject decided to forget about it. ... (p. 47, original emphasis)

Freud argues that this defensive measure cannot be totally successful; neither the incompatible idea nor its associated affect—the "sum of excitation"—can be eradicated. However, the powerful idea may be transformed into a weak one and robbed of its affective loading. The question now is—what happens to the detached affect?

> Up to this point the processes in hysteria, and in phobias and obsessions are the same; from now on their paths diverge. In hysteria, the incompatible idea is rendered innocuous by its *sum of excitation* being *transformed into something somatic*. For this I should like to propose the name of *conversion*. (p. 49, original emphasis)

In obsessions and phobias the deployment of detached affect is quite different:

> If someone with a disposition [to neurosis] lacks the aptitude for conversion, but if, nevertheless, in order to fend off an incompatible idea, he sets about separating it from its affect, then *that affect is obliged to remain in the psychical sphere*. The idea, now weakened, is still left in consciousness, separated from all association. *But its affect, which has become free, attaches itself to other ideas which are not in themselves incompatible; and, thanks to this "false connection," those ideas turn into obsessional ideas*. This, in a few words, is the psychological theory of obsessions and phobias mentioned at the beginning of this paper. (p. 51-52, original emphasis)

As Strachey points out, this account of the displacement of affect foreshadows Freud's later discussion of repression.

What is the source of conflict and the subsequent affect which now enjoys a "false connection"? Freud is quite explicit:

> In all the cases I have analyzed it was the subject's *sexual life* that had given rise to a distressing affect of precisely the same quality as that attaching to his obsession. (p. 52, original emphasis)

In 1895, Freud published "Obsessions and Phobias" (*S.E.* III, pp. 74-82). This adds little to the first paper where theory is concerned, but it presents eleven illustrative case summaries. These make fascinating reading because they include readily recognizable examples of types of obsessional states which have become classical, and which are commonly met with today. They include: (a) a young man who, like Mr. D. in our own series, reproached himself for having killed his cousin, etc.; (b) a woman who, like our Mrs. G., found herself obliged to count such items as floor-boards; (c) various cases of *folie du doute* who, like our Mrs. R., had doubts about the reliability of their memories; (d) a young woman who collected bits of paper, just as our Mr. J. collected bits of glass; (e) a woman who, like our Mr. E., was constantly washing her hands and would touch door handles only with her elbow.

Freud precedes his examples by emphasizing the point that "*the emotional state, as such, is always justified''* (p. 75, original emphasis). The "pathological mark" lies only in: "(1) *the emotional state persists indefinitely*, and (2) the associated idea is *no longer the appropriate original one, related to the aetiology of the obsession, but is one which replaces it, a substitute for it*" (p. 75, original emphasis).

In Section II of his "Further Remarks on the Neuro-Psychoses of Defence" ("The Nature and Mechanism of Obsessional Neurosis," 1896, *S.E.* III, pp. 168-74), Freud makes some interesting observations about what we have termed the "modes" of obsessional experience, beginning with the claim: "There are two forms of obsessional neurosis, according to whether what forces an entrance into consciousness is solely the *mnemonic content* of the act involving self-reproach, or whether the self-reproachful *affect* connected with the act does so as well" (p. 170, original emphasis). In the first form, the content of the obsessional idea is distorted in two ways. The sexual nature of the original, unacceptable experience is replaced by something asexual. The historical placing of the original experience (which actually took place in childhood) is distorted by making it contemporary. The associated affect is unpleasant, but not one of self-reproach; unlike the obsessional ideas, it does not "engage the patient's attention."

In the second form of obsessional neurosis, what forces its way into consciousness is not the "mnemonic content", but the affect. The repressed self-reproach may be transformed into any other unpleasant affect, which then emerges into consciousness. It may become shame, hypochondriacal anxiety, social anxiety, religious anxiety, delusions of being noticed, or fears of temptation. Now the ego seeks to fend off these distressing derivatives by developing "secondary defences." If these protective measures succeed in forcing the re-repression of the symptoms, then: "the obsession is transferred to the protective measures themselves and creates a third form of 'obsessional neurosis'— *obsessional actions*. These actions are never primary; they never contain anything but a defence—never an aggression" (p. 172, original emphasis).

Secondary defence against *obsessional ideas* may be effected by stress upon thoughts containing contrary content, which accounts for *obsessional brooding* (which is usually concerned with abstract ideas in contradistinction to the sensuality of the repressed idea). Or the patient attempts to master his obsessional ideas by "logical work," which accounts for *obsessional thinking*, a *compulsion to test things*, and *doubting mania*.

Secondary defence against *obsessional affects* may include *penitential* measures (numbering and ceremonials), *precautionary* measures (phobias, superstitions, pedantry, etc.), measures to do with *fear of betrayal* (collecting bits of paper, seclusiveness), or *numbing measures (dipsomania)*.

With what is the original self-reproach concerned? At the beginning of Section II, in an oft-cited passage, Freud flatly asserts:

The nature of obsessional neurosis can be expressed in a simple formula. *Obsessional ideas* are invariably transformed *self-reproaches* which have re-emerged from *repression* and which always relate to some *sexual* act that was performed with pleasure *in childhood*. (p. 169, original emphasis)

The source of the problem, then, is pin-pointed by Freud quite clearly—it is guilt due to juvenile sexual activity. But Freud is even more specific, discriminating between the *type* of sexual activity precursory to obsessional neurosis as opposed to that precursory to hysteria:

Sexual experiences of early childhood have the same significance in the aetiology of obsessional neurosis as they have in hysteria. Here, however, it is no longer a question of sexual *passivity*, but acts of aggression carried out with pleasure and of pleasurable participation in sexual acts—that is to say, of sexual *activity*. (p. 168, original emphasis)

In a typically Victorian manner, Freud equates sexual activity with males and sexual passivity with females, a view which would not be accepted unequivocally today. He goes on to argue that for this reason obsessional neurosis is more common among males, which is simply incorrect. His argument was repeated in "Heredity and the Neuroses" (1896, *S.E.* III, pp. 141-56), where, in comparing the aetiology of obsessional neurosis with that of hysteria, he states:

There is only one difference which seems capital. At the basis of the aetiology of hysteria we found an event of passive sexuality, an experience submitted to with indifference or with a small degree of annoyance or fright. In obsessional neurosis it is a question, on the other hand, of an event which has given *pleasure*, of an act of aggression inspired by desire (in the case of a boy) or of a participation in sexual relations accompanied by enjoyment (in the case of a little girl). The obsessional ideas, when their intimate meaning has been recognized by analysis, when they have been reduced, as it were, to their simplest expression, are nothing other than *reproaches addressed by the subject to himself on account of this anticipated sexual enjoyment*, but reproaches distorted by an unconscious physical work of transformation and substitution." (p. 155, original emphasis)

This confident "finding" was based upon the reports of thirteen cases of hysteria, three of whom Freud diagnosed as being mixed cases of hysteria and obsessional neurosis, plus three cases of "pure" obsessional neurosis. Freud anticipated that his "seduction theory" might encounter skepticism and recognized the "tendency to lies and the facility of invention" of hysterics. But he was confident of the validity of what he had elicited from his handful of patients, because the information had not been offered spontaneously, but only elicited under "the most energetic pressure of the analytic procedure" (p. 153). During the subsequent decade, however, he seems to have realized that human "recol-lectons" should be taken with a pinch of salt. Particularly is this so, it may be suggested, when the informant is submitted to "energetic pressure." Nowadays we are familiar with the vagaries of memory and recognize that it is a dynamic and reconstructive process. What is reported as a memory may reveal more about the subject's fantasy life and desires than it does about historical facts. And when it is painfully dragged forth in the way Freud describes, its content may well reflect the subject's level of suggestibility and his interpretation of his interrogator's expectations. So that a certain over-enthusiasm is betrayed by Freud's initial acceptance of his patient's reports at their face value. In a footnote added in 1924 to Section II of the "Further Remarks" paper he acknowledges: "This section is dominated by an error which I have since repeatedly acknowl-edged and corrected. At that time I was not yet able to distinguish between my patients' phantasies about their childhood years and their real recollections. As a result, I attributed to the aetiological factor of seduction a significance and universality which it does not possess" (p. 168).

Thus, Freud found it necessary to abandon both his aetiological cornerstone and its specific application to obsessional neurosis. His "Obsessive Actions and Religious Practices" (1907, *S.E.* XIII, pp. 117-27) makes no mention of the "seduction theory"; instead, it refers to the repression of instinctual impulse as the "primary fact": "A deeper insight into the mechanism of obsessional neu-rosis is gained if we take into account the primary fact which lies at the bottom of it. This is always *the repression of an instinctual impulse* (a component of the sexual instinct) which was present in the subject's constitution and which was allowed to find expression for a while during his childhood but later suc-cumbed to suppression" (p. 124, original emphasis).

The theoretical sections of "Notes upon a Case of Obsessional Neurosis" (1909, *S.E.* X, pp. 221-49) carry on directly from the 1896 paper, beginning with a criticism of the definition there presented in Section II. But, although this is one of Freud's longer papers, he does not offer an integrated development of his theoretical views as outlined thirteen years before. Instead, he raises spec-ulative questions derived from the consideration of the case under examination (the "Rat Man") and of various other patients. At the same time, he makes a number of insightful and thought-provoking observations. For instance, in dis-cussing the "secondary defensive struggle," he points out that patients combat their obsessional thoughts with rational analysis and reasoning, while simulta-neously accepting some of the pathological premises of the obsessions being fought. He then makes the interesting point that "the patients themselves do not know the wording of their own obsessional ideas" (p. 223). The wording of the secondary defensive thought is a distortion of the original and may be unrec-ognized and incomprehensible. It is this distortion which allows it to be successful in defence and which accounts for its persistence. But traces of the original thought still exist in the distorted form, often quite explicitly, and are amenable to translation (or de-coding) during psychoanalysis. The same applies not only to obsessional thoughts but to protective formulas, and Freud gives some neat examples of the elucidation of apparently meaningless words used as protective measures. He goes on to give clinical examples of self-fulfilling prophecies, the need for uncertainty, the omnipotence ascribed by obsessionals to their thoughts, and their attitude to death. He ends with a lengthy discussion of the conflict in the patient between love and hate and its relation to compulsion and doubt.

So far, this summary has been concerned with Freud's views about obsessional neurosis. But he also discussed the etiology of an associated personality type— the so-called "anal character." In "Character and Anal Erotism" (1908, *S.E.* IX, pp. 169-75), he reports his observation that a number of patients display a combination of three personality characteristics (each one subsuming various traits)—orderliness, parsimony, and obstinacy. He discusses the development of these characteristics as *sublimations* of anal erotism. They are formed, we are told, during the conflicts aroused by toilet training in infancy, which psychoanalysts stress as the first situation in which the child may, in response to the environment, postpone or renounce direct instinctual gratification.

The trait of orderliness—which includes neatness, punctuality, propriety, meticulousness, etc.—is taken to be a displacement of compliance with parental demands regarding defecation. In neurotics these obedience reflectors are reaction formations which may be broken, alternated, or permeated by the underlying opposite impulses. Abraham (1923) reports several examples of polar inconsistency in obsessional behaviour, such as persons who are scrupulously neat and clean about their top clothing and dirty and untidy about their underwear.

Parsimony—frugality, thrift, or downright meanness—represents a direct continuation of the habit of retaining faeces. This, it is postulated, is originally motivated by the erogenous pleasure achieved when evacuation is eventually engaged in. Just as orderliness is an elaboration of obedience to toilet-training requirements, so obstinacy is an elaboration of refusal to comply with such demands. Obstinacy or stubbornness may be seen as an inactive form of aggression. By his passive refusal to relax his sphincters the infant is able to spite his parents. Later the method may be used to combat the individual's own super-ego. By provoking unjust behaviour in others the stubborn individual attains a feeling of moral superiority which is required to heighten his self-esteem in the face of an over-demanding super-ego.

In the 1908 paper no mention is made of any association between anal erotism and obsessional neurosis. This was not explicitly suggested until 1913, in "The Disposition to Obsessional Neurosis" (*S.E.* XII, pp. 317-26). The purpose of this paper was clearly indicated by its sub-title: "A contribution to the problem of choice of neurosis." Putting aside the general question of why people develop neuroses, the problem to be discussed was why an individual should develop one particular neurosis rather than another. Briefly, Freud argues that the neuroses involve regression to "fixation points" which have disturbed the smooth and orderly maturation of psychical functions—particularly those to do with sex and ego-development. "Thus," he summarizes, "our dispositions are inhibitions in development" (p. 318). The symptoms of hysteria appear first in earliest childhood, and those of obsessional neurosis between the ages of six and eight years. This suggests that the problems in both cases lie in later phases of libidinal development. To determine at exactly what point an obsessional neurosis might originate, he examines the case of a particular patient who suffered from compulsive hand-washing and protective measures against injuring others. Both these symptoms Freud interprets as *reaction-formations against her own anal-erotic and sadistic impulses*. And these, he argues, are the two instincts which dominate the pre-genital organization of sexual life: "The extraordinary part played by impulses of hatred and anal erotism in the symptomatology of obsessional neurosis has already struck many observers and has recently been emphasized with particular clarity by Ernest Jones (1913). This follows directly from our hypothesis if we suppose that in that neurosis the component instincts in question have once more taken over the representation of the genital instincts, whose forerunners they were in the process of development" (p. 321).

Thus, both the anal character (personality structure) and obsessional neurosis derive from anal erotism. But in sharp contradistinction to Janet and such later authorities as Schneider, Freud differentiates between the personality and the neurosis. In a later section of the same paper, he observes that the same "instinctual forces" contribute to both character development and the neuroses: "But a sharp theoretical distinction between the two is necessitated by the single fact that the failure of repression and the return of the repressed—which are peculiar to the mechanism of neurosis—are absent in the formation of character. In the latter, repression either does not come into action or smoothly achieves its aim of replacing the repressed by reaction-formations and sublimations" (p. 323).

In other words, whereas neurotic behaviour reflects a failure of adaptation, with conflict due to a failure to completely repress unconscious material, the personality develops in the context of successful repression, aided by reaction formations and sublimation.

THE NEO-KRAEPELINIAN APPROACH: KÜRT SCHNEIDER

To all intents and purposes Schneider is completely unknown to English-speaking psychologists. This is strange because, although he was primarily a clinical psychiatrist, his viewpoint regarding personality disorders is readily reconcilable with that of psychological personality theorists. His writings are devoid of statistical content; nevertheless his assumptions are basically the same as those of dimensional and factorially minded psychologists.

Schneider's greatest contribution to psychiatric thought was in the field of personality disorder. His book *Die Psychopathischen Persönlickeiton* (1923) has had considerable influence in Europe although it has only been recognized in British psychiatric circles since its translation into English in 1958. Written to be comprehensible to the non-psychiatric reader, the book is lucid, readable, and unambiguous. This is partly due to its uncompromising adoption of one approach—that of the classical German (or, to be more exact, the Heidelberg) school, with its stress on a precise phenomenological method and meticulous diagnosis.

Schneider defines his use of the term "personality" as "an individual's unique quality" including "his feelings and his personal goals" but excluding intellectual and physical factors. He grants the close interrelationship of the latter factors with his topic but claims that for purposes of discussion it is not difficult to discriminate among the three.

By "abnormal personality" he means deviations from "factual averages," i.e., from statistical norms. He offers the following definition:

> ... abnormal personality is a variation upon an accepted yet broadly conceived range of average personality. The variation may be expressed as an excess or deficiency of certain personal qualities and whether this is judged good or bad is immaterial to the issue. The saint and the poet are equally abnormal as the criminal. All three of them fall outside the range of average personality as we conceive it so that all persons of note may be classed as abnormal personalities. (1958, pp. 2-3)

Schneider points out that "abnormal personalities" in this sense must be numerous. The category includes two groups which he terms as of "psychopathic personality." He defines these two groups by simple operational criteria: "abnormal personalities who either suffer personally because of their own abnormality or make the community suffer because of it" (p. 3). He acknowledges that this is a practical rather than a scientific definition; he also points out that it is clinical and implies no moral judgement.

Schneider goes on to examine various views of what is implied by the word "illness." He concludes that: "Mental phenomena should in our opinion only be associated with illness when they are conditioned by some actual morbid change in the body, or by defective structure" (p. 9).

He then flatly asserts that the schizophrenics and cyclothymias as well as the organic and toxic psychoses may properly be entitled illnesses although as yet little is known about their underlying physical conditions.

On this basis he points out that psychopathic personalities cannot be termed "illnesses." He considers as equally inappropriate the use of such concepts as neuropathy, degeneration, or "impoverished stock."

Schneider believes that personality and even more so psychopathic personality are both constitutionally determined—"the primary aetiology is a genetic one." However, he does not discount environmental influences and is careful to stress development as the process of maturation of inborn characteristics conditioned by experience and education.

In psychopathy the main concern is with characteristics of the individual's total disposition (*Anlage*). In neurosis, however, the concern is with the effect of experience on the disposition. Abnormal phenomena or symptoms may result from abnormal experience in a normal personality. Usually, however, there is an interrelationship with different degrees of emphasis on personality and environment. The psychopathic personality, Schneider implies, is predisposed to neurotic behaviour caused or precipitated by the environment. Schneider himself avoids the word "neurosis" because of its original neurological implications. He prefers the term "abnormal reaction"—the reaction occurring in response to external events or to inner tensions and conflicts.

After considering a number of classificatory approaches Schneider discusses the rationale of typology. He warns against thinking of personality "types" as diagnoses: "The human personality cannot be labelled diagnostically as we label mental or physical symptoms. Human qualities may be indicated, emphasized and perhaps isolated as distinguishing characteristics, but this is not committal to some diagnostic statement about a symptom" (p. 51).

He stresses the relativity of personality descriptions. Only certain traits are considered and again those are sometimes basic to the individual and sometimes more peripheral: "People are infinitely varied and we must not forget how fundamentally diverse they are underneath the clinical label" (p. 52).

The clinical labels, he reminds his readers, are merely convenient descriptions of observed phenomena in accordance with certain medical and social criteria. Whereas differential diagnosis in the psychoses relies on the examination of formal disturbance, content is of paramount importance in the consideration of psychopathic personality. But the individual nature of content precludes generalization.

In the second part of his book Schneider presents "an unsystematic typology of psychopathic personalities." He feels that the existing systematic typologies are unconvincing or incomprehensible: "Clinical facts are ignored in order to prevent the system of classification breaking down. Many terms are clinically insignificant and seem to be inserted in the scheme solely for classification's sake" (p. 50).

As a practical clinician he is opposed to classifications which strain after symmetry or neatness at the expense of clinical facts. He is particularly suspicious of unwarranted contrasts of positive and negative attributes. Clearly, in this sense he would have vigorously disapproved of the psychological habit of postulating dimensions ranging, for instance, from "the obsessive" to "the hysteroid." His own classificatory groups are empirical and clinical. Ten categories are offered:

1. Hyperthymic Psychopaths
2. Depressive Psychopaths

3. Insecure Psychopaths—Sensitives and Anankasts
4. Fanatic Psychopaths
5. Attention-seeking Psychopaths
6. Labile Psychopaths
7. Explosive Psychopaths
8. Unfeeling Psychopaths
9. Weak-willed Psychopaths
10. Asthenic Psychopaths

No type, we are told, is quite exclusive, although certain qualities appear to cancel out while others cluster together. Schneider's awareness of the complexity of human attributes and the range of individual differences leads him to admit that relatively few patients can be allocated to appropriate types. However, this does not seem to apply to the type with which this study is concerned. The characteristics of the insecure type are "fundamental and deep-rooted within the personality." The same applies to the unfeeling or affectionless type, the attention-seekers, and possibly the fanatics. But with regard to the other types the descriptions "relate to more peripheral traits and do not reveal anything so central to the personality. They describe the façade of outward behaviour only."

The group termed "Insecure Psychopaths" by Schneider includes what other writers have called "obsessional personalities," "anal characters," or "obsessoids." This, in fact, is the disorder with which this study is primarily concerned, and Schneiderian criteria had been employed in the classification of the subjects discussed herein.

The "insecure" group includes two very closely related sub-groups—the "sensitives" and the "anankasts." The first are sensitive in Kretschmer's sense—i.e., they have a "conscious retention of affect-laden complexes" but little capacity for the expression or outlet of affect. Such persons are chronically unsure of themselves, which may be reflected in withdrawal or in ambitious pride. They have high moral standards coupled with an awareness of their own shortcomings. They are "men of conscience" who are over-scrupulous and beset by ethical considerations. These are frequently in constant conflict with intense, and often abnormally directed, sexual drive, so that intermittent failures in repression result in shame and self-reproach. Compensatory or over-compensatory activities may include unusual formality and "correct" behaviour. Apparent forecfulness may conceal acute timidity and anxiety.

The term "anankastic" is often used as synonymous with "insecure," so subsuming the "sensitive" traits described above. The grammatical reason for Schneider's selection of the term "anankast" has been given above. A further reason is that the word "obsessional" has now acquired connotations of "neurosis" or reaction to external stress, whereas, as has been seen, Schneider is concerned with psychopathy, with the degree to which the individual or his society is afflicted by his own abnormality of personality. In his description of the anankast Schneider concentrates primarily on compulsivity. His differentiation between compulsive personality factors and symptoms is one only of degree: "Compulsion only becomes abnormal above a certain degree of intensity. In theory we can isolate it but in practice it is integral with other modes of experience ... "(p. 89). Compulsive thoughts, impulses, and sentiments are involved in the insecure person's experience; psychic control varies in inverse relation to the relative strength of the emotional impulse: "The emotional or affect-charged state becomes the conditioning factor, just that which Westphal wanted to exclude from his concept of compulsive ideas" (p. 90). Thus, the affect-charging of the insecure personality may be responsible for the associated intensity of compulsions. These, however, are not usually compulsive feelings: "Compulsive feelings are rare but compulsive ideas (or thoughts) are very much a part of insecure personality. We might logically expect this. There are persistent underground feelings of guilt and inadequacy which give rise to sudden compulsive ideas. Insecure personalities live in a continuous anxiety state lest they have omitted something or brought about some disaster or that something vague but ominous is about to take place" (p. 90).

It will be noted that the identification or classification of a person as an anankast in terms of the criteria mentioned so far require *phenomenological* examination. The characteristic attributes are ones of subjective awareness and cannot be *directly* examined by the observation of behaviour or by objective test techniques. Schneider goes on to describe similar attributes—fears of misfortune, scruples, and anxieties. He proceeds to compulsive urges—"vague misgivings lest one may do some harm, e.g. kill one's child, but without the presence of any real urge to do so" (p. 91)—and compulsive, anxiety-accompanied ideas. The only statement made regarding observable characteristics is as follows: "To the onlooker anankasts appear as carefully dressed people, pedantic, correct, scrupulous and yet with it all somehow exceedingly insecure. The compensations they reach after seem unnatural and constrained. Sometimes anankasts will go to much lengths to protect themselves against contact and develop such bizarre habits and rituals that they turn into very odd individuals although it may only be personal insecurity that underlies all the oddity" (p. 92).

9

Some Non-Psychiatric Theorists

The ''approaches'' summarized so far have been those of the major psychiatric theorists. They were selected, in fact, as being nominal influences upon current psychiatric thinking. Many other major figures in psychiatry have made studies of, and pronouncements about, the subject of obsessionality. But it is fair to say that these have all been merely modified versions of one or other of the three presented here. All the current Western European and American views of the problem reflect one or other of those views or a combination thereof. Contemporary British psychiatric views are predominantly eclectic. Eclecticism has many clear virtues; but it can veer dangerously close to confusion. And it seems probable that the muddling of concepts which is so clearly discernible in English-language publications on this subject is directly attributable to Henderson and Gillespie's (1950) uneasy admixture of German classifications, Freudian dynamics, and Mayerian social interrelationship theories.

One of the purposes of presenting summaries of the great psychiatric ''school'' approaches was to examine why some working clinicians confuse the concept of obsessional symptomatology and obsessional personality. But to examine the development of ideas about obsessionality in general it is necessary also to look at the work of a number of theorists who are or were not strictly psychiatrists. Their views have probably had relatively little influence on general psychiatric thinking. But no academic study of this field can afford to ignore them.

THE REFLEXOLOGICAL APPROACH: IVAN PAVLOV

Pavlov was, as he stressed, neither a psychiatrist nor a psychologist, but a physiologist. And one of the almost unbelievable things about this great scientist is that he was almost eighty when he began to apply his concepts to psychiatry, which necessitated clinic observations and intensive study in a completely unfamiliar field. (His contributions on obsessional disorder were made when he was about eighty-four, some two years before his death.) But for many years before he turned his attention to the relevance of his laboratory work to psychiatry and psychology he had been concerned with the behavioural variations shown by his experimental animals.

Pavlov's typology is based on his postulation of the twin cortical processes of excitation and inhibition. Both of these processes are seen as active properties of cortical tissue. At first he considered only the *balance* between these two processes. Subsequently he developed his theoretical framework to include also their *intensity* and their *lability*.

In the early 1920s Pavlov had remarked upon individual differences in conditionability between his experimental dogs. And in his attempts to systematize these differences he was soon to note parallels with Hipprocrates' classical types. Thus, in 1930 he summarized: "From our thirty years of work we find our dogs fall generally into the four classical type of temperaments of Hippocrates: the extreme excitatory and inhibitory and the two central types of quiet and lively" (Gantt, II, p. 64).

The parallel here was developed to include the criteria of intensity and lability, so that by 1935 he was to divide his animals into two major groups of "*strong*" and "*weak*" (referring to the intensity of the basic excitatory and inhibitory processes of the nervous system). The "strong" animals were further divided into "*balanced*" and "*unbalanced.*" The strong, balanced group were then further subdivided into "*labile*" and "*inert.*" Thus, finally, Pavlov offered the following fourfold classification (Gantt, II, p. 177):

Strong, unbalanced with excitation predominating: The "Choleric" type.
Strong, well-balanced, inert: The "Phlegmatic" type.
Strong, well-balanced, labile: The "Sanguine" type.
Weak, inhibitory: The "Melancholic" type.

It will be noticed that the three criteria allow for twenty-four possible combinations, thus:

	Strength		Weakness	
	Balanced	Unbalanced	Balanced	Unbalanced
	$e = i$	$e > i\ i > e$	$e = i$	$e > i\ i > e$
e and i inert				
e and i labile				
e labile, i inert				
e inert, i labile				

MacMillan (1963) has discussed the logical reasons why this mathematically possible number must be reduced. The main reduction is that all twelve possible "weak" types are subsumed under the "melancholic" category and, in fact, only one "weak" type has been experimentally observed. Pavlov himself explained this:

> And, lastly a weak type of animals which resemble most the melancholic temperament distinguished by Hippocrates; their common prevalent feature is their liability to inhibition, owing to the constantly weak and readily irradiating internal inhibition, and, particularly, to external inhibition produced by the action of different alien stimuli which in themselves may be of no great significance. In other respects this is a less uniform type than all the others. ... The cause of this lack of uniformity lies, of course, in the fact that animals of the weak type; just as those of the strong types, may be distinguished according to other features besides the energy of their nervous processes. However, the prevalent and excessive weakness of either inhibition alone or of both the processes nullifies the vital value of variations according to other features. (Gantt, II, p. 177).

In his attempts to apply his laboratory findings to human behaviour Pavlov introduced the concept of "the second signalling system"—speech. This he considered to be the attribute which distinguishes human beings from animals. For, whereas animals can only react to "external agents," human beings can also react to abstractions in the form of words. The cortical development of a first signalling system allows, by means of conditioned connections and associations, a much greater adaptation than that permitted by sub-cortical unconditioned responses. But the higher activity facilitated by the second signalling system (in the frontal lobes) enables man to create the highest adaptation in the "complex correlation of the organisms with the surroundings."

Pavlov considered that in any given individual the two signalling systems could be balanced in their development or one could predominate. He suggested that an individual whose first signalling system predominated over the second would be an "artistic type." The opposite situation would result in the "thinking type." The application of Pavlovian typological method to humans therefore involves the interrelating of the balance–intensity–lability triad with this new theory of intersystem balance. The full implications of this do not seem to have been worked out, but Pavlov presented the following derivations of the "weak" type:

(a) Hysterical personality: Occurs in the weak general type with "artistic" predominance of the first signalling system.
(b) "Constitutional neurasthenia": Occurs in the weak general type with balanced ("intermediate") signalling systems.
(c) Psychasthenia: Occurs in the weak general type with "thinking" predominance of the second signalling system.

In 1934 Pavlov published a paper entitled "An Attempt at a Physiological Interpretation of Obsessions and of Paranoia" (Gantt, II, pp. 150-61). Here he introduced the idea of "pathological inertness," referring to a pathological weakening in the inhibitory function of brain cells. He had deduced this impairment of process from experiments in which attempts had been made to reverse the effects of stimuli of "opposite conditioned significations"—i.e., the stimulus to which an excitatory response had been conditioned was now applied without reinforcement while the original inhibitory stimulus was now reinforced. "Weak" and castrated dogs appeared to respond to this change but subsequently reverted to their original responses. Further experiments demonstrated that the animals' cortical excitatory processes were now less yielding to the inhibitory processes, so that extinction did not take place. In other cases a negative instead of a positive effect was produced. The first effect is an example of "the paradoxical phase," the second of "the ultra-paradoxical phase."

Meanwhile, however, the animals were producing normal responses to other stimuli. Pavlov postulated, therefore, that under certain conditions "*pathological points*" could appear in the cerebral cortex, precise areas of inertness.

Pavlov postulated that in man "the symptoms of *stereotypy*, reiteration, and perseveration, as well as in obsessive neuroses and paranoia, the fundamental patho-physiological phenomenon is one and the same, namely ... 'pathological inertness'." The first three symtoms reflect inertness in the motor area of the cortex, while "in obsessive neuroses and in paranoia we have similar inertness in other cortical cells relative to our other sensations, feelings and conceptions."

After pointing out that psychiatric opinion was divided as to whether paranoia and obsessionality were, in fact, clearly differentiable, Pavlov goes on to examine various aspects of his theory. It transpires that the obsessional is not necessarily of weak nervous type. In fact, "pathological inertness of the excitatory process in a strong type must be considerable." Indeed, at one stage he implies that obsessionality will more usually occur in strong types: "As to the predisposing factor, it will be a common one in *obsessional neurosis* and in *paranoia*, i.e., a nervous system inclined to disease, as in our laboratory data. It may be, however, the weak type of the nervous system as well as the strong but unbalanced one" (Gantt, II, p. 157).

It would thus appear that, while the psychasthene is of weak type, obsessional disorder due to pathological inertia can appear in both the weak and the strong unbalanced types.

In this paper and in an open letter to Janet (to whose work Pavlov makes several respectful references), Pavlov interpret's Janet's "*Sentiments d'emprise*" (obsessional feelings of being dominated) as the result of the ultra-paradoxical phase which is "the base of the weakening of the idea of the opposite of our patients" (Gantt, II, p. 148). He postulates that response to a positive conditional stimulus and a negative stimulus, although in opposition, are "united by association and at the same time subdued by reciprocal induction, i.e. one ... stimulates and reinforces the other" (Gantt, II, p. 148). If the positive stimulus activates a weak cell or "sore point" it causes inhibition. This in turn induces "in the other half" a state of excitation instead of inhibition, so that the stimulus with which it is associated does not now cause inhibition but excitation. Thus "the patient is persecuted exactly by the things he is most eager to escape ... "(Gantt, II, p. 182).

Compulsions are postulated to be due to pathological inertia *of the excitatory process* which "persists even in the face of conditions which should normally convert it into the inhibitory process. ... Such a pathological condition may result from a continually increasing tension of the excitatory process or through its collision with the inhibitory process" (Gantt, II, p. 164).

The reader begins to have the uneasy suspicion that Pavlov is either trying to explain too much with too little or is guilty of loose organization of his psychiatric concepts. Perhaps as a result of his enthusiasm, or possibly because of ambiguities in translation, there seems to be a shifting of terms as Pavlov develops each of his arguments and applies them to specific examples.

First, although Pavlov stresses that his experimental production of pathological inertia occurred in weak, disturbed dogs, it turns out that the phenomenon can occur in *any* type.

Second, whereas his description of pathological inertia specifically refers to a weakening of *inhibitory* process, he later uses it in connection with the pathological change in *excitatory* process.

Third, it is not clear whether "sore points" in the cortexes of animals are due to "disease," constitution, or experimental/situational conflicts. In the case of humans the suggested aetiologies are suspiciously diffuse—"irregular development, occasional accentuation of one or another of our emotions (instincts), disease of some internal organ or a whole systems. ... Strong and overwhelming life experiences" (Gantt, II, p. 156).

Thus, of the concepts crucial to the Pavlovian explanation of obsessional disorder, only the "ultra-paradoxical phase" remains unchanged. Unfortunately this is not an explanatory mechanism at all but merely a descriptive term referring to observable behaviour.

With regard to the differential problems of symptoms versus personality Pavlov is fairly definite. Clearly his "types" are personality structures. His psychasthenic personality is that described by Janet. When he discusses obsessional disorder, he uses a term translated as "obsessive neurosis." This is referred to as "a nervous system inclined to disease," as a "disease," and as a "morbid form." The general presumption seems to be of constitutionally determined structure, but: "Naturally, besides an inherent predisposition one meets with cases of unstable or fragile nervous systems incapacitated by unfortunate occurrences, such as trauma, infections, intoxications and violent emotions'' (Gantt, II, p. 154).

Pavlov's attempts to apply his theories to actual cases drawn from Kretschmer are not very convincing. He himself admits his limitations in the final paragraph of the ''Obsessions'' paper: ''I am no clinician (I have been and remain a physiologist) and, of course, at present (so late in life) would have neither the time nor the possibility to become one. ... I dare not aspire to sufficient competency from a clinical point of view ... '' (Gantt, II, p. 161). But with a mixture of modesty and confidence he ends by saying: ''clinicians, neurologists and psychiatrists, in their respective domains, will inevitably have to reckon with the following patho-physiological fact: the complete isolation of functionally pathological (at the aetiological moment) points of the cortex, the pathological inertness of the excitatory process, and the ultra-paradoxical phase'' (Gant, II, p. 161).

THE DIMENSIONAL APPROACH: HANS EYSENCK

For more than thirty-five years the field of abnormal psychology in Britain has been dominated by the brilliant, controversial figure of Hans Eysenck. During that time his output of research has been consistent and formidable and, with the possible exceptions of Sir Cyril Burt and Raymond Cattell, he has been the most prolific writer in psychology. It would be quite outside the range of this book to attempt any close examination of his work but, fortunately, his basic tenets are few and straightforward. The mass of his investigations have been aimed at the testing of predictions drawn from the central theory, while most of his theoretical and review studies have been examinations of external evidence in the light thereof. From the present point of view the limits of appropriate review are narrowed even more because, as far as can be determined, Eysenck has neither investigated obsessional disorder as such, nor made more than the most passing pronouncement upon it.

Eysenck's central objective has always been the establishment of a hypothetico-deductive theory which could account for known facts about mental abnormality in terms of an objectively established dimensional framework. He reported his basic work in this direction in *Dimensions of Personality* (1947) and *The Scientific Study of Personality* (1952). Starting from a hierarchical view of personality structure and usually using large-scale psychometric methods, he demonstrated that the various levels of personality organization can be defined operationally in terms of correlations. Thus, the lowest level of generality in human behaviour can be expressed by test reliability correlations, the level of ''traits'' by inter-test correlations, and the highest level—that of ''types'' or such second-order concepts as ''neuroticism'' or ''g''—by inter-trait correlations. He postulates that mental abnormality is only quantitatively different from normality, that is to say that a given sort of abnormality represents the extreme of a continuous variable or variables. Thus, while he accepts the use of such terms as "types" (which represent a convenient way of referring to a given degree of variation from the norm or a constellation of such variations), he objects to the allocation or diagnosis of psychiatric categories instead of the determination of the underlying "dimensions" followed by the quantitative estimate of the patient's position on those "dimensions."

In *The Structure of Human Personality* (1953) Eysenck conducted an intensive review of the literature to demonstrate how other work could be reconciled with his own approach. He concluded that the two most fruitful and well-established dimensions which could be used as a basis for further development of his theory were neuroticism and extraversion–introversion. Neuroticism is regarded as a constitutionally determined level of autonomic nervous lability (or, to be more precise, a drive related thereto). Extraversion–introversion is seen as related to the degree of excitation and inhibition in the central nervous system, a balance which again is largely constitutionally determined. This view, which is based on Pavlov's postulations, can be combined with Hullian theory to allow the derivation of predictions and explanations regarding conditioning, learning, socialization, and the behavioural effects of stimulant or depressant drugs.

A mass of experimental studies have produced evidence for the association between behavioural measures and the above theory. As the Eysencks (1964) have pointed out, these refer to personality in its *genotypic* aspect. Interaction with the environment produces *phenotypic*, descriptive differences in extraversion–introversion which, claim the Eysencks, can best be measured by questionnaires. The questionnaire devised by Eysenck to measure N and E was the Maudsley Personality Inventory (MPI) and its later refinement, the Eysenck Personality Inventory (EPI). These are too well known to require description here. Suffice it to say that they possess outstanding construct validity and are highly reliable, well-standardized instruments from which separate scores for E and N may readily be derived. The two dimensions are claimed to be quite independent of each other. Interpretation (and, it is claimed, the results of both standardization and subsequent validation studies) involves the well-known quadrants—High Introversion/High Neuroticism, High Extraversion/High Neuroticism, High Introversion/Low Neuroticism, High Extraversion/Low Neuroticism. It is claimed that, in accordance with Eysenck's theory, hysteric patients give responses which place them in the High Extraversion/High Neuroticism quadrant, while "dysthymic" patients figure in the High Introversion/High Neuroticism quadrant. "Dysthmyics," in fact, are introverted neurotics. And it is in this group that obsessionals appear, along with "anxiety states," "depressives," and "mixed neurotics." It is clearly relevant to enquire: (a) how Eysenck defined an "obsessional" and (b) how sound the evidence was which indicated that "obsessionals" are members of the "dysthymic" class.

Although Eysenck's works are lucid and detailed, it is difficult to trace the development of his assertion regarding obsessionality. The basic academic detective work has, however, been published by Hamilton (1957a). Eysenck's earliest major study (1947) began by testing the hypothesis that extraversion–introversion vary independently of neurosis. Thirty-nine items covering patients' social history, personality, and symptoms were obtained for 700 male service in-patients at the Mill Hill Emergency Hospital. They suffered "from the mainly reactive types of mental illness," the majority of Mill Hill patients having been described by Slater (1943) as exhibiting "not so much an illness as a simple failure to adapt to army routine and discipline. ..." The thirty-nine items had been abstracted from comprehensive item-sheets completed for each patient by the psychiatrist in charge. Eysenck (1947, pp. 3-8) presents a "selection of items" from this sheet along with the percentage occurrence of each item for 5300 male and 2000 female service patients separately. Among this selection figure "Obsessive-compulsive symptoms" (with a frequency of 5% each for males and females) and "Obsessional state" (frequency of 2% each for males and females). But in the list of the thirty-nine items selected for study (p. 35) appears only the word "Obsessional." Subsequently (e.g., p. 36) he uses the term "obsessional tendency." So, *ab initio* it seems clear that Eysenck failed to differentiate between obsessional symptoms and obsessional personality, nor indeed, had he the necessary information to make such a differentiation had he so desired. If the "Obsessional" item in the short list refers to symptoms, then the significance of the resultant data must be open to doubt. If, on the other hand, it referred to the "Obsessional state" entries on the original item-sheets, then the 700 patients selected for study are unlikely to have included more than 14 such individuals.

Whatever the case may be, Eysenck proceeded to factor analyse the correlations among the thirty-nine items, and in the table of factor loadings the item "obsessional" appeared in the same quadrant as "anxiety," "depression," and "apathy." (It is of interest to note that in the same quadrant there also appeared "cyclothymia," "dyspepsia," and "somatic anxiety.") From this analysis Eysenck concluded that there were two main factors: "(1) A general 'neuroticism' factor, and (2) the dichotomous division between hysteria and dysthymia" (Eysenck 1947, p. 37). A footnote to the same page informs the reader: "The term 'Dysthymia' is used throughout this book to characterize the syndrome of anxiety, reactive depression, and obsessional tendencies found in our analysis. It was considered necessary to introduce a new term for this syndrome as none of the existing terms were found adequate."

On the basis, therefore, of one non-defined item, it would seem that Eysenck included "the obsessional" in his new "syndrome." To make matters worse, as Hamilton (1957) points out, "obsessional" had a zero loading on the orthogonal factor of neuroticism, which suggests that the obsessional feature under consideration was unrelated to severity of neurosis. In view of all this, it is surprising that in all Eysenck's subsequent work on those lines it has been the practice to subsume obsessionality under the concept of "Dysthymia" and the homogeneity of the latter has never been further examined. Thus, in Hildebrand's (1953) unpublished but much-cited thesis, the overall differences between neurotic sub-groups were tested but not separate within-group differences. Hamilton reports that on several tests (the Maudsley Medical Questionnaire, Annoyance Questionnaire, Extra-Punitive Humour, and the Static Ataxia Test) Hildebrand's obsessionals' scores were closer to those of the hysterics than to those of the anxiety states, while on a number of others the anxiety states' scores were closer to those of the hysterics than to those of the obsessionals.

In his reports of the MPI standardization data Eysenck (1959b) maintains that "those suffering from anxiety, reactive depression, obsessional/compulsive symptoms, phobias, etc." have high scores on neuroticism and on introversion, but the data for all these "dysthymics" are lumped together so that no check can be made on the results of specific sub-groups. It is to be noted, however, that his reference is now to symptomatology rather than "obsessionality" or "obsessional states." The same general claim is made by the Eysencks (1964) regarding the EPI. Here they present standardization data for the sub-groups separately which appear to support the claim. However, the group under consideration is now termed "obsessional" once more and consists of ten men and thirteen women (from a total abnormal standardization group of 483). No details of the criteria employed in selecting this small sample seem yet to have been published.

Eysenck has developed, with enormous energy and scholarship, a convincing research-provoking theoretical structure. But his treatment of obsessionality appears superficial, to say the least. The fact that the weakness is obvious is highly suggestive, because it is quite untypical of Eysenck to leave any errors showing; it has been his policy—as with, e.g., "reactive inhibition"—that attack is the best form of defence. Vulnerable flanks have not only been defended, they have literally bristled with high-level theorizing and research developments, as well as consolidation of evidence. That the opposite state of affairs exists here suggests that obsessional disorder represents a chink in Eysenck's massive armour of erudition. As will be seen later in this chapter, it may be that his stringent view of what constitutes a "neurosis" leads him to deny nosological validity to "types" of neurosis other than the hysteric/dysthymic dichotomy. But this can not account for his failure to discriminate between obsessional personality and obsessional symptoms.

In summary it may be said that Eysenck handles the problem of obsessional disorder simply by lumping it in with anxiety states and depression in the category of "dysthymia." His treatment of the subject is characterized by:

(a) A failure to define the terms "obsessional," "obsessionality," "obsessional state," and "obsessional tendency" which appear to be used interchangeably.

(b) A failure to differentiate between obsessional symptoms and obsessional personality or to discuss whether he considers such a distinction to be useful.

His assumption regarding obsessionality as an undifferentiated sub-group within "dysthymia" rests upon:

(c) The consideration of data from a very small number of cases.
(d) A single, undefined item on a checklist, the significance of which is unknown but which probably bore reference to secondary symptoms.
(e) The subsequent acceptance of data produced for another purpose and based, as far as obsessionality is concerned, on results from similarly ill-defined and undifferentiated cases. (Even had these data been valid for the present purpose they had not been statistically treated as such and appear to offer dubious support.)
(f) Results on the EPI drawn from 23 out of 483 members of the abnormal standardization group. The clinical status of these patients has not been defined, nor, once again, has any discrimination been made between symptoms and personality.

THE BEHAVIOURAL/LEARNING APPROACH: HANS EYSENCK AND JOSEPH WOLPE

The most radical shift in the study and treatment of mental disorders during this century, at least, has been professional acceptance of the validity of approach from the viewpoint of normal learning. This is not the place to examine the social, theoretical, and pragmatic antecedents of that revolution in attitude and practice; a number of excellent accounts are available, and the reader is particularly referred to Kazdin (1978), Rachlin (1980), and Krasner (1982). The new movement was in a direct line from classical behaviorists—Pavlov, Watson, and Hull. And its emergence was preceded by the work of several researchers who had studied conditioning, anxiety, and neurosis (e.g., Salter, 1949; Spence, 1956) or who had applied learning concepts to the examination of Freudian theory and used them in psychotherapy (notably Mowrer, 1950; Dollard and Miller, 1950). But its full flowering may be said to date from an influential address by Eysenck (1959a) which surveyed the evidence and argued for a fundamental change of approach. The article does not focus upon obsessional–compulsive disorders *per se*, but it prepared the ground for a new approach to those disorders, as to all neurotic problems.

Eysenck's position (which, incidentally, has remained consistent in the interim) seems, upon re-reading after more than a quarter-century, to be remarkably modest and acceptable. This must be taken as a sign of its basic appeal and the aptness of its timing. For, like many other paradigm shifts (*cf.* Freud's early work) it has now been assimilated into both professional and lay thinking. At the time, it was regarded as blatantly provocative and succeeded in raising a furor in both psychiatric and psychological circles.

Eysenck begins his article by dismissing Freudian theory as unscientific and pointing out that there is little evidence for the practical efficacy of Freudian or eclectic psychotherapy. The psychologist's contribution to psychotherapy, apart from intelligence testing, is limited to the administration and interpretation of projective tests, which are unreliable and invalid. He goes on to make a number of points, which may be summarized as follows:

1. Neurotic reactions, like all others, are *learned*, and must obey the laws of learning, derived by psychologists from laboratory studies of learning and conditioning.
2. Modern learning theory would claim that:

    (a) Neurotic symptoms are learned patterns of behaviour of an unadaptive kind. (The paradigm cited is the establishment of a phobic fear of white rats in Watson's little Albert.)

    (b) There are individual differences in conditionability (both in speed and strength of conditioning). The most readily conditionable individuals are most prone to develop phobias and anxiety.

    (c) There are also individual differences in autonomic reactivity which determine the degree of response to reinforcement. The more reactive the individual, the more likely he is to produce strongly conditioned fear reactions and anxiety.

    (d) Individual differences in conditionability and autonomic reactivity have been conceptualized as producing the two personality dimensions of introversion and neuroticism respectively.

    (e) The combination of high *I* and high *N* produces the "dysthymic" individual, who is "almost predestined to suffer from anxieties, conditioned fears and phobias, compulsions and obsessions, reactive depressions and so forth."

    (f) Some conditioned responses are adaptive and, indeed, indispensable; socialization probably depends upon conditioning. Anxiety acts as a powerful mediating drive. The individual with low *I* but high *N* is likely to be psychopathic or hysterical.
3. This theoretical approach differs from the psychoanalytic one in a variety of ways, the most crucial being:

    (a) Freudian theory regards neurotic symptoms as "the visible upshot of unconscious causes." Learning theory denies the latter—symptoms are simply unadaptive conditioned responses (learned habits). It is not a question of a neurosis underlying the symptoms—the symptoms *are* the neurosis. Removal of the symptoms means the elimination of the neurosis.

(b) The Freudian model is not amenable to experimental study, quantification, objective tests, etc. The learning model is; the mass of research into conditioning has produced elaborate laws of learning from which precise deductions can be made.

4. The use of behaviour therapy derived from the learning model will encourage the positive use of the special knowledge and competence of psychologists, who can now play a central role in psychotherapy. Who actually carries out behaviour therapy, once a scientific program for each patient has been prescribed, is unimportant.

Eysenck's article touches only lightly upon the practical implementation of the learning approach, but this was ably summarized by his colleague Jones (1958), a pioneer in the actual techniques of early behaviour therapy. However, the main inspiration for a surge of interest among practitioners was Wolpe's stimulating book *Psychotherapy by Reciprocal Inhibition* (1958), which detailed the application of learning postulates to clinical practice.

The technique of reciprocal inhibition (or systematic desensitization, as it came to be termed) requires the construction of a graded hierarchy of variants of the primary fear. The patient is trained in progressive muscular relaxation (often with the aid of tranquillizers or hypnosis). Then, while in a state of deep relaxation, he is presented on successive occasions with each item in the hierarchy, commencing with the most innocuous. Should anxiety be reported at any stage, the session is aborted, and item presentation subsequently recommenced at a lower level in the hierarchy.

Wolpe based his approach on the assumption that the reduction in autonomic reactivity associated with relaxation would reciprocally inhibit the anxiety induced by the fear items. This theory has been subjected to considerable criticism, as have the alternative explanations of counterconditioning, habituation, and extinction. In a chapter entitled "The Birth, Life and Death of Systematic Desensitization," Yates (1975) has provided a survey of arguments and findings which seem to devastate Wolpe's original approach. He presents ample evidence that the same therapeutic effects can be achieved without any of what Wolpe stressed as the crucial elements of his technique—relaxation, the painstakingly. constructed gradient, and the avoidance of anxiety by careful ascent of the gradient. Yates impishly enquires "Can we meaningfully continue to refer to the Cheshire cat when only its smile is left?" (1975, p. 163).

Despite the highly unsatisfactory status of systematic desensitization, and the many spirited attacks upon it, the method has been employed with considerable success, particularly in the treatment of monosymptomatic phobias. At the same time, Wolpe's (1958) original book includes the first claims of behaviour therapy's success with obsessional problems among reports of an "apparently cured" or "much improved" rate of about 90% in a series of 88 patients. Wolpe devotes several pages to discussions of the applicability of his methods to obsessional problems. But his own data do not provide very convincing evidence for this. From his Table 1 (pp. 208-13) it appears that:

(a) Of the eighty-eight patients in the series only six were "obsessional" (although in summary Table 2 [p. 216] Wolpe reports that there were eight).

(b) Only *one* of the six appears among the twenty-eight (or 32%) cases regarded as "apparently cured."

(c) *Three* of the remaining five appear among the fifty (or 57%) cases regarded as "much improved."

(d) The other *two* appear among the ten (or 11%) cases regarded by Wolpe as failures.

On the basis of those data alone Wolpe can scarcely claim to have had as much success with obsessional cases as with non-obsessionals. The data become even less impressive when the composition of this "obsessional" group is examined more closely. Table 1 gives no clinical details other than sex, age, and "Salient Clinical Features." The latter are as follows:

Patient Number	Salient Clinical Features
21	Paranoid obsessions.
41	Interpersonal anxiety; multiple phobias; severe obsessional state.
53	Obsessional ideas; phobia.
56	Interpersonal anxiety; obsession.
80	Obsessions.
86	Severe obsessions.

It is impossible to tell from this whether these "features" refer to symptoms or to personality. In view of Wolpe's consistent emphasis on symptoms it seems most likely that it is these that are referred to. No further details are given in the section concerned. But as it happens, case 21, the only one to be graded as a "cure," is described in the text.

The "Paranoid Obsession" turns out to be a case of a young man who was unreasonably jealous in regard to his fiancée. No evidence is presented of any obsessional–compulsive symptoms or personality features, and it seems likely that the case would have been classified by a phenomenologist as one of "Abnormal Psychogenic Reaction," non-specific regarding personality.

Another case discussed at length by Wolpe is described as one of "compulsive mimicry." On page 90, the case is cited, however, as an example of a "borderline case" displaying both hysterical and obsessional reactions; and on page 188, this case is described as one of "Hysterical Compulsion" and is included in a series of "Cases Illustrating Therapy of Low-Anxiety Hysteria."

Budding suspicions as to a degree of non-conformity in Wolpe's nosological procedures are not allayed by the other cases put forward in the text as examples of obsessional disorder. They include: (a) a "Kleptomaniac" with "a history of more than 100 undetected thefts of money" (p. 93); (b) an exhibitionist who had "exhibited to school-girls particularly frequently and with special relish" (p. 94); and (c) an "eating obsession", i.e., a woman who found irresistible a number of "delectable food" items which happened to be either of high salt content or fattening, both being contra-indicated by her cardiac insufficiency.

On the evidence Wolpe presents, only three of the cases in his series or among those discussed in the text are indubitably obsessional—either in symptomatology *or* in personality. One of these cases is described in the text as being a young woman who was preoccupied with formulating "problems" and their solutions; no mention is made of the outcome in this case. The other two cases are numbers 80 and 86 in the series. Number 80 had a long-standing obsessional fear that he had left objects such as razor blades and needles lying about where children might find them and injure themselves. Number 86 was "plagued by unwelcome thoughts" and eventually could not perform simple movements such as sitting down unless "favourable thoughts" were in his mind. *Significantly enough both these latter cases figure among the series "failures."*

Wolpe made (and continues to make) an invaluable contribution to the behaviour therapy movement. But, as we have just seen, his otherwise impressive therapeutic achievements cannot be taken to include success in the treatment of obsessional disorders. We shall discuss more recent work in a later chapter.

Where general principles are concerned, Eysenck's and Wolpe's positions, and that of the behaviour therapy movement in general, have been vigorously criticized on theoretical grounds (notably by Breger and McGaugh, 1965) and in terms of whether the therapeutic procedures are in fact behaviouristic (Locke, 1971). The debate, in fact, still continues. But despite divergences of opinion as to its theoretical bases, the behaviour therapy (BT) movement took off in the late 1950s, gathered momentum at a meteoric rate, and was accepted and well established by the mid-1960s. It is now regarded as a standard, conventional form of psychotherapy.

Before leaving the topic, several theoretical points are worthy of mention:

(a) Eysenck has been criticized for his bland and confident use of the phrase "modern learning theory." This suggests that there is one such theory generally accepted by psychologists, which, of course, is very far from being the case.

(b) He clearly favours some variety of S-R behavioural learning approach, quite overlooking the competing claims of cognitive learning theories.

(c) His constant references to "conditioning" seem to refer only to classical conditioning, which overlooks the fact that even within the behavioural-learning group there exist several quite different paradigms.

(d) The s in s-r approaches is usually taken to refer to environmental stimuli. In general, behaviour therapists have assumed that neurotic responses are triggered by specific external events.

(e) In the tradition of classical Watsonian behaviourism, early behaviour therapists at least tended to take "responses" to refer to observable behaviours.

(f) Behaviour therapy was intended to replace semantic therapies, with the latter's reliance upon cognitive features.

(g) Despite the manifest successes of BT in several areas, it is only during the last fifteen years that substantial advances have been made in its application to obsessional disorders. And in view of (f) above, it is ironic that, as we shall see in a later chapter, these advances have co-developed with an increasing recognition of the importance of cognitive factors.

10

Theoretical Views of the Relationship Between Obsessional Symptoms and Compulsive Personality

As we shall see, some authorities regard obsessive–compulsive states or neuroses as extensions of the compulsive (obsessional, anankastic) personality. Others do not accept that symptoms can be traits developed beyond some threshold of individual or social acceptance. Generally, these writers are those who follow the conventional medical model and do not relate an illness or syndrome to the pre-morbid state of affairs. That is to say, their nosological categories are more discrete and geared only to the current clinical picture.

Others may accept this but emphasize that, in some cases at least, obsessional symptoms may manifest themselves in people who do not possess obsessional personalities. What they deny is not that there can be an association between traits and symptoms but that any such association exists, at least to a significant degree, in the case of obsessional disorder.

It might be assumed that such a controversy should be amenable to empirical analysis. Clearly, it should be. There are several reasons why empirical studies have so far been contradictory and generally unconvincing.

Most importantly, there are discrepancies in the precision of individual clinicians' diagnostic techniques. For instance, considerable phenomenological subtlety is required to distinguish between the experience of compulsion and that of schizophrenic insertion. An over-valued idea may be misclassified as an obsession. The fact that a patient is verbally fluent, coupled with his hypochondriasis, may lead to him being labelled as "hysteric."

Second, even where diagnoses are made with care and consistency, the nosological *criteria* employed by individual clinicians still vary widely. For instance, one clinician, emphasizing the anxiety and depressed mood evinced by the new patient, will label his condition as that of "anxiety neurosis." Conversely, another clinician, observing the facial twitches of a tense and anxious patient, will label him as suffering from "obsessional neurosis." The experienced clinician, recalling that many of his previous patients who originally appeared to be suffering from obsessional problems subsequently turned out to be schizophrenic, may cut a corner by opting for the label "schizophrenia" in *all* such cases.

The data for determining pre-morbid personality are by definition historical. This immediately brings up well-known problems relating to the unreliability of human recall and the validity of reports. To elicit relatively objective reports of the patient's previous characteristics and behaviour is a lengthy and highly skilled task. Furthermore, it usually requires informants to make comparative judgements for which they have insufficient experience ("Would you say he was less thoughtful than other husbands, Mrs. Smith?" "So you think that throughout her life she has worried more than most people?") Again, the clinician's elicitatory techniques may not be above reproach. Clinicians naturally tend to "lead their witnesses," not only by the questions they ask, but by the way in which they ask them. And finally, their assessment of the "evidence" they receive tends to be distorted, both by hindsight and by the nosological approaches they favour. However high their integrity, they would scarcely be human if this were not so. But this is particularly the case in the present instance. The diagnosis itself may not be in dispute; the therapeutic regime may be clear; in other words, the patient's welfare and treatment are not at stake. The question to be answered— whether or not this patient, currently suffering from obsessional disorder, did or did not originally manifest an obsessional personality—seems to have few immediate consequences. It is basically of theoretical interest, being research-inspired rather than of direct relevance to the patient's needs.

As stated above, where the relationship or association between obsessional/compulsive *symptoms* and obsessional/compulsive *personality* is concerned, the standard psychiatric literature reflects wide disagreements. But authoritative, published opinions will be found to fall along certain main lines of approach.

First of all, there are writers who do not differentiate between symptoms and traits or whose theoretical approaches involve the consideration of symptoms alone. Thus, Henderson and Gillespie (1950) are concerned with the Meyerian concept of "psychoneurotic reaction types" so that, in the earlier editions of their textbook, the obsessional personality as such is not mentioned.

A second group of authorities regards both symptoms and traits as products of some common underlying factor which is probably genetically determined. Janet (1903) considered both to reflect a degenerative weakness in psychic integration, while Pavlov (1941) saw them as the outcome of a particular type of nervous system conditionability. Rado (1974) carefully differentiates between "obsessive attacks" (symptomatology) and "obsessive traits" (personality). But in his subsequent discussion he treats both as components of "obsessive behaviour."

A third group view the symptoms as being neurotic *extensions* of the traits. Thus, Jung (1920) credited Binet with the observation that "the neurotic only accentuates and shows in relief the characteristic traits of his personality.'' Masserman (1946) and Noyes (1954) postulate that the thinking and behaviour of the person of obsessional personality are defensive in nature. When these defences become so extreme that they are recognizably deviant the individual may be termed an obsessional neurotic. Reich (1949) believed that the difference between ''character attitudes'' and obsessional symptoms is one of degree, while Michaels and Porter (1949) go a step further by arguing that obsessional neurosis is only an exaggeration of several socially desirable normal personality traits such as orderliness and cleanliness. All these approaches, then, regard the personality traits as preceding the symptoms, which are extensions, exaggerations, or exacerbations of the traits. Such theories usually postulate some threshold of breakdown, but there is disagreement as to whether the underlying obsessional traits *necessarily* develop into obsessional symptoms after the breakdown. The extreme view here is that of Rapaport (1948), who may be interpreted as believing that the breakdown of an obsessional personality automatically involves the development of obsessional neurosis: ''Clinical experience indicates that the obsessive-compulsive *neurosis*, in full-fledged form, represents a breakdown of a previous compulsive *adjustment* ... '' (p. 196).

It will be noted that this third group are writers who are psychoanalytically oriented. Freud himself classically observed the correspondence between obsessional personality or anal character and obsessional neurosis. But he postulated a slightly different relation. In the development of the anal character, he claimed (Freud, 1913), the repression of threatening unconscious material is achieved with the aid of mechanisms such as reaction-formation and sublimation. The obsessional neurosis is due to a *failure* in repression. Thus, as Fenichel (1945) points out, the development of an anal character structure *may* protect the individual from the development of a neurosis: ''Not much is known, however, about what determines whether a compulsive character is developed simultaneously with compulsive symptoms as a part of a compulsion neurosis or whether this character structure wards off (and replaces) definite compulsive and obsessive symptoms. Both types occur'' (p. 531).

A fourth group of writers, mostly representing the ''classical'' or mainstream school of European psychiatry, regard the obsessional personality as providing a ''fruitful soil'' for the development of obsessional illness with its attendant symptoms. They do not, however, regard the symptoms as being exaggerated versions of the traits. Nor do they assume that the breakdown of an obsessional personality *necessarily* leads to the appearance of obsessional symptoms. Some of these writers merely note a degree of coincidence, without inferring anything other than a statistical relationship: ''Obsessive and compulsive phenomena are most frequently encountered in persons who are overconscientious, shy, pedantic, punctilious, painstakingly addicted to minutest orderliness and symmetry, not satisfied until everything is 'just so' '' (Kanner, 1948, p. 621). Others imply a more direct, even aetiological relationship: ''When we consider matters from an aetiological viewpoint, we note that there is a group of *persons, commonly called obsessional,* showing a constitutional syndrome, a well-marked constellation of character traits, who tend to suffer from a variety of illnesses, in which compulsive symptoms are usually prominent'' (Slater and Roth, 1969, p. 127, original emphasis). ''In the majority of cases the [obsessional] illness seems to arise from a certain character structure whose basic feature is inner insecurity and a feeling of inadequacy'' (Anderson, 1964, p. 183).

Here there is a shift of emphasis from the symptoms to the traits, which reflects a basic theoretical difference. This is pointed up by Schneider, in his discussion of the ''insecure psychopath'': ''Compulsions flourish on such a personality base, and in this respect we prefer the term anankastic or compulsive psychopath to such a term as compulsive neurotic. These personalities are easily gripped by compulsive ideas ... '' (Schneider, 1959, p. 21).

Schneider is stressing obsessional states as the products of *personality disorder* in which actual compulsive symptoms are secondary. The individual with a personality disorder manifests certain normally distributed traits to a statistically extreme degree. The degree of extremity is reflected in the degree of illness and, therefore, the incidence of symptoms: ''Compulsive symptoms are likely to flourish in persons of a certain sort of personality, and the more marked the personality deviation, the more likely is it that symptoms will occur. The qualities of this personality are in themselves normal, and are shown to some extent by the majority of healthy individuals ... '' (Slater and Roth, 1969, p. 130).

The writers in this fourth group are well aware that individual obsessional symptoms are not confined to obsessional illness or personality disorder but may occur in many illnesses and conditions. Nor do they claim that *all* persons of obsessional personality will show obsessional symptoms should they become mentally ill. But they do seem to suggest that obsessional symptoms are the most typical phenomena shown by such persons should they require psychiatric treatment. In each of the quotations above, it will be noted, the statement is made, albeit cautiously, that either (a) obsessional symptoms are most frequently observable in patients of obsessional personality (Kanner, 1948; Anderson, 1964; Slater and Roth, 1969) or (b) persons of obsessional personality tend to suffer from obsessional symptoms (Slater and Roth, 1969, Schneider, 1969).

A fifth group of writers, who otherwise are in general accord with the previous group, dispute one or other of the above statements by stressing the exceptions rather than the generalities. Thus, with regard to the first statement, Curran and Guttman (1949) are at pains to point out: ''True obsessive–compulsive states may develop in personalities with little or no evidence of obsessional characteristics in their previous make-up'' (p. 193). With regard to the second statement, Fish (1964) in discussing the obsessional personality, states: ''Some of these people have minor obsessional symptoms, such as counting and touching compulsions and habits of re-checking. ... Relatively few of these individuals develop obsessional states ... (p. 71).

Perhaps the most distinguished English-language writer to express skepticism about any one-to-one concordance between obsessional personality and symptoms was Sir Aubrey Lewis. During thirty years (e.g., Lewis, 1936; Lewis, 1965), he stressed that doubt must be cast on any suggestion of a clear-cut relationship by the fact that at least two quite different personality types (the obstinate, rigid, irritable type and the passive, vacillating, timid type) may be discerned among patients suffering from obsessional states. Furthermore, he points out, not only are the so-called obsessional traits as commonly in evidence among non-obsessional patients, but they are sometimes not to be observed among the latter.

> Of course many obsessionals have shown excessive cleanliness, orderliness, pedantry, conscientiousness, uncertainty, inconclusive ways of thinking and acting. These are sometimes obsessional symptoms themselves, sometimes character traits devoid of any immediate experience of subjective compulsion. They are, however, especially in the latter case, just as commonly found among patients who never have an obsessional neurosis. ... The traits are also, of course, common among healthy people. They are, conversely, sometimes undiscoverable in the previous personality of patients who now have a severe obsessional neurosis. ... (Lewis, 1935, p. 328)

In summary, the vast majority of reputable psychiatric writers in this field do differentiate between (compulsive) *personality* and obsessional *symptoms*. But while most European writers regard the obsessional or compulsive personality (anal character, anankastic personality, etc.) as being deviant from, or more extreme than, the statistical norm, certain American writers regard it, or its component traits, as normal and even desirable.

Where the *relationship* between personality and symptoms is concerned there is a wide range of differing, though overlapping views which reflect differing aetiological and nosological standpoints. Several strands may be identified:

1. Writers who, in regarding neurotic behaviour as reactions to environmental stress, tend to emphasize the symptoms and concern themselves more with the stress than with the particular personality suffering the stress.
2. Writers who see both symptoms and personality traits as being the common products of the same condition.
3. Writers who see the symptoms as being maladaptive exaggerations of pre-existing personality traits.
4. Writers who see the personality as offering a "fruitful soil" for the development of the symptoms but do not postulate any necessary causal or other one-to-one relationship.
5. Writers who stress this lack of one-to-one relationship, implying dubiety as to any clear connection between the personality in question and the symptoms.

To understand this confusing divergence of opinions it is necessary to consider the theoretical standpoints which they represent. An embarrassment of such lines of thought exists in the literature; fortunately, most of these are merely developments or modifications of the seminal authorities whose views have already been examined.

11
Compulsive Personality Traits: A Conceptualization

Before proceeding to analyse and conceptualize the traits listed in Chapter 5, it may be as well to attempt to justify this. For it could be claimed that if the observations are valid, in the sense that they reflect responsible clinical observation, then there is no reason why they should not be accepted as they stand, at their face value. There are two replies to this. The first is simply that advances in theory development can only be made by the assessment and ordering of empirically derived observations. No theory could be constructed if "facts" were left "as they stand." The second reply involves a consideration of the nature of clinical observations. At one level—that involving the observers' skill and honesty—there is, of course, no justification for any reassessment. But at another level, subjective observations demand considerable study and qualification before their value for scientific work can be assessed. A few comments are relevant here.

First, it seems possible that a number of clinical descriptions are merely different ways of looking at the same phenomena. Second, it is possible that some clinical observations, however carefully made, are unreliable for a number of reasons:

(a) Aspects of behaviour, or verbal reports thereof, may be elicited by one clinician but not by another. This might reflect different levels of professional skill or interest. But it might also be argued that elicitation is a function of the elicitor as well as the elicitee. Like workers in many other fields, a given clinician may gain particular information because he is looking for it and wants to find it. His patient, wittingly or unwittingly, may collaborate in this because he wishes to please his doctor.

(b) The observation may be valid but have no differentiating significance. The observation "Anankasts display attribute x" may be quite correct. But it adds little to our knowledge of anankasm unless it can be shown that anankasts possess more (or less) of attribute x than the population in general or than persons suffering from other personality disorders. Clinical psychiatrists have little opportunity for subjecting samples of normal, healthy people to the sort of phenomenological investigation they carry out with their patients. The knowledge that patient A scrubs her doorstep twice a week regardless of its condition, or that patient B regards sexual intercourse as "dirty" is of little value unless these findings can be set against a verified background of social norms and pressures.

(c) It is possible for clinical observations to cancel each other out, and this is particularly the case in the field of obsessional disorder, which has attracted a wealth of clinical descriptions and generalizations and yet in which, as has been seen, considerable divergences of opinion exist. For instance, it has been claimed that the individual of obsessional personality is characteristically *immature* (Yde, 1950), *timid* (Luxenburger, 1930), and *self-deprecating* (e.g., Petrilowitsch, 1956). It has also been claimed that he is characteristically *mature* (Michaels and Porter, 1949), *aggressive* (Stekel, 1927) and *arrogant* (Abraham, 1923). Such contradictions are far from uncommon in the literature. They may be due to differences of opinion as to what constitutes an obsessional personality, to different levels of interpretation, or simply to errors in observation. Or they can be justified as reflecting the ambivalence, "bi-polarity," or "counter-personality" of the obsessional. But there is also the disturbing possibility that the group of patients labelled as of "Obsessional Personality" includes the same wide variety of personality attributes as the population at large.

(d) Diametrically opposed conclusions may be drawn from the same piece of behaviour because of varying interpretations by clinicians, even when the latter are of the same persuasion. Thus the writer has heard the promiscuous activities of a female patient described by one eminent clinician as being proof of her "shallow affect and loose morals" and by another as indicating "an anankastic searching for perfection."

(e) Subjective assessments sometimes ignore intra-subject reliability. Clearly a person may generally behave in a consistent manner in a given situation but react quite differently in another. Thus, the fact that a certain patient invariably appeared at the clinic immaculately dressed and groomed, his shirt spotless and crisp, his jowl and shoes shining, his suit perfectly pressed, and his hands manicured was ascribed to his anankastic personality. What was not fully appreciated was that the clinic visits took place during the working day and that personal appearance was an integral part of the patient's business activities. On one of his days off he made an extra visit to the clinic to change an appointment. He was dressed in a dirty old sweater and jeans. His boots were muddy, he was unshaven, and his hands were covered in sump oil.

In short, while it would be an impertinence to doubt the face value of the clinical observations, it would be equally unwise to allot undue significance to them individually. Each observation must be seen in the perspective of the whole corpus of observations. Only with reference to the whole can the value of an individual statement be assessed.

A PSYCHOLOGICAL/SEMANTIC SYNTHESIS

In Chapter 5 we assembled a list of thirty-three traits reported by psychiatric authorities as characterizing the compulsive or anankastic personality, a list which at first sight seems so heterogeneous as to defy summary or synthesis. However, there is considerable overlap between some of the listed traits, and certain ''themes'' are discernible. Meanwhile, three important points about these clinical observations should be borne in mind:

(a) It is conceivable that several of the observations refer to different aspects of the same phenomena.
(b) The observations are of differing orders or levels of description.
(c) The differences between them may be more reflective of interpretative assumptions and value judgements than of denotative meaning.

For example, ''conscientiousness'' and ''perfectionism'' refer to modes of activity which behaviourally are practically identical. Furthermore, both terms are value judgements implying approval on the part of the observer. The mode of activity described as ''Perseveration'' could well be subsumed under either of the previous two headings. But this term is one of mild disapprobation. Similarly, ''Stress on Orderliness'' and ''Routine'' refer to the same sort of behaviour patterns; but whereas the first term has positive, constructive connotations, the second implies a passive approach.

These problems were to be expected, of course, in view of the subjective and often intuitive nature of clinical descriptions. The descriptions themselves are not impugned. But, before the phenomena to which they apply can be examined objectively, it is necessary to define them in operational or less affectively toned terms.

A careful analysis of the observations reveals that, despite their superficial heterogeneity, they have much in common. At a different level of analysis the observations can be re-categorized in the following way:

Category 1: Doubt, Inconclusiveness, Indecisiveness, and Scrupulosity. The first three of these are clearly related. Doubt and inconclusiveness refer to the absence of that sense of satisfaction or completion contingent upon the solution of a problem, the determination of an appropriate act, or the making of a choice. Indecisiveness refers to the failure to achieve resolution, select an act, or make a choice. Scrupulosity refers to doubts and hesitations with regard to questions of conscience. Thus, all four may be said to reflect an inability to categorize and balance competing alternatives, whether these be to do with information, arguments, or moral issues.

Category 2: Accuracy, Concentration, Detail, Meticulousness, Precision, Reliability, and Thoroughness. At first sight, these seven characteristics, although reconcilable, seem to have little in common as a group. However, upon reflection, it becomes clear that their differences are largely due to the varying *levels* of comment involved, coupled with different densities of connotative loading.

To note that an individual is very accurate and precise in his performance of a task and shows due concern with the details thereof while concentrating upon the job, is a relatively neutral assessment. It would normally reflect objective observations of the individual at work. The assessment of him as being thorough or reliable involves judgements of much wider application, along with positive value attribution in regard to the individual's character, social worth, and integrity. To term him "meticulous" lies somewhere between the two, because this is not an objective observation, yet it is not as value-laden as the last two descriptive judgements.

However, operationally the seven characteristics have much in common. They all derive from the same referent—they are observations about a particular style of behaviour displayed in the performance of a task. An individual described by any or all of these terms is seen to engage in the task with close attention, taking great care to comply with the requirements of the undertaking.

Category 3: Aspiration, Conscientiousness, Perfectionism, Perseveration, and Persistence. Here again, we are dealing with an apparently divergent group of characteristics, whose diversity is due only to different levels of application and connotative loadings.

Perseveration, as noted earlier, is a term implying mild disapprobation, but it reflects the objective observation that a sequence of behaviours is repeated or continued. Persistence means almost the same, but bears the connotation of strength of character and implies the use of will-power. To display a high level of aspiration, to be conscientious or perfectionist all connote traits which in our society are considered worthy and laudable. The use of these terms reflects value judgements of a very positive kind. What the individual thus described is actually doing is exactly the same as the behaviour of those described as perseverative or persistent. What differs is the observer's judgement of the value of the activity and his interpretation of the subject's (assumed) motivation.

All five observations, in fact, refer to behaviours which accompany or emphasize *reluctance to complete a task.* The observer may opt to interpret this continuing activity as reflecting perfectionism or conscientiousness. Indeed, subjects may "explain" what they are doing in these or similar moral terms.

Clearly, the behaviours described here have much in common with those in Category 2. But whereas the latter referred to the way in which a task is performed, these are to do with marking or determining the point at which the task can be regarded as completed.

Category 4: Ambiguity, Categorization, Patterning, Symmetry, and Tidiness. These five observations describe the ordering of ideas or visual input. They suggest that the anankast strives for clear limits and class boundaries. He tends to over-define categories and attempts to balance, smooth, and simplify the components of his visual field.

Category 5: Propriety, Punctiliousness, Punctuality, Rectitude. These observations refer not so much to moral principles as to the acceptance of the forms of social behaviour. They describe individuals who are sensitive to prescribed codes of behaviour and strive to act in accordance with them.

Category 6: Control, Discipline, Orderliness, Pedantry, and Rules. The connotations of these terms vary considerably, from discipline, which is often used in an approving sense, to pedantry, which refers to a fussy concern with the *minutiae* of regulations. Control is used approvingly if it has reference to oneself but less approvingly if it refers to control over others. But all five observations refer to a predilection for, and compliance with, regulations, prescriptions, and codes of conduct.

Category 7: Obstinacy, Rigidity, Routine. Once again, the differences among the members of this group can readily be recognized as ones of value judgement rather than denotative meaning. Obstinacy is regarded as a type of character which is not warmly regarded yet must be accorded respect. To be bound by routine describes a much more prosaic sort of individual—one who is dull and plodding but not necessarily difficult to co-operate with. Rigidity has more negative connotations but not such vivid implications as obstinacy. But all three terms point to the same sort of behavioural pattern—one which is characterized by a reluctance or inability to change or adapt to changing circumstances or task demands.

A further synthesizing of what originally seemed to be a rag-bag of disparate characteristics can now be achieved by the realization that these new categories are all related to the *structuring* of experience.

Category 1 observations are to do with an inability to tolerate the *absence of structure*—of clear-cut categories, limits, criteria, and guide-rules.
Category 2 observations are to do with the structuring of *performance*, involving a characteristic style of handling tasks.

Category 3 observations are to do with the structuring of *task completion—the determination of terminal limits*.

Category 4 observations are to do with the structuring of *cognition*—perceptual input and ideational content.

Category 5 observations are to do with the structuring of *social codes* and compliance therewith.

Category 6 observations are to do with compliance with general prescriptions, *rules and regulations*.

Category 7 observations are to do with the *maintenance and solidification* of prescribed structures.

Clearly all these observations are versions of the same central psychological phenomenon. Their apparent variety is due only to differing areas of operation and to the connotative toning of subjective observations. The descriptions, in fact, tend to be *content* orientated, whereas the underlying *form* is constant. The central, formal phenomenon may be seen as a striving towards boundary fixing or the setting of limits in cognition and performance. The problem seems to lie in difficulties of *spontaneous* categorizing and integration. This leads to the *over-structuring* of input, of fields of awareness, of tasks and situations.

If this conceptualization holds true, then it would appear that the problems experienced by those suffering from obsessional–compulsive personality disorder are rooted in their characteristic mode of processing and schematizing information. In other words, their disorder is primarily *cognitive* in nature. Furthermore, while characteristic content themes may be traced—contamination, filth, perfection, etc.—the basic impairments are to do with *structural organization* or *form*.

Having arrived at this point in the analysis, the next step is an obvious one. Given that formal cognitive characteristics underlie the problems associated with the personality disorder, may they not also be responsible for the state or neurosis? If the personality disorder reflects the operation of exaggerated *traits*, is it not at least possible that the *symptoms* are simply pathological extensions of those already exaggerated tendencies?

It is recognized, of course, that the above line of argument will not be acceptable to the large majority of contemporary authorities—neither clinical practitioners nor theorists.

From their various points of view, Freudians, phenomenologists, and learning theorists have always regarded obsessional problems as *affective* disorders. Particular emphasis has traditionally been placed on the central role of anxiety. Similarly, all schools of thought—even some German "mainstream" psychiatry—have always accepted the validity of tackling obsessionality through its *content*. Freudians have been concerned with its symbolic nature, mainstreamers for its evidence of intra-psychic conflict and self-insecurity, phenomenologists for its clues to the obsessional world, learning theorists for its apparent identification of what has been learned.

As we have seen, the Freudian view is that the personality and the symptoms are independent. Indeed, the traits are defences which must break down before the symptoms make their appearance. Some learning theorists explicitly disavow the very concept of "personality"; others would regard traits as determining the type of learning involved in the production of symptoms. Both groups would reject the suggestion that symptoms might be simply the products of exaggerated traits.

The writer is not abashed; he would merely point out that he is in good company. Prior to Freud, writers tended to focus upon the volitional aspects of obsessional disorders, rather than the affective while, as we have seen, Janet was what would nowadays be termed a cognitivist. As for the relation between obsessional symptoms and traits, Janet, Pavlov, and Schneider all took substantially the same line as that suggested here.

The remainder of this book will focus upon applying a cognitive approach to obsessional phenomena. We shall first consider the primary experience of compulsion itself, then the role of anxiety. Each of the classical symptoms will be examined and found to be amenable to study from a cognitive viewpoint. Experimental evidence regarding the cognitive characteristics of obsessionality will be reviewed, and the development of recent psychological remedial techniques will be traced. Finally, a summary chapter will present a theoretical synthesis and some therapeutic implications.

12
The Experience of Compulsion

But it was neither my dislike of the thought, nor yet any desire
and endeavour to resist it that in the least did shake or abate
the continuation, or force and strength thereof; for it did always,
in almost whatever I thought, intermix itself therewith in such
sort that I could neither eat my food, stoop for a pin, chop a
stick, or cast mine eye to look on this or that, but still the
temptation would come. Sell Christ for this, or sell Christ for
that; sell him, sell him.

John Bunyan, *Grace Abounding to the Chief of Sinners*, 1666.

It also does not infrequently happen, that patients will declare,
that certain notions are forced into their minds, of which they
fear the folly and incongruity, and complain that they cannot
prevent their intrusion.

John Haslam, *Observations on Insanity: with Practical Remarks*
on the Disease, 1798.

As we saw in Chapter 1, the experience of compulsion is the crux of obsessional
disorder, its primary criterial attribute. Unless a thought, doubt, fear, image,
affect, urge, or action is characterized by the sense of compulsion, it cannot
technically be termed obsessional or compulsive. The experience of compulsion
is, then, at the very heart of our topic. So it is more than a little disconcerting
to realize that this central phenomenon has been scarcely touched upon in the
literature. In psychological terms, what is it? What is its source? What are the
psychological mechanisms involved? Why does it operate only in certain modes
or channels of expression? During any given bout, what stimulus or process
initiates it? At the conclusion of a bout, what accounts for its diminution? Or is
it that it is in continuous operation but that its intensity varies? If so ... ? Dozens

more such questions spring readily to mind, but few answers have been offered, and those are notable neither for their coherence nor for their plausibility.

It would be far beyond the conceptual resources of the present writer to develop an all-encompassing answer. The modest aim of this chapter is to survey such sketchy explanations as have been proposed or implied and then offer a re-emphasis which may clarify or dispense with a number of questions.

A convenient starting-point would be some widely accepted presentation or discussion. Unfortunately, neither psychological, psychiatric, nor philosophical textbooks make any attempt to elucidate or analyse compulsion itself. The normal ploy is simply to ascribe the adjective "compulsive" to such nouns as "ideas," "thoughts," or "impulses." Attention is then given to the noun-referents, side-stepping the adjective. The *meaning* of "compulsive" is never examined; it seems to be regarded as so self-evident as to be unworthy of study or exposition. Oddly enough, this avoidance is shared by the great majority of seminal authorities and theorists. This is, indeed, puzzling, to say the least. It might well be enquired how it is possible to study a phenomenon without first examining the very factor that defines it.

It may well be, of course, that it has become the normal practice to accept implicitly the dictionary definition, without pausing to realize the psychological questions raised by the definition. What exactly *is* the conventional dictionary definition? Immediately, we face another difficulty. Most standard dictionaries define the word "compulsion" with the synonym "compelling." The majority of technical dictionaries and glossaries of medicine, psychiatry, and psychology interpret "compulsion" as a compulsive act, adhering to the translators' convention mentioned in Chapter 1. What is then defined is not the nature of the experience of *compulsion*, but the nature of such *acts* as can properly be termed "compulsive." Thus, the words "compulsion" and "compulsive" are not defined. Furthermore, the suspicion of circularity is introduced by some definitions which inform us that a compulsion is an act which is characterized by compulsion. However, a few dictionaries do take the semantic bull by the horns. Thus, Wolman's *Dictionary of Behavioral Science* (1973) offers us definitions of "compulsion" both as a compulsive act *and* as the experience itself:

> *compulsion* 1. The state in which the person feels forced to behave against his own conscious wishes and judgement. 2. The force which compels a person to action against his own will or forcing a person to act in this way. (p. 71)

The second of Wolman's definitions clearly provides us with a starting point. It has the added advantages of being clear and succinct. Furthermore, it is fair to say that the formulation would be acceptable to most clinicians and is implied by the majority of writers in the area.

A compulsion, we are told, is a "force." And it is our unquestioning acceptance of this single assumption, it may be suggested, that accounts for the conceptual confusion and obfuscation that shrouds the whole topic of obsessional disorder. Why do we accept such an idea without enquiring as to the plausibility of the concept of this mysterious "force"? Perhaps the concept possesses its own mythic significance which renders it sacrosanct and not open to rational examination. Certainly it has persisted over many centuries, quite immune from criticism because this has never been advanced. One is reminded of religious precepts and dogmas, which are maintained by a faith which condemns criticism as heretical or blasphemous.

The concept of a "force" which directs the actions of an individual against his own will is, of course, quite reasonable in any culture which believes in the existence of malign or punitive spirits which can invade the bodies of human beings or take control of their volitional processes. There still exist cultures which encourage such beliefs, and these were the norm in Europe, certainly from the Classical era through to the end of the Middle Ages. And contemporary acceptance of the "controlling forces" represents direct descent from the pre-scientific period of psychiatry. Paracelsus, the sixteenth-century Swiss physician, added to his four categories of mental disorder a possible fifth: "—obsessi, *qui a diabolo variis modos occupari solent.*" The "force" was conceived of as controlling from within by invading and occupying its victim's body. Such "possession" was routinely treated in Paracelsus' time, as it sometimes is in our own, by the formal rites of exorcism.

Modern psychiatrists and psychologists, of course, no longer believe that compulsive "control" is exerted by a force which originates outside the sufferer. But for the most part they accept the central idea of a "force." The only intellectual diversion from the standpoint of our forebears is that nowadays it is accepted that the "force" comes from within. Indeed, it is exactly this feature which is at the centre of Fischer's (1950) definition:

> By compulsion in general, we denote the phenomenon of a person being forced to do something by some stronger power against which he defends himself internally or externally. In psychopathology the expression compulsion means that this power or influence stems from one's own personality. (p. 135)

In other words, the only difference between the ordinary definition of "compulsion" as a "force" which surmounts the individual's will and its technical usage is that the latter presumes the inner origin of the force.

It will be noted that most accounts, by making the assumption that compulsion is a "force," place emphasis upon the latter, rather than upon its victim. They stress, it could be said, the demonic invader, rather than its host. Without examining the possible psychological nature of such a "force," they nevertheless assume that it: (a) operates positively; (b) is active and dynamic; and (c) is powerful enough to subjugate its victim. And this bundle of assumptions is implicit in the writing of such few theorists as have discussed the question.

Psychoanalysts have postulated an irresistible force, surmising that this is a manifestation of unconscious anal–sadistic drive derivatives. Phenomenologists also postulate the irresistible force, but regard it as an unanalysable upthrust of psychic energy. Learning theorists have not been concerned with the *experience* of compulsion, but most have interpreted compulsive behaviour as powered by some combination of high drive and habit formation. Thus, as the present writer (Reed, 1977c) has pointed out, "it is only a slight exaggeration to claim that contemporary views of obsessional experience savor of medieval thinking. There is more than a hint of some vile demon rising from the primordial sludge of the sufferer's unconscious, or of 'possession,' by an evil spirit."

Freud himself did not discuss the *experience* of compulsion but the nature of the compulsive *idea* (i.e., the "invader"). Basically he was concerned with the question of why certain ideas, impulses, etc., acquired their compelling power. To explain this, he relied upon examination of the content of the ideas in question, rather than the form of the experiences themselves. His original explanation (1896b) of the source of such ideas ran as follows:

> *Obsessional ideas* are invariably transformed *self-reproaches* which have re-emerged from *repression* . ... The next period, that of the illness, is characterized by the *return of the repressed memories*—that is, therefore, by the failure of the defences. (*S.E.*, III., p. 169, original emphasis)

The compelling power of the ideas derives directly from their source:

> Obsessional ideas have, as it were, a compulsive [obsessional] psychical currency, not on account of their intrinsic value, but on account of the source from which they derive. ... (*S.E.*, III, p. 171)

Whether it is well-founded or not, Freud's hypothesized explanation is probably the most internally consistent and developed theoretical approach yet published. However, it does not examine the flavour of the experience of compulsion. Nor is much added by Freud's distinguished expositor Fenichel (1945). Fenichel points out that, in all psychoneuroses, ego control is impaired: "In conversion symptoms, the ego is simply overthrown; actions occur that are not intended by the ego. In compulsions and obsessions, the fact that the ego governs motility is not changed, but the ego does not feel free in using this governing power. It has to use it according to a strange command of a more powerful agency, contradicting its judgement ... " (p. 268).

But what, we may ask, is this "more powerful agency"? Fenichel does not answer this directly, but he does tell us, one might argue, what it is *not*. Feared or forbidden impulses, urges, or drives are "warded off." Obsessions are *derivatives* of such warded-off impulses. The force of the impulses is not reflected in the intensity of the derivatives. Fenichel goes on to apply this line of argument to obsessional avoidance of phobic fears, to counter-phobic attitudes, and to the transformation of instinctual drives into compulsive urges. He then propounds what he describes as a "contradictory statement": "Compulsion can be described as a command from within. The idea of 'being commanded' certainly is rooted in the child's experiences with grownups who used to 'command' him, especially, in our culture, in experiences with the father. In compulsions this father commands from within; and an 'inner father representative' is called superego." (p. 269).

Fenichel presents the Freudian view with elegance and sophistication. But the reader may be forgiven for detecting a certain circularity in the argument. For instance, the insertion or substitution of the word "ego" in the statement "The individual does not feel free" cannot be regarded as explanatory. Likewise, to add the words "from the superego" to the statement "The indvidual experiences an inner command ... " does not advance our understanding. For it may reasonably be argued, at least in this context, that "ego" and "super-ego" are simply colourful metaphors rather than explanatory constructs.

Salzman (1980), although directly in the Freudian tradition in most respects, betrays an interesting divergence from the conventional Freudian analysis in his account of compulsion:

> ... obsessional ideas can exert profound effects on behaviour by demanding full attention all the time in the most severe cases or by distracting usual activities by an insistent intrusiveness in other cases. The obsessional individual cannot identify the source without help or guidance, since the thoughts are alien, unacceptable and grossly discordant with his public personality patterns of thinking and behaving. He therefore describes them as outside of his own self and as unwelcome intruders into his functioning. (p. 16)

This account, it will be noted, explains the ego-dystonic nature of obsessional thoughts by the suggestion that they are discordant with the sufferer's publicly presented image. He therefore describes them as being ego-dystonic and intrusive. Although Salzman does not make the point explicitly, it could be argued that the same line of approach might apply as well to compulsivity in general as to intrusiveness. In other words, a repugnant thought might be termed "compulsive" by its holder simply to provide himself with an alibi against any accusation that he is willingly harbouring it.

However, a page later, Salzman describes compulsion as something much more profound and mysterious. Having pointed out that only a limited range of human behaviour is determined by instinct, Salzman avers that most of the individual's behaviour, concerns, interests, values, and ideals are within his deliberate and conscious choice: "Obsessions and compulsions interfere and, at times, absolutely prevent such choices because their imperious demand, the source of which the individual cannot identify, must be acknowledged and pursued" (p. 17).

It would appear possible that Salzman shares some of this inability to identify the source of compulsive thoughts, for he goes on to simply assert: "In fact, compulsions and obsessions are evasive, relentless efforts to give a person an illusion of power by strength and control; he must achieve a state of perfection which can sustain the illusion of invincibility and omnipotence" (p. 17).

Salzman develops this theme throughout the book, with subtlety and elegance. But its introduction at this juncture allows him to side-step the question of what constitutes compulsivity, a central theoretical issue to which he does not return.

While it is consistent with Freud's theoretical position that he and his followers should be interested in the content of compulsive experiences rather than their form, it might be expected that those employing an avowedly phenomenological or existentialist approach would concentrate upon the flavour of the experience. But in fact this does not appear to be the case. Straus (1948) neither describes nor even mentions the experience of compulsion. Section IV of von Gebsattel's (1958) classical paper is entitled: "The Defensive Side of the Compulsion-Syndrome and the Nature of Compulsion." But the nature of compulsion is not examined at all.

Unlike Freud and most "dynamic" or eclectic theorists, Jaspers (1923) differentiates sharply between form and content and might therefore be expected to analyse the formal nature of compulsion. He does, in fact, offer a detailed account of the flavour of the compulsive experience. But nowhere does he examine its causes or the psychological mechanisms involved. Indeed, he opens his section on "compulsive phenomena" with the flat statement: "Experience of psychic compulsion is an ultimate phenomenon" (1963, p. 133). In other words, he asserts, the experience may be described, but it is not amenable to theoretical analysis.

Jaspers goes on to describe the normal phenomenon of feeling overpowered by external events, other people, or one's own "perceptions, anxieties, memories and dreams." These can be surrendered to instinctively or because of voluntary choice. However, " ... should the self be no longer master of its choice, should it lose all influence over the selection of what shall fill its consciousness, and should *the immediate content of consciousness remain irremovable, unchosen, unwanted*, the self finds itself in conflict faced with a content which it wants to suppress but cannot. This content then acquires the character of a psychic compulsion" (p. 133, original emphasis).

This, and the ensuing discussion, merely serve to differentiate between normal attentiveness to something that we choose to be interested in and the psycho-pathological equivalent which is marked by an absence of choice or control. Such a distinction is clinically important, of course; however, there is no discussion of volitional processes or the absence thereof. And instead of tackling this, Jaspers immediately goes on to discuss, first of all, content, and then compulsive affects, compulsive beliefs, and compulsive urges. All of this provides crucial pointers for the clinician. But it does not address itself to the psychological factors involved in the compulsive experience.

Prior to the recent work of Parkinson and Rachman (1981 a and b) on intrusive and repetitive cognitions, the only empirical studies of relevance to our present topic had been those of Horowitz and her associates (e.g., Horowitz, 1975; Horowitz and Becker, 1971). Horowitz derived her predictions from the psychoanalytic observation that compulsive repetitions in thought and action follow psychic traumata. They are recapitulations of insufficiently processed stimuli, and reflect attempts to master and adapt to such traumata. Stress was experimentally induced by the well-known method of displaying appropriate films. Normal subjects reported significantly more intrusive thoughts and images after watching films of a moderately disturbing nature than after watching innocuous ones. Wilner and Horowitz (1975) found similar results, using a depressing film.

The studies conducted by the Horowitz group have been original and thought-provoking. But in relation to our present interest, some reservation must be expressed as to whether the intrusive thoughts and images reported are directly comparable with the clinical symptom of compulsion. They do not seem to share the phenomenological flavour of the classical compulsive experience, lacking as they do the paradoxical admixture of personal significance and ego-dystonic repugnance. As Rachman and Hodgson (1980) have pointed out, Horowitz has not clearly distinguished between obsessions and preoccupations. At the same time, the method of study used does not allow for intrusive thoughts of an anticipatory nature (e.g., ''What if I were to kill my baby?'').

More recently, Rachman (1981) has contributed a very interesting discussion of unwanted and intrusive cognitions in normal people, which he maintains are at least connected with or similar to clinical obsessions. This view had been supported by the results of a questionnaire given to normal subjects by Rachman and de Silva (1978), their findings being confirmed and extended by interviews with another sample of normals (Parkinson and Rachman, 1981a). Both these studies indicate that the contents of intrusive thoughts are strikingly similar to those of clinical obsessions, the most common themes being those relating to death and to possible harm to the individual, his friends, or his family. However, the degrees of distressfulness, unpleasantness, and unacceptability reported were lower than those associated with the obsessional experiences of psychiatric patients. Parkinson and Rachman (1981b) also studied the intrusive thoughts of a group of mothers whose children were about to undergo surgery, as compared with those of a control group of mothers. As might be expected, the experimental group reported heightened anxiety, which was accompanied by a greater number of intrusive thoughts and images.

It will be noted that, although they spring from very different theoretical standpoints, both the Horowitz *et al.* studies and those of Parkinson and Rachman are content-oriented. Furthermore, they both associate intrusive cognitions with arousal and anxiety. The Horowitz studies focus upon the question: "What sort of perceptual experiences will subsequently be recalled intrusively and repetitively, with vividness and intensity?" As with earlier writers, the emphasis is laid upon the idea or image that is recalled, rather than on the form of the compulsive experience itself. The Rachman studies focus upon the question: "Why do these thoughts persist, despite their unpleasant nature?" (Interestingly enough, it was the *answer* to that question, albeit from the psychoanalytic perspective, which had provided the springboard for the Horowitz studies.) While recognizing that a significant proportion of intrusive thoughts have no identifiable trigger, their discussions emphasize the important role of external precipitants or stimuli, and the central role of anxiety, reflecting their behavioural/learning perspective.

In the present writer's opinion, the Rachman studies represent the most stimulating and promising attacks to date on the general topic of unwanted, intrusive thoughts and images. But so far, it can scarcely be claimed that they have succeeded in deriving a direct answer to the problem of what constitutes the compulsive experience.

In summary, the experience of compulsion has not been satisfactorily examined to date, the majority of writers having simply not discussed the matter. They seem to have accepted the dictionary definition of compulsion as an active, ego-dystonic, overpowering "force" which originates within the individual. They have avoided the psychological questions raised by such a definition. It would seem most unlikely that the questions have simply not been recognized. We are thus left with the suspicion that "compulsion" is such a slippery concept that its elucidation has baffled some of our best brains over several generations. To be more precise, however, it is not the concept itself that presents difficulty; it is simply that it does not gel with our present state of knowledge of human psychology and physiology. In the same way, we have no difficulty in appreciating the concept of a centaur, but we should face problems if we were required to incorporate the concept into our knowledge of zoology or veterinary science.

Another possibility exists, though only the present writer (Reed, 1977c) has so far had the effrontery to advance it. That is, that the evidential material from which the concept was derived has been misapplied in some way. In the present case the "evidence" consists of the verbal reports of their subjective states given by patients regarded as suffering from obsessional disorder. The question, of course, is not whether they suffer from the experience of compulsion; the question is simply whether they describe the experience in terms of an overpowering "force."

The present writer had available to him verbal reports from over sixty such patients in response to the question: "What does it [the compulsive experience] feel like?" For various reasons (mixed diagnoses, inability to respond, etc.) this list was reduced to the series of fifty referred to in the early chapters of this book. Categorization of the fifty responses presented considerable difficulty, mainly because some of the replies were clear but over-inclusive, while a few others tended to offer ''explanations'' rather than descriptions. But it proved possible to discern five main groupings. They are presented here, with representative examples for each group.

1. *An impairment of will-power.* The majority of descriptions referred to are respondents' feelings of weakness of will, ineffectiveness, submission, etc. Thirty-five of the fifty (70%) replied in some such terms.

> I keep wondering, and then I can't get it out of my mind. I know it's stupid, but I haven't got the will-power to push it out. *(A 21-year-old student with ruminations about the possibility of being attacked, and crippling doubts.)*

> I can't stop doing it. It's as though I need to sort every little detail out. I just haven't got the will-power to stop. *(A 25-year-old man suffering from compulsive counting and checking.)*

> I'd be all right if I had more self-control. I should be able to stop wasting my time like this and start living. *(A 32-year-old woman suffering from obsessional fears and checking.)*

> I'm ashamed of myself. I keep doing these things, yet I know that they're completely pointless. I know I'm intelligent and I could be doing something useful. But I go on like this. ... I'm just weak. *(A 27-year-old woman suffering from obsessional fears and ''touching'' rituals.)*

> I'm real soft, I know that. I just worry about everything and I can't get things out of my mind. ... *(A 49-year-old woman with ruminations, obsessional fears, and checking.)*

> One of the thoughts will come into my head. It just pops in, and I should pop it out again and go on to something else, shouldn't I? But no, I don't seem able to summon up the will-power. And then I'm afraid I'll shout it out loud. ... *(A 32-year-old man with compulsive thoughts and impulses.)*

> The thoughts go round and round. I can't cope, somehow ... . Guess it's lack of character. *(An 18-year-old girl, handicapped in her studies by obsessional doubts.)*

2. *The glutinosity of the experience.* Eight of the respondents (16%) emphasized that their experiences were *sticky*, using such analogies as ''glue.'' They did not describe the compulsions as powerful, but rather that they could not extricate themselves from their subjective situation, thus implying (and sometimes stating) that their efforts to escape were ineffectual:

> I can't make a decision—I'm *stuck*. It's a terrible paralysed feeling. I can't move on because I can't convince myself that I've finished what I'm doing. *(A 37-year-old woman suffering from grossly compulsive hand-washing and associated rituals.)*

My mind gets clogged up—it starts working all right and then it's as though it was being oiled with glue. Doubts and then more doubts about the doubts. ... *(A 22-year-old man suffering from incapacitating doubts and indecision.)*

It's like trying to wade through a sea of mud. ... *(A 45-year-old man suffering from severe obsessional ruminations and self-reproach.)*

3. *"Functions" attributed to experiences.* Reports in two cases (4%) focused not so much on the experiencing of compulsions as upon what the respondents took to be the functions of the compulsions:

I number to complete actions—to convince myself they're finished. I feel that, without numbers, nothing registers. I can't be sure what's real somehow—it all goes through my head—so I need numbers to make them register. ... *(A 28-year-old woman suffering from compulsive hand-washing, contamination fears, and "numbering" rituals.)*

4. *Bemusement.* To some extent, as might be expected, perplexity was expressed in regard to their compulsive experiences by all respondents. But in three cases (6%) their descriptions of the experiences highlighted their bemusement, accompanied by a sense of helplessness:

I can't make head or tail of it. It's the daft little things that get me down. I can do the work—I know I can. Maths, for instance—it's not the answers. It's soppy things like the way the pages are curling up, or checking that I've really turned over. ... *(An 18-year-old student with obsessional doubts and ruminations.)*

I know the thoughts aren't important; mostly, they're just silly. Why can't I think about things I *want* to think about? *(A 30-year-old man with continuous obsessional ruminations.)*

5. *Power of the compulsions.* Two of the respondents (4%) laid major emphasis upon the power and implacability of their compulsions, and they perforce also mentioned their own weakness in the face of such domination:

The idea is overwhelming. It just keeps coming back, and there's nothing I can do about it. ... *(A 19-year-old man with obsessional ruminations, fear, and doubts.)*

The fears just take over. They blot everything else out. ... *(A 28-year-old woman obsessed by fears and ruminations.)*

Clearly, the differences among the above five categories are merely ones of emphasis, and there is considerable overlapping. Indeed, categories (2) and (4) may be simply variants of the large category (1), while the two respondents in category (3) were technically not answering the request to describe the experience. But one thing is quite clear—the vast majority of these respondents did *not* emphasize the unusual power of a compulsive "force." They laid the stress upon the other side of the coin—their own weakness or ineffectiveness in countering, controlling, or expelling the compulsions. They reproached themselves for their lack of "will-power," "self-control," or "character" in failing to switch their attention, to think of other things. Similarly, those patients displaying reiterative compulsive behaviours did not view them as responses to powerful forces which demanded their continuation. Rather, they were concerned with feelings of helplessness in being unable to switch their patterns of activity.

In other words, respondents who were preoccupied by unwanted doubts or fears and tormented by recurring thoughts did not stress the *positive strength* of the thoughts, but the *negative strength* of their will-power. In short, the obsessional–compulsive experience, to judge by the evidence of these respondents, is characterized not so much by an awareness of a powerful, compelling force as by a feeling of inadequacy in volitional process. The problem seems to be related not to a pathological intensity of *excitation* but to a relative failure of *inhibition*.

This shift of emphasis immediately makes the problem more amenable to study in psychological terms. The problem can be seen as an imbalance of malfunctioning in negative feed-back. What the sufferer experiences is then analogous to positive feed-back or to a mechanical system after failure of the governor. This possibility was expressed vividly by a ruminator from the above series: "I just go on and on. Like an engine you can't switch off. Or the steering wheel has come off, so I can't change direction."

An important outcome of acceptance of this re-emphasis is that the focus of attention ceases to be the "force" of the "invader" and becomes the individual victim or "host." We can cease to be concerned with the compelling power of compulsions and concentrate upon the weaknesses of the victims. There is at least one classical precedent for this apparently novel switch of approach. Unlike Freud, Janet (1903) concentrates upon the *form* of the compulsive experiences rather than upon their variegated *content*. Again, unlike Freud, he concentrates not on why the obsessional idea returns to the sufferer, but on *why the sufferer returns to the idea*. He uses the homely but vivid analogy of the way in which we constantly probe the affected tooth with the tongue when we suffer from toothache.

For Janet, then, compulsivity is not a discrete psychological phenomenon, but yet one more example of the impaired functioning associated with reduced mental "tension" in psychasthenia. And the psychasthenic, with his characteristic indecisiveness, is, of all people, the least able to resist such an urge as probing an aching tooth. Indeed, Janet uses the word "temptation" (*tentation*) to describe what should be resisted. Thus, Janet's approach is diametrically opposed to that of Freud. Stress is placed not upon the overriding power and irresistibility of the obsessional thought, but upon the weakness of resistance of the obsessional person. It need scarcely be pointed out that this view coincides exactly with the subjective accounts given by the patients in the present series. But this way of looking at the problem seems to have been overlooked for many years, during which the Freudian approach, warts and all, has become the norm.

13

Anxiety, Depression, and Resistance

ANXIETY AND ANXIETY-REDUCTION

Conventionally, obsessionality has been regarded as an affective disorder—that is to say, one whose sources are emotional in nature. It should be pointed out, however, that this aetiological assumption has become the norm only since the acceptance of Freudian theory. Nineteenth-century authorities categorized it as a disorder of will, while Janet (1903), although detailing the accompanying distress, traced the basic problems back to what we would nowadays refer to as cognitive defects.

For the majority of writers, the affective component in question has boiled down to *anxiety*. The basic assumption of psychoanalytic writers has been that obsessional phenomena spring from the anxiety associated with the emergence of taboo material from the unconscious. Anal-erotic characteristics reflect the psychic defences recruited to prevent this emergence, while the neurotic symptoms express the anxiety or unavailing attempts to cope with it. At the other extreme of theoretical standpoint, those of a behaviouristic persuasion, while denying the relevance of any concept of an unconscious, also depend upon anxiety as central to their explanation of obsessional activities. For them, the function of compulsive behaviour is to reduce anxiety. As we have seen, they analyse compulsions in terms of the avoidance behaviour of animals in learning experiments.

Thus, both of the major groups of theorists allot a central role to anxiety in their approaches to obsessional disorder, but with the subtle difference that in one case anxiety is seen as the *cause* of the activity, while in the other the activity is seen as an attempt to alleviate the anxiety. Before considering these two assumptions further, it should be mentioned that there appears to have been no satisfactory experimental attempt to confirm or disconfirm either of them. At first sight they would appear eminently amenable to empirical investigation. But in practice several profound, and sometimes insoluble, difficulties complicate any experimental attack:

(a) The clinical picture is invariably complex and confused. It is difficult to identify and extricate particular experiences or contributory features, never mind measure correspondences or interactions. As Solyom *et al.* (1969) discovered, by comparison with phobics, "the situations which may provide anxiety in the obsessive patient are less clear-cut, the number of cues capable of setting off anxiety is much greater, secondary elaboration is more evident, as the patient responds to them with any of his many obsessive symptoms ... ."

(b) The characteristics of the personality disorder may reasonably be expected to be manifested in the majority of situations, including those which are prosaic, routine, and not vested with personal significance. Obsessional symptoms, on the other hand, are presumed to be triggered or released by events or reflections with particular meaning for the individual. The neutral setting of an artificial or laboratory analogue is highly unlikely to elicit the pathological experiences under study.

Beech and Liddell (1974) used this latter point in their critical discussion of an interesting study by Hodgson and Rachman (1972) which had produced some results discrepant with a report by Walker and Beech (1969). The Hodgson and Rachman investigation was specifically designed as a direct test of one of the topics under discussion here—the anxiety-reduction hypothesis. Twelve patients who displayed washing rituals rising out of fears of dirt or contamination were studied. It was predicted that: (a) touching a contaminated object would produce increases in "anxiety/discomfort" and pulse-rate variability; (b) a reduction in these measures would occur with completion of a washing ritual; and (c) the interruption of a washing ritual after such contamination would produce increases in both measures. A neat design was used, wherein each subject was studied under each of four serial conditions, controlled for order effects. The four conditions were: (a) control measures being taken before and after the touching of a neutral object; (b) washing *immediately after* touching a "contaminating" object; (c) *delayed* washing after touching a "contaminating" object; and (d) after touching a "contaminating" object, washing *interrupted* at the start of the ritual.

Subjective ratings of "anxiety/discomfort" clearly supported the first two predictions; pulse-rate data showed a similar trend, though not at an acceptable level of statistical significance. The third prediction was not borne out, inasmuch as neither subjective ratings nor pulse-rate variability were affected by the experimenter's interruption of the washing ritual. Hodgson and Rachman took their findings as offering support for the anxiety-reduction hypothesis, while recognizing that the latter might not apply to all types of compulsive behaviour.

Beech and Liddell's (1974) rejoinder to this study was that the laboratory situation employed differed substantially from the real-life exigencies faced by obsessional patients. Not only was the contamination event artificially contrived by the experimenters, but as Hodgson and Rachman themselves had pointed out, their patients had known in advance that they would be allowed to carry out their washing rituals later.

A related factor, not mentioned by Beech and Liddell, is the *presence of the investigator*, which itself introduces an element of control and reassurance to the situation. Furthermore, this is not merely a question of a neutral presence; the investigator is not simply an uninvolved observer but a trusted person with special responsibilities for the patient. And, although the behaviour therapists prefer to term themselves "experimenters," they are primarily in a therapeutic role and form many of the same relationships with patients that conventional psychotherapists form. We have noted elsewhere the relief and solace afforded to obsessional patients by the opportunities to delegate decisions and responsibilities to trusted others. The clinical experiment is just such a situation: The patient feels that things are under control because the trusted figure of the experimenter can be relied upon not to let things get out of hand. The present writer found it impossible to elicit the compulsive urge to engage in ritual activity in four hand-washers in the present series. Having determined the most feared contaminants for each individual, specimens or simulacra were introduced and each patient was asked to touch, manipulate, or sniff the material in question. While expressing distaste for this experience, no subject evinced significant changes in anxiety levels, as measured both by self-reports and a battery of physiological measures of GSR, heart rate, and temperature. In each case, this relative equanimity was explained by the patient in terms of trust in the experimenter. "I knew you wouldn't give me anything really dangerous to hold." "You wouldn't let anything happen to me." "It must be all right, really—you handed it over to me."

Exactly the same phenomenon was reported by Rachman and his colleagues when they applied their technique to twelve compulsive checkers (Röper *et al.*, 1973). They found difficulty in eliciting discomfort, because the patients reasoned that the experimenter was unlikely, for example, to leave the gas taps on, and that even if this did occur, then the responsibility would be the experimenter's. Results from this experiment showed the same pattern as those of the washing study but much less dramatically.

Röper and Rachman (1976) replicated and extended their checking study in order to reduce the distorting effects of experimental artificiality. Twelve patients were tested either in their homes or in a therapeutic community. They tended to feel more disturbance during the experimenter's absence, feeling more tense and worried when they experienced the compulsive urges.

As we have stressed throughout, obsessional problems are primarily *subjective*. Fully satisfactory *objective* measurers or even indicators have not yet been devised. Indeed, by definition, it is unlikely that they exist. The quality of subjective experience seems to be largely determined by cognitive attribution, and any one-to-one correspondence with physiological states has never been identified. Thus, the psycho-physiological measures so beloved by experimental psychologists— GSR, heart rate, blood pressure—have proved to be disappointing in studies of obsessionality. While providing clear, objective evidence of physiological changes, their use even as indicators of anxiety is dubious. Clearly they indicate *arousal*, but whether this is isomorphic with any given experience is a different question. It should be borne in mind that physiological arousal accompanies subjective experiences which, far from being classifiable as anxiety-producing or distressing, are marked by the most pleasurable anticipations.

It should be noted that in the experiments outlined above, the objective measure of pulse-rate variability contributed little to the results. Whatever their expectations, the investigators had to depend upon their subjects' self-reports. And, despite such interesting psychophysiological studies as those of Boulougouris *et al.* (1974), investigators still have to rely upon their subjects' descriptions of how they feel.

It would seem that where obsessional doubts at least (as opposed to the concomitants of compulsive rituals) are concerned, patients do not feel that their emotional states cause the doubting. In surveying the results of intensive phenomenological interviews with four severely handicapped obsessional patients (in fact, the original four of the series referred to in this book), the present writer (Reed, 1968) reported that all four claimed that their emotional responses were the *result* of their doubts, not the cause. For example:

> Mr. D.: "I'll be feeling all right and then my thoughts get this fuzzy feeling. *It's when I find I can't sort them out that I begin to get upset. ...* "
> Mr. M.: "I only begin to feel disturbed when I find the vicious circle has begun. It's usually the *result* of finding I can't stop brooding, can't come to a decision."

Furthermore, the reports of Reed's subjects did *not* indicate that their compulsive rituals reduced anxiety:

> Mrs. G.: "By numbering, it sort of clicks in my mind. But it doesn't make me feel any calmer—*I get more and more anxious the more I have to number.*"
> Mr. D.: "So I start saying my words to try and sort things out. But that always makes me feel terrible. ... "

These reports seem to be diametrically opposed to the findings of Rachman and his associates reported above. It is possible, of course, that what applies to mental rituals such as counting or incantation does not apply to compulsive hand-washing. The four most severe hand-washers in the present series were observed while they were actually in the grip of their washing compulsions, being asked to report how they felt at regular intervals. There was no doubt that their distress *increased* during each session. In each case it began as they realized that they were unable to stop; this did not occur until several minutes had elapsed. The patients attributed their distress to their awareness of helplessness in the face of their continuing activity. It became more severe as the session went on, so that the longer they found it necessary to continue, the worse they felt. This, of course, is the exact opposite of what would be expected according to the anxiety-reduction hypothesis.

So does compulsive activity reduce anxiety? Walker (1973), in a closely reasoned submission, asserts that this is exactly what it usually does *not* do. In fact, she argues, this is one of the features that differentiate compulsive rituals from normal behaviours such as childhood rituals (e.g., not stepping on cracks in the pavement), superstitious acts (e.g., throwing spilled salt over one's shoulder), primitive tribal rituals (e.g., rain-making rituals and those associated with births and deaths), and religious rituals and ceremonies. All these latter activities seem to relate to threatening situations or possible events over which the group or individual can exert no control. It seems reasonable to assume that the "normal" ritual, while it cannot modify the objective situation, functions to reduce the associated anxiety. There are several possible explanations as to how this function could develop, including those invoking a learning approach and that which focuses on the symbolic significance of the acitivity. But the preoccupations of obsessionals are not objectively dangerous or threatening; they are usually improbable, trivial, or bizarre.

In summary, Walker suggests that the obsessional ritual differs from its normal counterpart in three ways: (a) It is performed in situations of subjective rather than objective danger; (b) it is repeated; and (c) it does *not* reduce anxiety.

Reed and Walker have not been the only ones to express doubts about the general validity of the anxiety-reduction hypothesis. Herrnstein (1969) criticized the model on theoretical grounds, while a number of clinicians and behaviour therapists such as Walton (1960), Haslam (1965), Walker and Beech (1969), and Mohlenkamp (1977) have pointed out that not all compulsive acts are associated with the reduction of anxiety. In fact, Wolpe (1958) himself discriminated between "anxiety-reducing" and "anxiety-elevating" rituals.

Meanwhile, it must be re-emphasized that the debate has usually been restricted to the consideration of compulsive behaviour. There has been no suggestion that the anxiety-reduction hypothesis could be used to explain obsessional experiences in general. Indeed, if obsessional experiences functioned as reducers of anxiety and distress, why would obsessional people seek psychiatric help?

However, there may be a problem of semantics here. For obsessionals do not usually describe their suffering as "anxiety." They are disturbed, worried, frustrated, angry with themselves, rather than anxious. They often do experience anxiety, it is true, but this is usually related to long-term apprehension rather than the immediate experience, and it is submerged in a morass of other affects. Mrs. R. expressed this vividly as she stood, sobbing, at the washbasin:

First, there's my Big Fear—that I'm going mad. Mixed up with that one is the fear that I'll never get better. And I worry about the effect this is having on my husband. Embarrassment, too—I'm embarrassed about what people will think. And I'm depressed about my weakness—furious, too, that I'm stuck here and can't just decide that enough is enough. ...

Mr. M., an articulate and educated young man, also emphasized the complex of emotional concomitants to the compulsive experience:

Anxiety? I wouldn't call it that. Fear, yes—in fact, terror sometimes. Where will it all end? But I would say it's more a mixture of frustration and bewilderment. Frustration because I can't make a simple decision. Bewilderment—why should this be happening to me? I'm totally tied up—under the net. ...

Most other members of the present series also described complicated emotional states, while de-emphasizing the role of anxiety as such—for example, Miss Q.: "Gloom, mainly. Gloom and irritation" or Mr. T.: "Annoyance with myself— you lose your self-respect. I fight it, but obviously not well enough. It's very depressing. ... And I have my job to think about."

Patients in the Rachman series also denied that what they were experiencing was anxiety. For that reason, the investigators decided to use the neutral term "discomfort." For their part, Beech and his associates emphasized "mood state" as opposed to anxiety. This phraseology may provide a closer fit with the subjective condition of obsessionals and invites closer examination.

The differences between "anxiety" and "mood" are subtle, ill-defined, and not widely understood or accepted. Both are generally regarded as *affects*. But whereas "mood" is usually briefly defined as "feeling-tone," "emotional attitude," or "frame of mind," a good technical dictionary like that of Campbell (1981) will devote many columns to defining "anxiety," its varieties, and its correlates. The basic differences seem to boil down to two:

(1) In clinical discussion, anxiety is usually taken to be relatively short term, being a direct "emergency" response to a perceived threat, psychic conflict, etc. Mood, on the other hand, is taken to be "enduring, but not permanent ... " (Warren). (It will be remembered, however, that some personality psychologists distinguish between "state anxiety," which is what is under consideration here, and "trait anxiety," which refers to the individual's characteristic threshold of anxiety. This is assumed to be lifelong and probably genetically determined.)

(2) Anxiety is an "affect that differs from other affects in its specific unpleasurable characteristics" (Campbell). Mood, on the other hand, can refer to any sort of feeling tone, including euphoria, depression, tranquillity, anger, etc.

Walker and Beech (1969) elected to use the term "mood state" because of (b) above. They observed, as has been done in this book, that the ritualistic behaviour of obsessional patients is accompanied by a complex variety of experiences. Over-simplified accounts, they argued, had led to inadequate theoretical models for the explanation of obsessional behaviour. Instead of the usual retrospective reports, therefore, direct observations and reports by two obsessional patients were used to study their experiences before and after their performance of hand-washing rituals. Several generalizations were induced, which were tested in a detailed and controlled study of a third patient. The first of several interesting findings was that anxiety is not the only affect associated with ritualized activity. Hostility and depression are also evident, and these three emotional components vary together. This concurs with observations made by the present writer. Patients in the present series reported similar complexities of experience, as witness the testimonies cited above. The affective concomitant most commonly reported by patients in this series was a depressive mood. If a common factor was to be found, it would be depression rather than anxiety.

In summary, there appears to be no convincing evidence that anxiety plays a significant role in obsessional disorders. It may figure among a variety of distressful concomitants, particularly in relation to ritualistic behaviour. But it is an over-simplification to regard it as predominant or at the core of the compulsive experience. And where it can be identified it seems to be a *result* rather than a *cause* of compulsive activity, being in many cases elevated rather than reduced by that activity. However, obsessional individuals often deny that their primary affective state can be described as anxiety at all. At the same time, depression is commonly reported; we shall consider this in the next section.

DEPRESSION AND THE QUESTION OF RESISTANCE

Although the precise nature of the relationship has not yet been satisfactorily determined, it has been known for more than 150 years that there is a close association between depression and both obsessional symptoms and the compulsive personality. Pritchard (1835), and Esquirol (1838) both commented upon the appearance of obsessions during depressive psychosis. Their observations have been confirmed by more recent writers, such as Lion (1942), Stengel (1945), and Ingram (1961a), and by the results of large-scale surveys conducted by Lewis (1934), Skoog (1959), Gittleson (1966a and 1966c), and Kendell and Discipio (1970). Rachman and Hodgson (1980) provide a recent and informative discussion. Again, it has been noted that depressed patients commonly show premorbid compulsive (anankastic) personalities. Abraham (1927) maintained that most depressives have pre-morbid compulsive personalities, and many other writers have discussed the relationship, including Muncie (1931), Stengel (1945), and Anderson (1964). Surveys by Kinkelin (1954) and Hopkinson (1964) reported that about 70% of patients suffering from depressive psychosis possessed pre-morbid anankastic personalities. (A short report by Vaughan [1976] of a survey using Maudsley Hospital item-sheets found that only 29 of 168 cases of depression had been noted as having obsessional personality traits. Vaughan's findings are atypical and may reflect simply the abbreviated and routine nature of her source material.) The general view has been that sufferers from depressive psychosis tend to be of compulsive personality, but it must be pointed out that empirical attempts to substantiate this have faced serious methodological problems (Snaith *et al.*, 1971). Whether the relationship between compulsive personality, obsessional symptoms, and depressive disorders is a causal one remains an open question; it is certainly not a simple matter. Not all depressives can be shown to have had pre-morbid compulsive personalities. Not all of them show obsessional symptoms; of those who do, some have shown them prior to the onset of depression, but some develop them only during the depressive episode. Of the latter group, most but not all lose their obsessions as their depression lifts.

Although a lot of investigation remains to be done, some substantial empirical evidence has been presented by Gittleson (1966), who made a retrospective study of the case notes of all the patients diagnosed as suffering from depressive psychosis who had been admitted for in-patient treatment to the Professorial Unit of the Maudsley Hospital, London, during the four-year period 1956 to 1959. Of a total of 398 patients, 171 (43%) were regarded as having had pre-morbid compulsive personalities (though not necessarily personality *disorders*.) Fifty-two patients (13%) had experienced obsessions prior to the depressive illness. Thirty-nine patients (10%) were "Keepers," who exhibited obsessions both before and during their depressive illnesses. Eight-five patients (21%) were "Gainers," whose obsessions appeared only after the onset of depression. Thirteen patients (3%) were "Losers," whose pre-depressive obsessions disappeared or were transformed during depression. Eleven patients (2.8%) experienced a permanent worsening of their obsessions after recovering from depression. Of these, 7 were among the 52 who had suffered from obsessions prior to their depressions. Similar findings to those of Gittleson's were reported by Kendell and Discipio (1970) who surveyed 92 in-patients, some suffering from neurotic (reactive) depression, others from depressive psychosis. The Leyton Obsessional Inventory (Cooper, 1970) was administered to patients at the height of their disorder, and again shortly after recovery. From responses to the Leyton inventory, four scores can be derived—an obsessional symptom score (number of symptoms), an anankastic trait score (number of traits), a resistance score (severity of symptoms), and an interference score (degree of disturbance produced by the symptoms). In 20 cases obsessional symptoms were detected at the initial, clinical interview. But 72% of the patients obtained higher resistance scores and 58% higher symptom and interference scores during their depression than they did after recovery. These figures are similar to those of Lewis (1934) and Gittleson (1966) and offer further evidence of the prevalence of obsessions in depressive disorders. But several other findings of interest were reported. Age and sex had little influence. Pre-morbid compulsive personality proved to very important but not in a clear-cut manner. On all scales, the scores of patients with obsessional traits proved to be much higher than those of patients without such traits. After recovery, the symptom and trait scores of the former group *did not fall at all*. Neurotic and psychotic depressives made almost identical scores on all four scales. But after recovery the neurotics made higher scores on all scales. In other words, psychotic depressives have fewer pre-morbid obsessional traits than neurotic depressives but have a greater tendency to develop obsessional symptoms during the depression. Their depression tends to be more severe than that of the neurotic group.

There is a vast literature on the topic of psychiatric depression, and it would be foolish to attempt even the sketchiest of summaries here. However, the reader may care to be reminded that the clinical picture subsumes both physical and psycho-motor features as well as the typical mental state. The first group includes: loss of appetite, accompanied by a dramatic weight loss; changes in the pattern of sleep, including most typically, early morning wakening; psycho-motor retardation or agitation; a pronounced diminution of libido; and such deteriorations in psychological functions as constipation and reduction of secretions. Of more immediate relevance to our present concerns are the characteristic features of the depressive mental state:

(a) *Depression* refers to the lowering of spirits and drive. In lay parlance "depression" is taken to be synonymous with "sadness." It must be emphasized that technically the term derives from *depressione vitalis*—a diminution of the level of vitality. Such phenomenological psychiatrists as Schneider have stressed the occurrence of *"depressio sine depressione,"* where dramatic symptoms may not be present and, where, more importantly, patients do *not* report sadness or unhappiness. Diagnostically of more clinical significance are patients' reports that "the life has gone out of everything," that "things look flat and have lost their colour," or that "there's no point to anything." (Such depressive feelings show diurnal variation. It has been claimed that reactive depression worsens as the day proceeds, whereas endogenous depression is worse in the early hours.)

(b) *Self-reproach* and feelings of guilt exist. The depressive regards himself as worthless—to his loved ones or society in general. He grossly under-values his personal qualities and skills and may judge his life history as lacking in moral value.

(c) Consciousness is clear, but there is a severe *diminution in concentration*, marked by slowness of thought and indecisiveness.

(d) Closely related to (c) above is the *lack of interest* in or responsiveness to other people and external events. The depressive's attention is self-focused.

(e) Related to (a) above, the depressive is *listless*; he lacks energy and enthusiasm and complains of fatigue.

(f) Delusional ideas develop into full-blown *delusions*—typically of worthlessness, ill-health, poverty, or persecution. These presumably spring out of (a) and (b) above.

(g) Associated with (b) above is the fact that the content of depressive thought is often to do with death and suicide.

The over-riding flavour of the depressive experience, then, is a compound of self-denigration, low spirits, and the sort of helplessness discussed by Seligman (1975). Depressed people feel as though they have "fallen from grace" and have lost any control over events. The reader will doubtless have noticed that these features also characterized the mood state described by obsessionals in the previous section, which included dejection, helplessness, self-criticism, worry, and despair. Furthermore, the self-reproach and feelings of helplessness bring to mind our earlier discussion of the experience of compulsion. It will be recalled that the obsessional stresses not so much the power of his obsession as his own weakness in failing to control or resist it. (However, a crucial point to be borne in mind is that, at least initially, he does in fact make strenuous attempts to do so.)

The phenomenological similarities between the obsessional's state of mind and that of the clinically depressed person do not seem to have been stressed in the literature. This may well be because of differences of content or, more likely, because readily identifiable obsessional features may mask an underlying depression. Whatever the reason for previous writers' silence upon the topic the close parallels remarked upon here obviously invite attention. But first it must be emphasized that it is not being suggested that obsessional disorders are simply depressions under a different label. Not at all. It is, of course, possible for misdiagnosis to occur. As suggested above, the presence of noticeable obsessional symptoms may mislead the clinician. But in general, the two disorders are readily discriminable; the obsessional person does not manifest such signs and symptoms of depression as the so-called "biological signs" listed above (weight loss, sleep pattern changes, etc.). What is being discussed here is simply the uncanny similarities of the mood states experienced in the two disorders.

Perhaps the most productive approach to this enigma is to enquire as to whether any determinable *differences* exist. And the answer may be hazarded that the only crucial difference seems to be *resistance*. The obsessional person, by definition, unsuccessfully resists his intrusive thought. The depressed person is too lacking in vitality, too subjectively helpless, to struggle with the morbid thoughts which preoccupy him. The psychopathological difference may best be illustrated by a real example. Mr. E.'s everyday life was severely constricted by his fear about the insidious spread of germs, disease, and corruption. He had unsuccessfully resisted this fear for several years, and it was described, quite properly, as an *"obsession."* Mr. A., a much older man, harboured a fear which was identical in content. But he made no attempt to resist it. His fear, again quite properly, was described as a *"delusion."* In view of other clinical features in his case, it was taken to be a delusion of the nihilistic variety which is not uncommon in depressive disorders. Technically, the crucial phenomenological difference between the two experiences is that in Mr. E.'s case the fear dominated his consciousness despite his attempts to repel it.

An important point here, as Gittleson (1966a) pointed out, is that in the course of time the change may take place within the same individual. After a long period of failure, the obsessional weakens in his resolve. The "fight is knocked out of him." It may well be that a vicious circle develops. It may be postulated that the more depressive the mood of the obsessional person the less able he feels to resist his obsessions. And the more helpless he feels, the more depressed he becomes. Thus, the more severe the disorder or the longer it has persisted, the more the passive response features will predominate.

Such an increase in depressive mood and, therefore, of subjective helplessness is probably the key to a problem hinted at in the first chapter of this book. As was emphasized there, internal resistance is by definition one of the three formal criteria of what constitutes an obsession. However, a few writers have argued that this is misleading and does not coincide with the phenomenological accounts given by obsessional patients. Walker (1973), in proposing a new definition of compulsive rituals, argued that a feeling of compulsion accompanied by resistance was neither necessary nor sufficient to define obsessional thoughts or actions. She cited as examples two cases where classical compulsive ritualization was *not* resisted. Similarly, Stern and Cobb (1978), in presenting the results of structured interviews with 45 obsessive–compulsive neurotics, reported that 15% of the patients asserted that they made no attempt to resist performing their rituals. A further 31% offered only slight resistance. Only 30% felt that they made great efforts to resist. However, the researchers pointed out in passing that these figures might have been different had the questioning referred to the past ("Have you ever in the past resisted your rituals?") rather than being restricted to the present ("How much do you resist your rituals at present?"). Herein may lie the key to this divergence of opinion regarding the importance of resistance.

Before going on to examine the question of fluctuations of resistance, it should be noted that the studies of both Walker (1973) and Stern and Cobb (1978) focus upon resistance to *the performance of compulsive rituals*. The primary definition of obsessions is concerned not with performance but with obsessional *thoughts*. As we have seen, compulsive behaviour is secondary to obsessional urges, fears, and preoccupations. So, in restricting their discussions to rituals, both the studies in question may have missed their mark. For example, a person may suffer from the obsessional fear that she is unduly susceptible to contamination, an idea which she struggles unavailingly to dispel. She resists it because intellectually she is aware that her alarm is grossly exaggerated. Among other "defensive" measures, she develops several cleaning rituals. And these she may not resist, considering them to be appropriate in view of the dangers which beset her. Indeed, Stern and Cobb elicited the interesting fact that when their subjects did report resistance in relation to their ritualistic behaviour, it was not the rituals themselves which were resisted, but their *repetition*. This coincides with the reports of the subjects in the present series. The most severe hand-washers— Mrs. G., Mrs. R., Mr. E., and Mr. F.—did not complain of their hand-washing as such, nor of its elaborate ritualization, but of the fact that they found it necessary to engage in it so repeatedly. Mr. A., Mr. N., Mr. U., Mrs. E., and Mrs. P. regarded their over-methodical checking itself as sensible and prudent; what they tried to resist was their inability to prevent themselves from prolonged re-checking. (It will be noted that this accords well with our conceptualization of compulsion as a diminution of inhibitory processes.)

Let us now return to the issue of fluctuations of resistance. In Chapter 1 it was pointed out that resistance can vary in intensity over time. In severe cases, or ones which have persisted over long periods, the sufferer's resistance may be worn down. He eventually submits to the obsession, not because he finds it any more acceptable or reasonable, but because he feels exhausted by the struggle and simply gives in. Similarly, an individual's degree of resistance may vary from occasion to occasion, reflecting his state of physical health, his morale, and various possible environmental factors. Thus, Mr. M. was able to dispel his obsessional ruminations for several days after receiving news that he was to be offered a coveted position: "I just feel on top of the world. I could handle anything. ... " On the other hand, Mrs. R., who had valiantly resisted her contamination obsession for many years, metaphorically ran up the white flag during her menstrual periods or when suffering from bowel trouble. As she was concerned to point out, this was not because the obsession was more powerful at these times but that she herself felt weaker: "There's too much stacked against me. ... It's bad enough fighting it at the best of times, but right now I feel helpless—I haven't the will-power to go on."

What is being argued here is that resistance is indeed a central component of the obsessional experience. Its abandonment as a definitional criterion would raise several insoluble problems of diagnosis. However, the intensity of resistance varies, as might be expected. Furthermore, it may now be suggested that the degree of resistance varies negatively with the level of depressive mood. When the obsessional individual's mood is elevated, he feels relatively confident and energetic; he resists his obsessions, even though it is a losing fight. But the more depressed his mood, the less energy he can recruit, the blacker the outlook appears, and the less point there seems to be in continuing the struggle. He may, in fact, surrender, by discontinuing his resistance. Some evidence supportive of this approach may be adduced from the fact that, as we saw in an earlier chapter, the only physical treatment of help in obsessional states is the use of *antidepressant drugs*. Again, of considerable significance for our present discussion is a very interesting report by Foa *et al.* (1983). In patients with obsessive-compulsive disorder who completed courses of behaviour therapy but failed to improve, there was a linear relationship between initial depression and negative outcome.

However, as is so commonly the case, an obdurate fly blemishes the creamy ointment of this argument. If increasing depression causes, or is associated with, a diminution of resistance, how is it that, as we noted earlier, depressive episodes are often accompanied by the emergence of obsessions? On the present argument, obsessions should decrease during depressive disorder, to be replaced by delusions. Furthermore, Kendell and Discipio (1970) reported that resistance scores were higher during depression than after recovery. There are several possible ways of swatting this particular fly. The first one is to postulate a spreading effect. With an increased depressive mood, it may be postulated, less resistance can be made to the original or "core" obsessions. But as a full-blown depressive disorder develops, perhaps a wider range of obsessions intrude, and it is these "secondary" phenomena which are experienced during the depressive breakdown itself. A second possibility is that whatever subsumes resistance steadily deteriorates, but varies in a cyclical manner, as do the classical affective disorders. It could also be, of course, that the present suggestion is simply ill-conceived. Whatever the case, there is clearly room for further research—phenomenological, empirical, and experimental.

14
Compulsive Checking

This chapter will be concerned with the excessive checking engaged in by many persons suffering from compulsive (anankastic) personality disorder. As we saw in Chapter 4, such checking is usually to do with everyday activities or conditions. Most commonly reported is the ascertainment that door bolts and locks have been properly engaged, gas and water taps turned off, and electric lights and gadgets switched off. In such examples, the checking appears to be aimed at ensuring that certain domestic routines have in fact been carried out by the checker. The checking often takes the form of repeated visual inspection; but in many cases it may involve re-doing the task in question. Another common group of instances is related to the ensuring of a prescribed order or organization, which may be quite idiosyncratic. Kitchen shelves are checked to make sure that utensils are "properly" aligned, cupboards to ensure that their contents are "correctly" arranged, wardrobes to determine that clothes are hung in the "right" order. A third group includes checking which is less "meaningful" and directive than the examples noted above. Here, the checking seems to be aimed at re-affirming casual observations, such as the number of motifs in the wallpaper pattern or the layout of flagstones in the yard.

All the examples cited above are drawn from the domestic sphere; but checking of all types is not uncommon in occupational areas. The locking of drawers, filing cabinets, and workshop or office doors may be checked, as may the layout of tools, the filing of documents, and the arrangement of desks. A well-known example is the repeated re-checking of tabular totals or other computations.

Examples in the first two groups noted may all have a familiar ring; most careful people would probably recognize the sorts of instances where they themselves check. Behaviourally, the only differences are the amount of checking carried out and the regularity with which it is undertaken. But there are crucial differences in the associated *experience*. Anankastic checking must be differentiated from the prudent but undemanding routines of normal, conscientious people. Normal checking may be said to involve confirmation (that a task has been carried out, that a recollection or understanding is valid), reassurance (that some situation prevails), and assessment (of the appropriateness of a situation or the outcome of a completed task). It may be described as a "one-off" procedure. Confirmation is sought that a given task has been accomplished or that a desired condition obtains. Once confirmed, the matter is closed, the question resolved. The anankast, on the other hand, seldom achieves a complete feeling of closure. Compulsive checking fails to provide satisfactory confirmation, reassurance, or assessment, which is one aspect of the obsessional's *sentiment d'incomplétude*. The checking failure leads to further checking and the checking of the checking itself, so that a vicious circle of uncertainty develops. Sometimes, no amount of checking will succeed in fully allaying this uncertainty; the subject may well have recourse to accepting the results of some arbitrary number of checks. Again, anankastic checking has a *compulsive* quality, in as much as the obsessional person experiences some subjective resistance to his activity. Much of the time, he may be aware that his checking is unnecessary and finds his need to check and re-check irritating, inconvenient, and even disturbing.

Unelaborated, personality-bound checking of the sort under discussion is seldom the primary cause for psychiatric referral. The symptoms reported by patients suffering from obsessional–compulsive illness often include checking, of course. But in such cases it is much more pervasive and elaborated, figuring as part of the complex of compulsive ritualization. Mundane checking of the types outlined above may continue during the course of the illness; but by then it is overshadowed by the bizarre and preoccupying nature of the symptomatology. Thus, in general, simple checking is recorded not in the clinician's account of the "present illness" in the case notes, but in the "pre-morbid history" section.

To indicate the range of types of checking and prepare the way for some attempts at classification, let us look at some examples from the series of patients referred to in earlier chapters.

Mr. A., a 41-year-old café proprietor, had always suffered from pronounced feelings of inadequacy which had been exacerbated by worries about his business. Among several compulsive symptoms were his excessive checking of locks and switches, both at home and at work.

Mrs. E., a 49-year-old housewife with anankastic ruminations, had always been fussy and house-proud. She carried out her housework according to fixed routines, checking each completed chore seven times.

Mrs. O., a 43-year-old housewife, suffered among other things from phobic fears of electrical appliances and switches, the positions of which she checked repeatedly.

Mr. N., a 25-year-old clerk, suffered from compulsive doubts and fears. He could not retire to bed without checking all the household bolts, locks, and switches, a task which took at least an hour each night.

Mr. U., a 38-year-old local government officer, had a long history of compulsive symptoms. He had been a compulsive checker since childhood, and his work performance was handicapped by his repeated checking of ledger entries and schedules of routine visits.

Mrs. G., a 28-year-old laboratory technicican, had suffered from compulsive hand-washing, ruminations, and rituals for five years. She was preoccupied with obsessional fears of contamination, which were reflected in continual checking of clothing, cutlery, linen, etc.

Mrs. N., a 33-year-old typist, had suffered from overwhelming obsessional fears of thunderstorms for four years. She was extremely house-proud, a perfectionist who found it necessary to check and re-check all doors and the fireguard.

Mrs. P., a 39-year-old housewife, had suffered a life-long dog phobia, which was now incapacitating. She had always checked doors and under the bed, but in recent years had found it necessary to continually check the doorstep, garden paths, and lawn for any sign of canine excrement.

Mrs. F., a 28-year-old typist, suffered from an increasing obsessional fear regarding the spread of illicit drug abuse. She found it necessary to compulsively check with hospitals, police, and newspapers to assure herself that there had been no local drug-related catastrophe.

Mr. D., an 18-year-old student, suffered from continual obsessional ruminations, the most intrusive being the possibility that he had murdered two elderly neighbours by cutting out their livers. He compulsively checked the whereabouts of the ''victims'' at intervals throughout each day in attempts to assure himself that they were alive and well.

Clearly, to bring some order to such a rich and variant group of activities, a variety of classificatory approaches is possible at different levels. Some possible classifications will be offered here. But first of all, a basic distinction must be made.

To allow for any rational study of checking behaviour and avoid the confusion contingent upon comparing conceptual apples and oranges, it is important to be quite clear about the difference between: (a) the original actions, outcomes, situations, arrays, etc., which are subject to checking, and (b) the checking itself. Failure to recognize this distinction can lead to misunderstanding, confusion, and circular reasoning in discussion of the topic. It should be borne in mind that what is of interest in the present context is the phenomenon of compulsive checking itself, which is a formal matter. The paucity of theoretical studies of the phenomenon may be due largely to writers' being distracted by the content features of (a) above. Understandably, psychoanalytic writers have been preoccupied with questions of content and have thus failed to attack the problems inherent in (b) above. Oddly enough, researchers in the behavioural/learning tradition have followed the same route, as we shall see.

Among the many ways in which examples of the items subject to checking may be classified are:

(a) Given that checking concerns a desirable state of affairs, the latter may consist of:
   (i) The presence of desired attributes (e.g., among the examples cited above, Mr. A. and Mrs. E.)
   (ii) The *absence* of *undesired* attributes (e.g., Mrs. O. and Mr. N.)
(b) The desirable state of affairs may refer to:
   (i) Naturally occurring situations, events, arrays, etc. (e.g., Mrs. G., Mrs. N., and Mrs. P.)
   (ii) The outcomes of tasks or activities (e.g., Mr. A., Mrs. E., Mr. N., and Mr. U.)
(c) The tasks referred to in (b, ii) may be:
   (i) Simple—consisting of a single action such as turning a key (e.g., Mr. A. and Mr. N.)
   (ii) Sequential—consisting of several actions done in order (e.g., Mr. U and Mrs. P.)
   (iii) Complex—consisting of several simple or sequential acts appropriately integrated (e.g., Mrs. F. and Mr. D.)
   It will be noted that some "tasks" requiring checking are themsleves checks.
(d) In temporal terms, the desirable state of affairs may be:
   (i) Current—the present state is the desirable one (e.g., Mr. A., Mrs. E., and Mrs. O.)
   (ii) Prospective—the desirable state will continue (e.g., Mrs. F.)
   (iii) Retrospective—the desirable state occurred in the past (e.g., Mr. D.)

To date, it does not seem to have been recognized that there are at least three distinct types of *checking*. They differ according to the situations checked, the purposes ascribed to them by the checkers, and the sorts of behaviour involved in the act of checking:

a) *"Confirmatory" checking by inspection*: This type consists simply of inspections (usually visual) to confirm that some desired situation exists. The "situation" may involve the presence or the absence of something but often is evidence that some task has been completed. The checker describes his activity in this case in terms of "making sure" (that a job has been done, etc.) or in terms of compensating for shaky recall: "I can't be sure that I locked it, so I check to make sure"; "I *think* I locked it—I always do. But I can't quite remember. ... " Tasks to which class (a) checking would be applied include those requiring a single act—e.g., turning a key, pressing a switch, shooting a bolt—or sequential tasks where satisfactory completion can be confirmed by inspection—e.g., typing a letter, finishing a jigsaw puzzle.

b) *"Verificatory" checking by repetition*: This may be a compound variant of class (a). It involves confirming that some task has been completed satisfactorily. But here the check is conducted by re-doing the task in question. The checker describes his activity in terms of "making sure," not in terms of suspect recall. The emphasis is placed upon the correctness of the outcome, not simply upon the completion of the task: "I'm just making sure it's right." Tasks to which class (b) checking would be applied are those involving a series of steps or components, each of which must be completed appropriately if the final outcome is to be correct or satisfactory and where correct performance of the components cannot be verified by inspection alone, e.g., tuning an engine, assembling a gadget. The general question of compulsive repetition will be considered in a separate chapter. There is considerable overlap, but the two phenomena are not identical. Not all compulsive repeating involves checking, whereas all compulsive checking involves repetition.

c) *"Verificatory" mental checking*: This is probably a version of class (b). All the same features apply, except that, in this case, the tasks are mental ones so that neither their performance nor the checking involve observable behaviour. Examples would include solving a mental problem, doing an arithmetic sum mentally, learning a speech, or rehearsing an argument. A variant of this class occurs where the checking is carried out mentally, although the action checked was behavioural: "I run through it in my head, to make sure I did it right."

Janet (1903) mentions checking briefly, under the heading of *"la manie des verifications."* He gives two examples, and then concludes: *"Il est inutile de rappeler les malades bien connus qui verifient indefiniment si la porte est bien fermée, si le gaz est eteint, si la lettre est bien dans la boite, etc."* (p. 114)— ["It is pointless to recall the well-known patients who check indefinitely whether the door is properly closed, whether the gas is turned off, whether the letter is really in the box, etc."] He does not discuss checking specifically, including it merely as another example of the vacillation, the indecisiveness, and the need for assurance, precision, and order which we have noted as characteristic of compulsive personality disorder.

Excessive checking is mentioned in almost every textbook account of compulsive personality disorder and figures in several published case studies. But it has received remarkably little attention at the theoretical level, by comparison with other obsessional–compulsive manifestations. There are a number of possible reasons for this neglect. Most major theorists seem to have dismissed it as merely one of the many facets of obsessional indecisiveness. There is considerable justification for this attitude. But it has led to the presumption that checking does not merit examination as a phenomenon in its own right, whereas other obsessional activities and experiences do. Psychoanalytic writers, being primarily concerned with *content*, have probably found little interest in the mundane nature and surface simplicity of unelaborated checking. They have preferred to examine more complex and dramatic manifestations which may be interpreted in terms of symbolic significance. In his classical account, Fenichel (1945) makes no reference whatsoever to checking as such. Even Stekel's (1927) massive study contains only one reference to checking (and that example refers to a patient whose checking was highly elaborated and ritualized). Likewise, phenomeno-logical writers have clearly been drawn to the examination of experiences with existential implications. Thus Straus (1948) does not refer to checking at all (though it may be implied in his discussion of "perfectionism"). Schneider's (1925) account of the anankastic personality outlines a variety of undramatic characteristics but checking receives no mention. What is more surprising is that the phenomenon—which may be studied at one level as a determinable, ob-servable piece of behaviour—has received little more attention from behavioural psychologists.

Almost the only recent writers to have examined compulsive checking from either a theoretical or a pragmatic (treatment) point of view have been Rachman and his associates. Over the last eleven years they have published several in-teresting studies of checking, as part of their major research program of behaviour modification with obsessive-compulsives (e.g., Röper *et al.*, 1973; Röper and Rachman, 1975; Rachman, 1976). These have reported a variety of stimulating findings and observations (summarized in Rachman and Hodgson, 1980), the theoretical basis for which is quite straightforward.

Using a behavioural/learning paradigm:

(1) Rachman's central assumption is that checking is an example of *active avoidance*, as opposed to cleaning (compulsive hand-washing, etc.), which exemplifies *passive avoidance*.

(2) Cleaning compulsions, like phobias, involve fear of an object or situation. But checking, we are told, is motivated largely by *fear of criticism*, including self-criticism or guilt.

(3) Whereas cleaning compulsions are *restorative*, checking is *preventive* in nature; it represents attempts to forestall unpleasant events, such as harm to the checker or family members.

(4) They are appropriately cautious, but, on more than one occasion in their book, Rachman and Hodgson (1980) argue that *indecisiveness* is not a crucial factor, thus taking a position diametrically opposed to that of Janet (and, incidentally, of most other authorities).

Unfortunately, each of these four central assumptions or conclusions seems to be open to damaging criticism.

In reference to (1) above, Rachman and Hodgson's (1980) application of passive avoidance to cleaners and active avoidance to checkers is not so convincing as they seem to believe. The distinction between the two types of avoidance is neatly drawn and quite clear: "For present purposes we will asume that in passive-avoidance training you get punished if you do; in active-avoidance training you get punished if you don't" (p. 118). Nicely put. Thus, under passive-avoidance training, the subject is conditioned *not* to respond, whereas in active-avoidance training he is conditioned to respond—to take evasive action. Are we then to understand that the tortuous and exhausting activities involved in compulsive hand-washing are *non*-responses by comparison with the action required to check whether a switch has been pressed? Surely not. And it cannot have escaped the notice of Rachman and Hodgson that the acceptance of checking as *passive* avoidance would have extricated them from the subsequent theoretical convolutions required to explain why checking persists even when it is punished by social criticism.

In reference to (2) above, what evidence is there for the claim that checking is motivated by *fear of criticism* or guilt? Admittedly, some actions which are checked may be interpreted in this way. The householder may be said to lock his front door because he is afraid that otherwise his wife will criticize him for leaving the house open to burglars. But how can the *checking* itself be interpreted in this way? It seems likely that Rachman and Hodgson have fallen into the conceptual trap, discussed earlier, of confusing the activity or situation which is checked with the checking itself.

Furthermore, as they themselves point out, most patients report that, far from avoiding criticism, their checking behaviour actually provokes it.

Regarding (3) above, in what way can checking be regarded as *preventive* in nature? Again, some original actions may be of a preventive kind, (e.g., the householder locks his front door to prevent burglars from walking in). But our concern here is with checking, the functions of which, as noted above are *confirmatory* or *verificatory*, rather than preventive.

Furthermore, some examples of checking have a retrospective object, as in class (d) (iii) on page 147. They concern events (or the absence thereof) which have already occurred. Thus, even the original action could have served no preventive function. Three of the ten examples given by Rachman and Hodgson themselves are of this type. One such case was that of a male nurse who found it necessary to check that nobody had been trapped in a manhole, that no babies had been dumped in dustbins, etc. Another example is that of a lady who repeatedly checked with the police to ensure that she had not caused any accidents. In neither of these cases could either the original or subsequent checks have *prevented* the unhappy events feared by the checkers.

As far as *indecisiveness*—(4) above—is concerned, Rachman and Hodgson honourably quell their misgivings to report that their checkers did in fact report doubts and indecision more than did the cleaners. "Checking rituals are prolonged and associated with excessive doubting because they are designed to anticipate, and indeed to prevent, some future event, and hence can have no end point, no obvious conclusion'' (p. 134). This account seems to overlook the distinction between checked actions and checking *and* its range of temporal referents described above.

However, there seems further support here for the view that checking is associated with doubts and indecisiveness. But how, it may be enquired, could it be otherwise? After all, checking is by definition a test of accuracy or completion, engaged in because these are matters of uncertainty. If uncertainty, doubt, indecisiveness, etc., did *not* prevail, then checking would not occur in the first place.

Close consideration of what is known about compulsive, unelaborated checking suggests that it cannot be as straightforward as it at first appears. To start with an obvious point, but one which is often overlooked, any checking is initiated by a query about *recall*. The normal person checks, for instance, that the back door is locked, because he is unable to remember whether he locked it earlier. He has asked himself the question "Did I lock the back door?" but not found an answer. He therefore goes to look (checks), and the condition of the backdoor lock provides him with an ostensive answer. Immediately, something paradoxical about compulsive checking is indicated. For the compulsive checker often reports that he knows that the door is locked *before* he checks. In other words, in his case the question seems to have already been answered.

Furthermore, the checking of the normal person has a direct relation to his previous experience of the activity or condition in question. It does not seem to have been previously observed that this is not necessarily the case with the compulsive checker. His checking seldom yields complete assurance; he finds it necessary to check again. Thus, in this regard, his question has not been fully answered. A conventional retort to this might be that it is exactly this sort of thing which makes him classifiable as an obsessive–compulsive. But this savours of circularity. To say that a compulsive checker re-checks because he is a compulsive checker does not advance the enquiry. It is probably correct to argue that obsessional problems are associated with difficulty in accepting evidence and/or a high threshold for the experience of assurance (e.g., Beech and Liddell, 1974). And this may well reflect high subjective probabilities of undesired outcomes (Makhlouf-Norris and Jones, 1971; Carr, 1974). But in the present case a more parsimonious possibility exists. The compulsive checker's doubts have not been allayed; his question, then, has not been answered. But, as his check *has*, in fact, answered the question of whether he had locked the back door, his continuing dubiety strongly suggests that *that was not his question*. But, it may be objected, if that was not his question, why did he attempt to answer it in the first place? The reply to that objection is that perhaps he didn't. Some sorts of questions have only one answer; but any one answer will fit many questions.

It seems likely that however undramatic the behaviour involved in unelaborated compulsive checking might be, the antecedent and associated experiences are highly paradoxical and merit closer study. We need to know more about the formal quality of the psychological processes involved, and the refined study of these must be preceded by some basic phenomenological investigation. The present chapter represents a preliminary ground-clearing exercise of this type.

A group of fifteen psychiatric patients who reported that they engaged in compulsive, unelaborated checking constituted the subject sample. The group included seven females and eight males, with a median age of 33 years (range 18 to 49). All of them had been classified as suffering from compulsive (anankastic) personality disorder; cases involving organic or psychotic complications were excluded. Presenting symptoms included compulsive rituals (four males, two females), obsessional ruminations (two males, three females), obsessional fears (two females), and profound feelings of inadequacy (two males). The unelaborated checking occurred in the following areas: locks, bolts, taps, and switches (two males, two females), cleaning and other household chores (four females), occupational routines (four males, one female), and the arrangement of possessions (two males). It should be emphasized, however, that in most cases checking was reported as occurring in more than one area. The above list refers to areas where the patients felt their checking was most extreme.

Subjects were asked to describe in detail the experiences they associated with their checking, starting with their feelings prior to the checking itself. Every one referred to the antecedent feeling of unsurety, using terms such as "making sure," "not certain," and "not quite convinced." The following excerpts are representative:

> I just feel uneasy about it. The feeling gets stronger until I just have to go back and make sure. ...
>
> It's very inconvenient, but I can't get off to sleep if I don't make sure. ...
>
> Somehow, I don't feel certain that it's all right. ...

But despite this feeling of uncertainty, six subjects reported that they knew prior to checking that the task had in fact been satisfactorily completed or that the desired condition obtained. Five others felt that they knew "most of the time":

> I usually know I've done it, but I'm not satisified. ... It's ridiculous, really. Pointless. ... In one way I'm quite sure there's nothing left on, so there's no reason to check. ...
>
> I know I've turned them off properly. In fact, nearly all my checking is a waste of time. I realize that, but. ...

In such cases, when the checker "knows" what the outcome of his checking will be, what is it that he is unsure of? The answer is indicated in the following complaint:

I'll say to myself, 'You know you did it right. You always do. Don't fuss!' But it's no good—*I can't convince myself that I'm remembering right.* ...

A number of other reports tended to confirm this hint. Indeed, the more articulate subjects tried to discriminate between the *flavour* or conviction of their memory images:

It's as though the memory is there, but it isn't *definite* enough. ...

I remember doing it in a way, but it's all fuzzy. ...

Usually I can remember that I've done it. But the memory isn't clear somehow. ...

What is unsatisfactory about the memory images? The following excerpts suggest the answer:

It's done, I know that—*but I can't see myself doing it.* ...

I think I remember all right. But it's blurry somehow—*as though I'm not there.* ...

I know they are o.k. When I think back I can see them in my head. The trouble is that I can't be sure that *it was me seeing them before.* ...

What such reports appear to be describing is some failure of *personalization.* They are attempts to differentiate between the neutral flavour of formal, factual recall and the richness of personal reminiscence. In that case, what does the checking accomplish? Only three of the subjects felt that it allayed their doubts completely. The remainder expressed considerable reserve. In one sense, checking (or re-checking) brought some relief; but none claimed that it resolved the ambiguous nature of their memory of the task in question.

My checking is like an alibi. If I think back, I'm still not sure. But I've checked. ... I try to think of something else. ...

Usually, one check does me. But if I'm feeling worried or browned off or anything, I often have to go back again.

The checking doesn't satisfy me much, as a matter of fact. But I know that if I go on doing it, I'll be up half the night. ...

I have to go and check, but then I'm not convinced about the checking. So I have to go and check that I checked properly. ...

In a very interesting recent study, Sher *et al.* (1983) set out specifically to examine the relationship between compulsive checking and memory dysfunction. Using questionnaires, they selected groups of checkers, cleaners, and non-cleaning non-checkers from a population of normal undergraduate students. Subjects were required to recall seven separate tasks which they had just completed. These included a test of "reality" monitoring adapted from the work of Johnson and Raye (1981), who have described reality monitoring as the process of distinguishing memories of imagined occurrences from those of actual occurrences. Sher et al.'s checkers showed poorer recall of their previous actions. But what is of even greater interest in the context of our present discussion is that while their performances on the actual reality-monitoring task were not inferior to those of the controls, they underestimated their abilities in this regard. This suggests that, for this task at least, they suffered from uncertainty and doubt as to their own effectiveness.

The testimony of the present respondents indicates that their need to check was indeed associated with a lack of certainty. What they were unsure about was not the factual content of their remembering, but the *quality of the remembering itself*. This seems to reflect a failure or attenuation of the personalized element. In psychological terminology, it is not storage or retrieval which are faulty, but the degree of *redintegration*, the development of which has been discussed from the cognitive viewpoint by the present writer (Reed, 1972), and which I have had recourse to in a study of obsessional disorder and remembering (Reed, 1977a).

If this is so, what checking presumably represents is an attempt to invoke a satisfactory level of redintegration. Normal experience suggests that this should achieve its purpose. (In everyday life, we establish richly redintegrative recall of a scene, a face, or a work of art by repeated observations.) But in fact, many obsessional patients seem to find only semi-satisfactory levels after checking, and several of the present subjects reported that they seldom achieved complete conviction. The point at which tolerable satisfaction is attained tends to be variable. It is strongly influenced by the patients' reactions to external events, coupled with their mood state. Some compulsive checkers attempt to legislate against unduly prolonging the search for surety by instituting a predetermined limit to the number of checks. One patient in the present series checked the completion of her household tasks exactly seven times at each session. Her reason was not that seven checks would satisfy her, but simply that she had to place a limit on her unsatisfying activity. And, as Röper et al. (1973) have pointed out, when satisfaction is not attained, continued re-checking may lead to an increase in the difficulty of knowing when to stop. Several of the present subjects reported that continued re-checking tended to make them more uneasy than ever. It could be that this "diminishing returns" experience is due to the fact that each check is itself a new experience, the recollection of which invokes the same uneasiness as the original one. A continuing series of checks may thus lead to a spiral confusion effect, accompanied by increasing uneasiness and indecision. After a time, a checker is checking on his checking. Indeed, such a vicious circle of indecision is one characteristic of obsessional disorder and typifies, in particular, the endless questioning of the classical ruminator.

The present findings, however tentative, reaffirm the writer's conviction—
that obsessional experiences cannot be assessed by behavioural descriptions which
ignore qualitative features (Reed, 1969b). And they add some support for the
present hypothesis that the formal characteristics of anankastic/obsessional cognition are directly related to impairment in the structuring of experience.

In conclusion, it is suggested that:

(a) Compulsive checking differs from normal checking, in as much as it is
    not destined to remedy simple forgetfulness.
(b) The uncertainty associated with compulsive checking is not necessarily
    so much to do with the factual content of recall as with the quality of the
    recalling itself. The qualitative weakness reflects unsatisfactory person-
    alization, which indicates that the problem may not be one of mnemonic
    storage or retrieval but of attenuated redintegration.
(c) Compulsive checking may therefore be seen as an attempt to alleviate
    uncertainty by accentuating the personal component of the experience. It
    may fail in this because each check constitutes a new experience, the
    recollection of which adds further uncertainty.
(d) The experiences associated with unelaborated compulsive checking are
    therefore anomalous and confusing to the checker. They may provide a
    paradigm for more complex obsessional phenomena.

The relative ignoring of *unelaborated* checking is regrettable. For, while at first
sight it appears prosaic and unenticing, reflection suggests that it might well be
examined as a paradigm for the study of obsessional cognition. It is suggested
that checking may fruitfully be regarded as a microcosm of the complex
manifestations of both compulsive personality disorder and severe obsessional
illness—self-questioning, doubts, indecision, procrastination, rumination, circumstantiality, and ritualization. The very mundanity and circumscription of
simple checking should facilitate its analysis. The absence of complex content
allows for (indeed, invites) the direct study of the underlying *form*.

15

Repetition, Stereotypy, and Rituals

Suddenly I found myself doing that which even at the time struck me as being highly singular; I found myself touching particular objects that were near me, and to which my fingers seemed to be attracted by an irresistible impulse. It was the table or the chair that I was compelled to touch; now the bell-rope; now the handle of the door; now I would touch the wall, and the next moment, stooping down, I would place the point of my finger upon the floor: and so I continued to do day after day; frequently I would struggle to resist the impulse, but invariably in vain.

George Borrow, *Lavengro*, 1851.

One of the most characteristic and bizarre features of obsessive–compulsive disorder is the way in which thoughts and actions tend to be repeated. In this chapter, we shall discuss repetitive compulsive behaviours, traditionally referred to as "rituals."

As we saw in discussing checking, repetition of certain acts may continue *ad infinitum*, or until exhaustion prevails, the sufferer complaining that he finds it impossible to achieve satisfaction. In most cases, however, a prescribed number of repetitions is developed in self-defence.

The fact that the repeater is striving for closure or satisfaction suggests that repeating has much in common with checking. Indeed, as was noted in the last chapter, there is a clear overlap in some cases.

A few examples may indicate the range of the repetition phenomenon:

Miss Q., an 18-year-old student of good intelligence and ability, suffered from anxiety, doubts, and an acute lack of confidence. Her school achievements were deteriorating, partly because she had begun to find it necessary to re-read every paragraph in her notes and textbooks up to eight times, despite the fact that intellectually she knew that she had mastered the material.

Mrs. X., a 55-year-old housewife, suffered from compulsive guilt feelings. She found it necessary to polish her floors and furniture three or four times each day.

Mr. C., a 19-year-old clerk, was plagued by obsessional ruminations and compulsive activities. The latter included brushing his teeth, combing his hair, and touching objects in his bedroom four times or in multiples of four. He felt that without these repetitions he might become insane.

Mr. I., an 18-year-old apprentice fitter, found himself unable to work because of obsessional ruminations and compulsive activities. The latter included saying "I am myself" three times. While walking in the street he would find it necessary to stop and turn round three times. He attributed this to what he described as a "silly idea" that the spirit of a dead workmate had come to live in him.

Clearly, compulsive repetitions range from what might be regarded merely as unnecessary fussiness in the performance of mundane tasks through to grotesque and neo-psychotic activities.

To capture the flavour and complexity of serious cases we may look in more detail at a classical textbook example of compulsive behaviour which had persisted for over ten years:

Mrs. R. was a 37-year-old housewife who was referred for psychiatric treatment on account of her compulsive hand-washing. She usually washed her hands four or five times per day, but each session lasted between three and four hours. She also washed her face excessively, and when first seen both face and hands were raw and bleeding. Compulsive repetition, it transpired, characterized many other of her daily activities. All doors, bolts, and locks had to be checked three times before she could leave her home. Electric switches for lights and appliances had always to be turned on or off twice. Her keys and purse had to be placed in her handbag twice. While dresssing, each piece of underwear had to be put on, taken off, and put on again three times. All outer garments had to be straightened twice as they were put on. Such household chores as she was still able to undertake, such as cooking, cleaning, laundering, and ironing, were each split into segments, each of which had to be repeated three or four times. She did not admit for some time that she also found it necessary to repeat everything she said three times—once aloud, twice *sotto voce*.

Each hand-washing session consisted of a full "cycle" repeated four times. Each "cycle" consisted of the following stages, each stage being repeated four times also:

(1) Soap taken between fingertips of both hands
(2) Hands and soap plunged in water

(3)   Hands and soap revolved on bottom of washbasin
(4)   Hands soaped vigorously in water
(5)   Hands out of water, soap put down
(6)   Lathering of wrists
(7)   "Gauntlet" lathering of lower forearm
(8)   Muttered counting and rocking motion, to establish the "right rythm"
(9)   "Ploughing" of water, fingertips together
(10) Hands plunged to base of washbasin
(11) Rinsing—hands flat—water splashed up forearms
(12) Hands out—forearms held vertically

Any particular stage might be "spoiled"—by "losing the rhythm," by external distractions such as footsteps in the corridor, or by the intrusion of a distressing thought. This would require starting the stage all over again. The omission of a stage or its faulty performance involved punishment—re-doing the stage in question $4 \times 4 = 16$ times.

Repetitions were ensured by counting aloud. If Mrs. R. was disturbed or distracted, she sometimes "lost her place." This would necessitate going back to the beginning of the cycle.

Sessions were preceded and succeeded by prescribed tasks. The washbasin had to be cleaned and the soap and towel carefully positioned before the initial cycle. The soap had to be rinsed and the basin cleaned immediately after the session. All these tasks had to be repeated four times, while the drying of her hands demanded almost as complex a routine as the washing itself, though of shorter duration.

Mrs. R. attributed her washing behaviour to her profound fear of contamination by germs. She explained her choice of 4 as an appropriate number of repetitions in terms of (a) an arbitrary limit: "I used to wash 20 times, but I didn't take so long. As it got worse—the feeling that I hadn't finished—I realized that I'd have to put a limit on it. Otherwise, I'd be at it all day and night" and (b) a practical number for ensuring optimal cleanliness: "I might miss a bit with only one wash—you couldn't be sure that all the germs were gone. I read somewhere that twice was better, so I thought 'Let's be on the safe side and double it.' "

PSYCHIATRIC THEORETICAL APPROACHES

The "repetition compulsion," a concept which has excited much subsequent interest among psychoanalysts, was first discussed by Freud in 1914 in "Remembering, Repeating and Working-Through." This is one of the many papers he wrote discussing psychotherapy and the techniques of psychoanalysis, and here his subject is the responses of patients in treatment. Thus he is not discussing the pathological behaviour with which the present chapter is concerned, although the idea he presents may have some relevance. Briefly, he is discussing how the analyst encounters resistance from his patient in the sense that the latter is unable to remember information because he has repressed it. Freud argues that although unable to recall material from his childhood and duly verbalize it, the patient will re-enact events and attitudes which are not accessible to conscious recall: " ... we may say that the patient does not *remember* anything of what he has forgotten and repressed, but *acts* it out. He produces it not as a memory but as an action; he *repeats* it, without, of course, knowing that he is repeating it" (*S.E.*, XII, p. 150, original emphases). For example, the patient may be unable to remember his defiant attitude towards his parents; "instead, he behaves in that way to the doctor."

Freud develops this idea further in *Beyond the Pleasure Principle* (1920), starting with the therapeutic situation, but going on to speculate that we possess an instinctual compulsion to repeat. This overrides the pleasure principle by revitalizing past experiences of an unpleasant kind.

Beyond this, Freud has surprisingly little to say about the activities of compulsive repeaters. But he opens a new line of attack in *Inhibitions, Symptoms and Anxiety* (1926). Here he argues that neurotics try to make the past non-existent, striving to "repress it by motor means": "The same purpose may perhaps account for the obsession for *repeating* which is so frequently met with in this neurosis and the carrying out of which serves a number of contradictory intentions at once. When anything has not happened in the desired way, it is undone by being repeated in a different way ... (*S.E.*, XX, p. 120, original emphasis).

Stekel (1927) refers to compulsive repetition throughout his study, stressing, of course, its symbolic nature and arguing that it is the usual outcome of irreconcilable desires, the "striving for recognition of a reality," the attempt to provide symbolic solutions to unsolved problems. At a more objective level, he describes it as: "*deriving from the anagogic tendency to improve everything, to repeat every action until it is perfect*" (1949, p. 293, original emphasis). This suggests a different approach from that of Freud, a suspicion reinforced by Stekel's earlier assertion that: "It is characteristic of all compulsions that, after their completion, the patient always doubtfully asks himself, 'Have I really fulfilled my program?' This leads to repetition compulsion. But even repetition does not succeed in eliminating the doubt ... " (p. 258).

In line with Freud's central tenets, Rado (1974) traces various elements of obsessional psychopathology back to the conflicts of childhood. He does this with compulsive repeating, but quite unlike Freud he suggests an explanation springing from everyday learning: "The obsessive patient excels in repeating the component acts of performance. Repetition enters as an organizing principle into his ritual-making, brooding, and, to some extent, the entire routine of his daily life. Its origin is unmistakable. Repetition is pre-eminently the technique employed in the learning process ... '' (p. 204).

Parents, Rado goes on, impose repetitions and practice upon their own off-spring. The future obsessional adult is an obedient but defiant child. He obeys instructions to repeat, but expresses his defiance by taking the repetitions to absurd extremes in a "travesty of the learning technique."

Monroe (1974) suggests that we attempt to determine the meaning of Being through "intentional acts," but that there is always a mysterious unknown beyond the horizon of our consciousness. The "mystery" may be viewed with positive hope, but the obsessional can only see it as threatening, leading to death and decay: "With this view of the world, it is not surprising that the obsessive has an intolerance for the indefinite, undetermined character of what is beyond the horizon and still beyond his intentional acts. He denies this mystery and, instead, fills his world with intentional acts that become increasingly mundane, repetitive, routine, and nonsensical. He hopes to control the mystery which he cannot face through the magic of rituals" (pp. 214-15).

It is very noticeable here how mundane repetitions are suddenly transmogrified into magical rituals.

In *Obsessive Actions and Religious Practices* (1907), Freud refers to obsessional acts as "ceremonials" and goes on to discuss them as pathological counterparts of "the sacred acts of religious ritual." He begins by observing that neurotic ceremonials consist of small adjustments of everyday actions, carried out in a stereotyped way—i.e., without change or with only methodical variations. These actions are meaningless to the patient, but he suffers intolerable anxiety if he fails to carry out each action in the prescribed manner.

Freud points out the resemblance between these neurotic ceremonials and religious rites—the qualms of conscience brought on by their neglect, the conscientiousness with which they are carried out in every detail, etc. But he is careful to point out that differences exist, "a few of them so glaring that they make the comparison a sacrilege" (*S.E.*, ix, p. 119). However, one apparent difference—the fact that religious ceremonials are replete with significance and symbolic meaning, whereas neurotic ceremonials seem to be senseless—disappears under psychoanalytic scrutiny. The rest of the paper is concerned with showing that compulsive acts do, in fact, possess meaning, but at an unconscious level. In general, "a ceremonial starts as an *action for defence* or *insurance*, a *protective measure*" (p. 123, original emphasis).

In this paper Freud is concerned, of course, with tracing the symbolic significance of the content of compulsive behaviour. He stresses stereotypy, but makes only passing reference to repetition, although these are the characteristics which define the very phenomena which he is discussing. In this respect, as in many others, he set the pattern for subsequent psychiatric theorists, almost all of whom seem to have been concerned with the content as opposed to the form of compulsions.

It is of considerable interest to trace how semantic factors have determined psychiatric discussions of the topic in question. Repetititive, stereotyped acts were described by Freud, as noted above, as "ceremonials." These he compared with religious ritual. The actions in question now began to be termed "rituals." The use of this term predetermined further discussion, because of its obvious connotations. An initial assumption was made simply by the use of a label which was taken to establish the aetiology of the phenomenon. Discussion became centred upon "religious belief," then upon "superstition." From there, it was an easy step to "magic." The original phenomenon—repetitive, stereotyped behaviour—dropped out of sight. This line of discussion has been followed by generations of Freudian and post-Freudian writers. And the assumption that compulsive behaviours have their roots in magic has been extended to include all obsessional experience. Thus, Rado (1974) states firmly: "We have shown that magic's deepest root is the infant's belief in his own omnipotence, in his primordial self which we view as the nucleus of the action self. From this source derive the obsessive patient's superstitions which he is reluctant to admit even to himself" (pp. 202-03).

The line of argument is shared by non-Freudians. For example, von Gebsattel (1958), having compared repetition as a part of healthy life with compulsive repetition, asks: "How should this performance of repetition be understood? ... We know this kind of repetition in the liturgic realm where formulas of prayers take on, through repetition, a meaning of conjuration. A kind of conjuring effectiveness also qualifies the anankastic repetition. ... it conjures up a kind of completion which purely practically it cannot achieve at all. It achieves this in the way magical acts achieve effectiveness, the effectiveness of an undefined sorcery ... (p. 181).

Here, at least, von Gebsattel is only arguing from analogy. But another existential phenomenologist, Straus (1948), goes beyond analogy and asserts: "The ritual is a counter-charm directed against the spells by which the patients are encircled. ... Obsessives are magicians of a brand of their own. They become adepts before they have been apprentices" (pp. 37-8).

Even Jaspers (1923), who, of all writers, would not be expected to confuse metaphor with actuality, concludes: "The world of the obsessional patient has two basic characteristics: It is a transformation of everything into threat, fear, formlessness, uncleanness, rot and death; and it is such a world only because of a magic meaning which supplies the content of the compulsive phenomena, but which is wholly negative: the magic is compelling, but the mind sees it as altogether absurd" (1963, p. 286).

At this point, let us stand back from these heady, theoretical potions and remind ourselves of what we are dealing with:

(a) Obsessionals tend to engage in circular and continuing cognitive and motor activity. Some of them repeat certain motor acts for no apparent reason. The way in which such acts are performed and the order in which they are performed appear to be fixed.

(b) This apparent stereotypy was likened by early writers to the ritualistic activities associated with religious ceremonials.

(c) Use of the word "ritual" encouraged speculations and discussion of the relevant behaviour in terms of "religion," "superstition," and "magic."

(d) Obsessional people are now often authoritatively described as "magicians."

Here, surely, we have a classical example of the logical fallacy of ascribing identity to a metaphor. A phenomenon is described in terms of an analogy or metaphor, and it is then presumed that one *is* the other or, at least, that some causal relationship exists. What was originally an "as if ... "description is now assumed to be a statement of fact. Further analysis and debate now revolves around the metaphor, the phenomenon itself being side-stepped.

LEARNING THEORY APPROACHES

Learning theorists, of course, have not been concerned with questions of content, symbols, and dynamics. But they have been intrigued by the formal phenomena of compulsive behaviour—its stereotypy and its repetitiveness. The first of these presents no problem—it coincides with the results of many animal studies which have reported a decrease in the variability of response of animals undergoing avoidance training. Yates (1962) reviews a number of findings which indicate that heightened arousal increases stereotypy of response. So the stereotypical nature of compulsive behaviour is reported as a fact, so predictable that it scarcely warrants discussion.

Compulsive repeating, on the other hand, has presented problems for learning theorists. The repetitions seem to be without purpose and produce no reward. In learning terms, the problem is to explain why behaviour should be repeated in the absence of reinforcement. Why does extinction not occur? This is particularly puzzling for the learning theorist when it is remembered that the behaviour itself is usually of an unpleasant and distressing kind and should therefore be classifiable as punishing or aversive.

Perhaps the majority of learning-theory approaches to compulsive behaviour have relied upon the paradigm of avoidance learning. But as several writers, such as Morgan (1968), have pointed out, there are difficulties in applying the concept of extinction to avoidance learning. Extinction is defined in terms of the diminution of behavioural responses after the withdrawal of reinforcement. In laboratory animal avoidance learning, the reinforcement is aversive; its withdrawal is accomplished by the experimenter switching off the electrical shocker. But the rat does not know he has done this. As far as the rat is concerned, its avoidance behaviour continues to be effective because no shocks are forthcoming. However, experimental findings show that, given time, extinction does usually occur.

Perhaps the most regularly cited theoretical model of avoidance learning has been Mower's (1960) "two-factor theory". This has taken several forms, but may be summarized as follows:

(a) Before the avoidance response has been established, the animal receives repeated shocks, each preceded by a warning signal. The latter thus acquires aversive properties and the animal becomes conditioned to react to it with anxiety.

(b) The avoidance response terminates the warning signal and thus reduces the conditional anxiety. The acquisition and maintenance of the avoidance behaviour is reinforced not by avoidance of the shock but by the reduction of the conditioned anxiety.

This model would be applied to Mrs. R.'s compulsive hand-washing in the following way: Imagined contamination of her hands evokes conditioned anxiety. Washing the hands reduces this anxiety. The reduction of the anxiety reinforces, and thus maintains, the hand-washing.

This interpretation faces several problems:

(a) To round out this interpretation, we must now postulate an "initial" punishment—the aversive stimulus that was being avoided in the first place. If contamination merely constitutes a "warning signal," what is the "shock" that is being signalled? Mrs. R. herself identified the awful condition that she was trying to avoid as being contamination, so for her that was the "shock." A Mowrerian theorist would presumably have to postulate a deeper fear as the true "shock"—perhaps some fearful disease envisaged as the outcome of the contamination. But to do this surely diminishes the pragmatic significance of the model.

(b) The model explains why the hand-washing is repeated. But does it explain why the component segments of each wash are repeated? Surely, if the function of the washing is to remove the source of the anxiety, the more rapidly this is done the better. To answer this involves recourse to Mrs. R.'s own argument—that she must feel convinced that each wash is efficient, and overall efficiency requires an appropriate level of performance of each segment of the task.

(c) Given the plausibility of the foregoing, this still does not fully explain why the activity should take so long. Many of the repetitions of components are undertaken as expiations. So we are now dealing with self-imposed punishments protracting the performance of a task, the function of which, we are told, is to reduce conditioned anxiety associated with the fear of punishment.

Despite these problems involved in applying it to a particular case of compulsive hand-washing, Mowrer's theory is an engaging one, which has stimulated both research and theorizing for many years. Unfortunately, it is not reconcilable with a number of experimental findings, such as those reviewed by Herrnstein (1969), Seligman and Johnston (1973), and Rachman (1976a), for example. Herrnstein's own argument reverts to the original assumption regarding avoidance learning—i.e., that what reinforces avoidance behaviour is the avoidance of punishment. The warning signal is just that—a discriminative stimulus signalling a situation in which the avoidance response will be effective.

However, neither the Mowrer nor the Herrnstein models seem to offer a direct and convincing answer to our original question—why does extinction not occur in the case of compulsive behaviours? As observed earlier, the majority of animal studies show that, in the absence of reinforcement, extinction takes place sooner or later and, indeed, this is predicted by the two-stage theory. One well-known exception to this is the study reported by Solomon and Wynne (1953), who used a "traumatic" shock of maximal practicable intensity. This suggested that the degree of resistance to extinction may be related to the intensity of shock employed, an idea questioned by several workers but supported by the findings of Boren et al. (1959). However, there have been many subsequent reports (reviewed by Gray, 1971) showing that avoidance behaviour can persist long after fear has ceased, and without traumatic training. The whole area of animal learning has been excellently reviewed by Mackintosh (1974), who includes scholarly discussions of avoidance and extinction.

The conceptual problems and contradictory findings of the behavioural/learning approach when applied to compulsive repeating suggest four alternative explanations:

(a) Reinforcement *does* exist, but of a covert nature not amenable to behavioural analysis.
(b) The compulsive behaviour is initiated by a traumatic experience. But there is no evidence whatsoever of this in clinical accounts.
(c) The "avoidance" hypothesis in whatever form is not the appropriate one for explaining the behaviour in question.
(d) Learning models in general cannot totally explain compulsive behaviour.

DISCUSSION—THE FUNCTION OF OBSESSIONAL REPETITION

How do compulsive repeaters themselves explain their apparently unnecessary and unwelcome activities? Explanations (rationalizations) vary, of course, according to the questions asked:

(a) *Why repeat at all?*
  (i) Easily the most common answer is that repetition is engaged in as an attempt to ensure that the activity in question has been properly carried out—i.e., to an appropriate level of effectiveness with no component skimped on or omitted.
  (ii) A few repeaters report that they engage in continual activity to avoid, or distract themselves from, disturbing compulsive thoughts.

(b) *Why repeat a prescribed number of times?*
  (i) Easily the most common answer is that *some* limit must be placed on the repetitions. The actual number is usually selected on some neo-rational basis. For example: "Just once more isn't good enough, and twelve times would take too long. So I split the differences and do it six times. ... "
  (ii) An answer which does not seem to be mentioned in the literature is that the repetitions are regarded as expiatory. They are a self-inflicted punishment or penalty engaged in as retribution for an error or oversight in performance. Analogies would be the 100 lines required of the schoolboy by his teacher, or the four Hail Mary's imposed upon the sinner by his confessor. There are at least two major differences, of course. First, in the examples the penalties are exacted by an outside authority. Second, they are imposed because of some determinable misdeed or omission. In the case of the compulsive repeater, the penalty is exacted by the guilty person himself, and his misdeed is not usually objectively determinable. If the "error" is repeated or a new one introduced during the "punishment" sequence, then the penalty is increased. Often the increase is a multiple of the original "sentence." The miscreant must start the segment of activity afresh and now instead of doing it six times he must do it thirty-six times.

Another problem regarding the nature of the repeated activities is whether in fact they represent repetition *per se*, or whether, in terms of cognitive analysis, something more complex is involved. For instance, it could be argued that the circular and ongoing series of behaviours represent the reconsideration of information related to any attempt to achieve optimal decision levels. The argument proposed here is that the indecisiveness of the obsessional is really a question of decisions about decisions. Whether this is true or not, a central problem for the obsessional is the search for decisions and the failure to find decision levels which satisfy him, however valid the decisions themselves may appear to be objectively. Now it could be that the repetition of thought or behaviour reflects the continual reassessment of relevant information leading to the particular level of decision. This might appear a somewhat tenuous argument. How, for instance, can washing one's hands be regarded as an activity leading to decision? However, the hand-washer usually talks in terms of reaching satisfaction. In one sense this is a striving for decision. Indeed, many hand-washers describe their basic problem as being their failure to achieve a satisfactory decision. Perhaps "decision" is not the word most suited for this purpose. However, a decision normally implies the achievement of balance or the attainment of a syllogistic solution.

A rather different approach to the problem of repetitiousness is to enquire whether obsessional behaviours *are*, in fact, usually repetitious. Are they replicative? Are they *stereotyped* as they are often described? Observation of compulsive hand-washers suggests that what might seem to be merely chains of stereotyped behaviours are actually very different, both in detail and in terms of their position in a sequence or overall pattern. This point was well made by Walker and Beech (1969). In the present example, Mrs. R. was *not* merely repeating the same act or series of actions. She seemed to be striving for a synthesis, or for an optimal level or pattern. If she failed to achieve the correct developmental rhythm, she would feel the need to start again—either the whole process or some component thereof. But she did not do exactly what she had done before. Indeed, if she did do exactly what she had done before, she would be facing renewed failure. The obsessional counter, engaged in continual counting of, for instance, the dots on the wallpaper, does in fact count them all and then count them again. He repeats only in the sense that he renews his journey towards perfection. He counts, but in a slightly different way, at least describing his activities in terms of an attempt to improve his performance. In an ironical way, the position is parallel to that of the person practising a component of a skill. The difference is that the person engaged in perfecting a skill has an objective target to aim for—he wishes to improve his drive or his back hand, for example. In the case of the obsessional, there is no such objective standard and indeed no determinable goal. But one might suggest that the continual nature of obsessional behaviour, as well as its apparent repetitiousness, could be regarded in terms of information through feed-back. A golfer improves his performance, or attempts to do so, by repeating his swing on the practice range and observing the errors he has made. The purpose of his repeated practice is to cut down the errors while establishing those elements of his performance which are considered appropriate. The mathematician attempting to solve a problem may attack the problem repeatedly, inserting different variables or constants in one or both sides of an equation. If we dispense with the idea of objective outcomes or levels of performance, then there may be a close parallel between what the golfer and the mathematician are doing and what the obsessional hand-washer and the obsessional ruminant are doing.

The golfer and the mathematician, as they repeat their activities, would not accuse themselves of lacking in decision. Then why do obsessionals reproach themselves? The answer is probably inherent in the very situation. The golfer and the mathematician both have determinable, criterial outcomes to aim for. The golfer's swing can be demonstrated to have improved by the length of his drive. The mathematician will eventually solve his problem or not, as the case may be. The obsessional, as we have just noted, is engaged in a task which has no objective target limits or outcomes. Thus, the problem for him is to decide the subjective levels of satisfaction or outcome. *This* is where he is indecisive. He is unable to decide what should satisfy him. It is not his behaviour itself that fails to satisfy him. It is the quality of performance required and the failure to determine that which poses the problem for him. A parallel might be the situation where the golfer is not informed of what constitutes improvement. Thus, he might find that his performance is in fact improving but he will not be satisfied because he will be unaware of whether the improvement is significant. An even closer parallel might be that where he is not given feed-back information. As he continues to swing he fails to receive any information as to whether *any* improvement is taking place. Thus, he has to determine his own subjective ideas of what constitutes an improvement in performance before he can gain any satisfaction from his practice. In a manner very similar to that of the obsessional, he might then feel dissatisfaction with his performance, not realizing that the performance itself might be quite satisfactory. It is the level of determination, not that of the performance itself, which causes him concern.

An intriguing point here is the function of feedback information in such a case. If the determination of a subjectively acceptable level of performance has not been made, then of what use is further information based on the ongoing performance? The answer to this, it may be suggested, is that in one sense the obsessional is in fact striving to determine an acceptable level. As with any other decision, the successive determinations are based on new information coupled with reconsideration of the old. In this situation, performance feedback information is not being utilized to make judgements about or improvements in the performance itself. It is being utilized to help in the determination of criteria which will provide subjective satisfaction. But presumably the performance itself is assessed in terms of these criteria. So now we have the circular situation where the criteria can only be determined when the performance has already attained criterial level. It is as though the golfer, on managing to drive 350 yards, said to himself: "That feels about right. I will accept my practice performance as being appropriate when I manage to achieve a drive of 300 yards." But he has *already* achieved a drive of that length. Indeed, it was only by achieving a drive of that length that he determined the acceptable criterion drive.

The problem cannot be quite as simple as this, however. For it would imply that the obsessional's criteria must be higher than other people's. Perhaps they are. The point would be that if the obsessional's criteria were reasonable or indeed low, then he would achieve satisfaction in his performance very rapidly and not suffer any obsessional problems. Is it merely then, that the obsessional has inappropriately high criteria? Or is it something to do with his categorical activities—his inability to discriminate between "satisfactory" and "unsatisfactory"? Or is it not a question of criteria as such, but a question of subjective satisfaction? Perhaps the obsessional is a person who can determine appropriate criteria but is merely unable to feel either conviction that they are indeed appropriate, or subjective satisfaction regardless of their appropriateness? If we use the term "will" in a neutral way, merely to signify our state of mind when faced with an unresolved syllogistic situation, then it is little wonder that the obsessional complains of his *lack* of will. It is not that he has less of whatever volitional processes constitute "will." It is merely that he is continually in situations which are unresolved and therefore suffers from a state of mind describable as "lacking in will" more often than other people.

Many clinicians have observed that the obsessional can be helped to a limited extent by some external determination of appropriate goals or levels. The therapist can assume the role of external adjudicator and thus take the "decision" responsibilities from the shoulders of the patient. In doing so, *he* is making these decisions. If this works, the patient's performance is not objected to by the patient.

To summarize the discussion, it may be said that, when stripped of interpretative extensions and colourful content, compulsive repetition may be taken to represent a striving towards the establishment of criterial levels of performance. They may then be regarded as aspects of the obsessional need for structure, coupled with the search for completion. They represent attempts to close off a sequence of activities.

But there is a corollary to the above approach. If compulsive repetitions serve to "finish" a sequence, they may also be said to *initiate* a new sequence. An everyday equivalent would be the formulaic utterance: "Ready ... set ... ". This can constitute a piece of verbal self-regulation accompanying a deliberate "winding-up" process preceding new activity, which is precipitated by the completion of the formula—"GO!" In other words, compulsive repetitions may reflect the obsessional's difficulty in switching to another line of thought or action.

It can scarcely be overlooked that this objective model of the function of compulsive repetitions offers a neat example of an earlier observation—that anankastic characteristics all seem to be related to the structuring of experience. The repetitions may be seen as attempts to establish categorical limits which carry conviction or a sense of completion. The obsessional finds it difficult to switch to a different activity or train of thought without this feeling of closure.

Finally, it should be observed that, as in our discussion of the experience of compulsion, the difficulty seems to be a question of impairment of inhibitory processes. The present argument would weigh against the view that compulsive repetition is the outcome of some self-generating energy. Instead, it would suggest that the problem is not one of the presence of something that makes the compulsive repeater go on, but of the absence of something to make him stop.

16

Indecision and Doubt

> *A scruple is a great trouble of minde proceeding from a little*
> *motive, and a great indisposition, by which the conscience*
> *though sufficiently determind by proper arguments, dares not*
> *proceed to action, or if it doe, it cannot rest.*
>
> Jeremy Taylor, *Ductor Dubitantium or the Rule of Conscience,*
> Vol. I, 1660.

In this chapter we shall discuss what all authorities mention, and some believe to be the core of obsessional disorders—indecision and doubt. It will be recalled that these figure both among the *symptoms* of obsessional disorder and among the *traits* characterizing the compulsive personality disorder.

Many writers have used both terms interchangeably, presumably regarding them as synonymous, which is quite incorrect because there are significant differences between the meanings of the two words. The dictionary definition (*S.O.E.D.*) of "indecision " is:

Want of decision; inability to make up one's mind; hesitation.

"Decision" is defined as:

The act of deciding ... settlement, determination ... a conclusion, judgement ...

The definition of "doubt" on the other hand, is:

1. The (subjective) state of uncertainty as to the truth or reality of anything; with *pl.*: a feeling of uncertainty as to something. ...

Thus, while there may be some overlap between the meanings of the two concepts, the differences are paramount. *Indecision* is a failure or hesitation in deciding, an inability to make up one's mind or come to a conclusion. Basically, it refers to *difficulty in choosing* between alternatives. *Doubt* is more pervasive and not limited to questions of choice. Basically, it refers to *uncertainty*. The uncertainty may be in regard to anything—its truth, its category, its status, or its very existence.

Now, it is true that one may have doubts about a decision, or about the alternatives which were considered in the process or arriving at the decision. Doubts may be entertained as to the validity or relevance of the alternatives taken into consideration. Or, indeed, one may have doubts as to the wisdom or appropriateness of making a decision in the first place. But the term "indecision" cannot be regarded as equivalent, because it has a much more restricted reference, having to do only with the decision-making itself.

In general, psychiatrists and psychoanalysts have spoken of the "doubt" suffered by obsessional patients. Doubting has been emphasized as a central component of the obsessional experience ever since the classical contributions of, for example, Maudsley (1895), Janet (1903), and Freud (1909). Psychologists, on the other hand, have preferred to talk about "indecision." Presumably, this is because "doubt" refers to a subjective state: Psychologists have been uneasy about using the term because it is scarcely amenable to objectivization and measurement. But "indecision" can be operationally defined. It can then be quantified in terms of, for example, the time taken to make a choice or decision, or the number of requests made for further information.

INDECISION

It is generally assumed that for the majority of normal people, the degree of difficulty experienced in arriving at a decision is a function of the variables to be taken into consideration. The number of competing variables clearly determine the level of complexity involved in the task of decision-making. In addition, there is the problem of allocating relative weight to the variables and the search for some sort of equation which can incorporate the relevant weights and provide a summary of *pros* and *cons*. Finally, in many situations, including those in which decisions are of most significance, we must discriminate between short-term and long-term gains and losses. The judgemental task is complicated by the fact that long-term assessments may require consideration of new variables or ones subject to change.

The above assumptions spring from the fact that we tend to assume that our decision-making is a rational process of analysis, trade-offs, and judgement. There are, of course, other theoretical models of decision-making, and one of these will be briefly considered later. But, for the time being, let us employ the conventional approach in our consideration of the difficulties experienced by obsessional people.

Obviously, there are pronounced individual differences in decisiveness, which are consistent regardless of the situation or task involved. This suggests a personality attribute, which may well be conceived as varying along a continuum or dimension. On the "rational" model, it might well be suggested that the crucial variable is the level of cognitive skill available for collating and assessing information, determining its relevance, allocating appropriate weights, and applying inferential logic in reaching judgemental conclusions. Clearly, all these tasks demand intellectual abilities, and it might therefore be suggested that differences in decision-making simply reflect differences in intelligence. There may well be some truth in this, although it should be noted that such a claim would apply most obviously to formal problems. However, it has never been suggested that obsessionals are of limited intelligence. On the contrary, several authorities have asserted that they are endowed with superior intellects, that they are logical to a fault, and that they are precise and articulate. These claims will be considered in another chapter, but meanwhile it can be stated that at least there is no evidence that the indecisiveness of obsessionals can be attributed to some inability to marshal evidence and assess it logically.

Another possibility is that obsessional people's indecisiveness reflects their exaggerated need for precise information. In assessing the information upon which a decision is to be based, they may be dissatisfied with either its amount or its quality. This would certainly fit in with several of the anankastic traits reported in Chapter 5. The anankast's perfectionism, accuracy, meticulousness, and insistence upon precision would all militate against the ready acceptance of data as evidence for decision-making. On this argument, obsessionals will, for instance, demand more input than other people before being prepared to make a decision. Such a prediction should be simple to test empirically, but there has been surprisingly little direct experimental examination attempted. Indeed, the only published report of this kind known to the writer is that of Milner *et al.* (1971). They compared the performance of six patients suffering from obsessional symptoms with that of eight control patients on a simple laboratory task, that of detecting faint auditory signals in white noise. In condition A, a simple "yes" or "no" response was required on each of fifty trials; in condition B, each of one hundred trials was repeated on request until the subject was prepared to give a definite answer. Tones were delivered on 50% of the trials on a random schedule. Using signal-detection methodology, Milner *et al.* found no difference between the groups on either signal detectability or response bias under condition A. Under condition B, however, the number of requests for repetitions of trials was much higher in the obsessional group (average 0.277 per trial) than in the control group (average 0.065 per trial). Results under condition A showed that this difference could not be attributable to lower detectability. Rachman and Hodgson (1980) have expressed reservations about this study, referring to Milner's (1966) thesis to show that only two of the subjects were diagnosed as obsessionals. However, as noted above, the Milner *et al.* findings are the best evidence available so far of obsessionals requesting additional information during the performance of a neutral, laboratory, and, presumably, content-free task. But, in any case, apart from clinical accounts, similar evidence has been reported in relation to "meaningful" tasks. For instance, the present writer (Reed, 1966) compared the performance of twenty anankasts with that of twenty controls (patients suffering from other personality disorders or abnormal psychogenic reactions) during their completion of a self-appraisal questionnaire. Subjects received individually a duplicated list of questions which they were required to mark as "True" or "False." Each sheet was headed by straightforward printed instructions which were repeated and amplified by a standard oral introduction. No less than thirteen of the anankasts asked for further instructions, some doing so throughout the session. Only three of the controls did this, a difference which is statistically significant at the 0.005 level.

This aspect of indecision accounts for the *slowness* shown by obsessionals in the performance of certain tasks (particularly those requiring sequences of choices). Thus, Foulds (1951) found that his obsessional subjects were slower in performing the Porteous Maze Test than any other group except depressives. Obsessionals' slowness is particularly handicapping, of course, in their performance of timed tasks, and differences may disappear if they are allowed to work at their own speeds. In a study by the present writer (Reed, 1977b), the scores of a group of matched controls were significantly superior to those of thirty obsessionals on a timed numerical "series" test. But this difference disappeared when subjects were allowed to continue in their own time. Rachman (1974) has discussed obsessional slowness in the performance of rituals; he suggests that, in a few cases, the slowness may be regarded as a "primary" dysfunction rather than secondary to, for example, repetitive checking.

The question of obsessionals' requiring more information (clarification, confirmation, amplification) before arriving at a decision is of high relevance to the cognitive "structuring" approach propounded in this book. The present writer (Reed, 1966, 1969b, 1977b) has demonstrated that obsessional indecisiveness is related to the degree of structure perceived in the task or situation. The obsessional experiences less indecisiveness in clear-cut, highly structured tasks and manifests most indecisiveness in open-ended tasks requiring an inductive, intuitive approach.

At least one further plausible argument regarding obsessional indecisiveness exists. The difficulties experienced and the caution deployed in making a decision vary according to its seriousness. In everyday life we generally require more relevant information and take longer to come to a conclusion about serious matters or ones of personal significance than we do about trivial matters. Before deciding which car to purchase we will defer a decision until we have studied brochures and road test reports, visited several dealerships, and consulted with friends.

Very little of this precedes our purchase of shoelaces or a bag of potatoes. In deciding questions of major significance such as proposing marriage, the most incisive person may suffer agonies of indecision and prolonged inner debate. So it is not unreasonable to suggest that the obsessional is indecisive because of two interrelated characteristics: (a) he has a lower threshold than other people for what is to be regarded as of consequence or personal significance and (b) he will, like other people, be more indecisive about questions of high significance. Therefore, it could be argued, he finds himself in situations conducive to indecisiveness more often than the non-obsessional. In other words, the obsessional's indecisiveness is just like anybody else's, but he manifests it more often because he is more ready to regard issues as important and is more easily disturbed.

There is some force in the above argument. As we have seen, obsessionals do tend to be worriers who take things unduly seriously. But there are three significant features of obsessional indecisiveness which the above formulation cannot account for.

First, there seems to be no consistent correlation between the degree of indecision suffered by obsessionals and the importance or significance of the issues in question. Their difficulties often occur in the context of problems which they themselves regard as prosaic and trivial. Indeed, it is their recognition of this, and the fact that they struggle with their unwanted feeling of indecision, that give the experience its compulsive quality. Again, issues may be so abstruse or ill-defined as to be obviously insoluble and therefore not amenable to rational decision—and this, too, is often recognized by the sufferers.

Second, there exists a large category of decision situations which require conscious choice but which are so unimportant or routine that we would not normally bother to collate information or consider trade-offs. This category would include such undemanding decisions as whether to put vinegar or ketchup on one's french fries or whether to have another cup of coffee. In such cases we seldom recruit inferential methods; we respond intuitively, reverting to appetite, habits, or ingrained personal preference. We may take time to determine a preference while, for example, studying a restaurant menu, but often we have a comfortable feeling of self-indulgence in so doing; we seldom reproach ourselves for being indecisive. And yet there can be no doubt that these instances are ones of decision-making, for they involve conscious choices made from among alternatives, judgements, and the act of deciding.

Obsessional people often complain of "indecision" with reference to choices of this trivial kind. But it would be hard to maintain that low threshold, for the perception of seriousness would be such as to encourage them to regard such choices as that between vinegar and ketchup as being of consequence. Indeed, they are often only too aware of the total unimportance of their choice dilemmas and reproach themselves bitterly for their inability not to waste time in pointless dithering. Mr. Y., for example, would sit miserably on the side of his bed every morning, trying to decide which sock to put on first. He was intellectually fully aware of the pointless foolishness of his agonizing inner debate, but it could totally preoccupy him for between two and four hours. Mr. F. was tied to the bathroom for several hours each day. Among other problems, he could never decide whether the toilet paper had been satisfactorily flushed down the lavatory.

Finally, and perhaps most significantly, obsessional indecision is often experienced in the context of activity which is not only insignificant but would not generally be dignified by the appellation "decision-making." Perhaps the majority of our everyday activities, both physical and mental, are of this type. The simple action of rising from a chair involves a complex and reciprocal sequence of skeletal and muscular adjustments. In walking from the chair, we must retain a vertical posture, placing our weight upon one foot while swinging the other forward. All these movements have long been automatized, and in good health we do not need to deploy any conscious attention to ensure their achievement. We do not describe ourselves as "making decisions" prior to their activation. And yet, in one sense, we are doing that, because other alternatives are available. At each stage, at some level, a choice has been made. We do not term this selecting of appropriate choices "decision-making" largely because the selecting was not deliberate. Being automatized, it does not demand conscious consideration.

It is in exactly this sort of activity that many obsessionals encounter their most grievous sense of indecision and uncertainty.

Thus, for example, Mrs. G. could never quite decide whether to rise from her chair in order to cross the room. To make matters worse, having actually crossed the room, she still felt uncertain as to what her decision had been. To afford herself some precarious relief, she devised a number of what she called "breaking-up actions." These marked the "working-up" to a decision, the making of the decision, the initiation of the consequent action, and its completion.

Again, one of the many reasons why Mr. E. became unable to continue at school was that while bicycling he found himself unable to decide whether he was pressing down with one foot on the pedal or raising the other. He was miserably cognizant of the foolishness of this—"I know it's not something you decide about. Other people just *do* it, don't they? Like I used to."

Two alternatives are suggested by the definitional problems posed by the three categories above. One is that the term "decision" should be defined with more precision, so as to exclude routine, trivial choices and the results of automatized activities. The other is that the "rational" model of decision-making is severely constrained in its applicability and certainly too narrow to use as a basis for the study of obsessional indecision.

THE CYBERNETIC APPROACH TO DECISION-MAKING

The term "uncertainty" has been used several times in this book. It may be noted that the reduction of uncertainty is the central principle in the cybernetic model of decision-making. Even the most summary of expositions of cybernetic theory would be well beyond the scope of this book. There is, of course, a vast literature upon cybernetics (and such related fields as systems analysis, information theory, computer science, and artificial intelligence) ranging from highly readable introductions, such as Sluckin (1960) and Apter (1970), to more technical treatments such as Arbib (1972) and Haugeland (1981). The relevance of the cybernetic paradigm to our present concern is that it is as applicable to the "trivial" and the "automatized" situations outlined above as it is to more formal decision-making.

Wiener's (1948) well-known book, which first established the term "cybernetics," defined it as the study of "control and communication in the animal and the machine." The central principle used in the study of control is "feedback," where the output of a system modifies the input in some way. The most useful type is "negative feedback," a term we used in our discussion of the experience of compulsion. Negative feedback controls the system by ensuring that output is kept within certain specified limits, thus achieving constancy and predictability. The classical mechanical example is the steam-engine governor, invented by James Watt in 1788. Here, two metal spheres rotate around a vertical shaft attached to the main shaft of the engine. As engine speed increases, centrifugal force swings the spheres apart, closing the throttle and slowing the engine. As engine speed decreases, gravity draws the spheres down and inwards, the throttle is opened, and engine speed increases. But feedback-control systems existed long before Watt's time. A homely example is the brick on the lid of the cooking pan. As steam pressure builds, the lid is raised to release the pressure; then, as pressure decreases, the lid falls again. This practice, still popular among outdoor enthusiasts, long preceded the modern pressure cooker. Automatic controls using negative feedback are extremely common today, ranging from such well-known domestic examples as thermostats, radio receivers, and servo-mechanisms like power brakes, right through to the technological sophistication of space vehicles. Whatever their differences in complexity, these all have the same characteristic: Each system exerts control over its own operation, limiting variability and therefore uncertainty. Once it is set, its decision-making is automatic.

What is important for our present concern is that the cybernetic principles which apply to mechanical and electrical systems also apply to biological organisms. Our bodies maintain homeostasis by the interactive functioning of hundreds of thousands if not millions of such feedback-control mechanisms— mechanical, chemical, electrical, and neurological. For example, body temperature, oxygen supply, blood sugar, and water content figure among the many bodily sub-systems which must function within determinable limits if homeostasis is to be maintained. They are controlled by feedback mechanisms associated with the autonomic division of the central nervous system. At this level, our bodies are making multifold decisions continuously throughout our lives, but we are not aware of such activity, at least while we are in good health.

It may reasonably be assumed that all these sub-systems are ordered hierarchically and that higher-order decisions are activated whenever malfunctioning occurs within any specific mechanism or sub-system. A more serious disturbance would be that caused by malfunction at a high level in the hierarchy. Control and co-ordination would then devolve upon lower levels, with a consequent diminution in overall integration. This suggestion is strikingly reminiscent of Janet's (1903) basic postulate. Janet, it will be recalled, attributed psychasthenia (which subsumes obsessional disorder) to the lowering of "psychological tension" or integration and control from one level of organization to another.

It could be argued that, while the cybernetic approach offers a way of looking at obsessional indecision in lower-level "automatic" activities, the conventional "rational" approach is still required in respect of obsessional problems in higher-order situations. However, a number of cybernetic theorists, notably Simon (1957), have argued cogently that the cybernetic approach can be applied equally well to formal decision-making and rational choice.

Whether or not the cybernetic paradigm is accepted as being more apposite for examining the range of situations in which obsessionals experience indecision, the present writer would argue that decision-making itself is not the crucial problem. The obsessional person is quite capable of making decisions at the intellectual level. This is particularly so if the problem or choice is of a routine nature and amenable to deductive reasoning. His problem is that he may fail to achieve a feeling of satisfaction or conviction. "Obsessionals often 'know' at an abstract level. But they cannot internalize the 'knowing'; they do not experience conviction or a sense of completion, and thus do not implement the intellectual decision. In other words, it is not so much *decisions* that cause difficulties for obsessionals as *decisions about decisions*" (Reed, 1976, original emphases).

The mention of implementation here invites further discussion. Some authorities have used the term "inconclusiveness" instead of "indecisiveness." This usage provides an important insight into the obsessional state. At first sight, the two words may appear to be equivalent, and several writers appear to have used them interchangeably. But they reflect different levels of description and analysis. Typically, "indecisiveness" has reference to *outcomes*, describing activity from an objective, behavioural viewpoint. We use the term "indecisive" when we deduce from a person's behaviour (including verbal reports) that he is unable to make decisions or is unduly slow in so doing. "Inconclusiveness," on the other hand, is not only a more general term, but one, it may be argued, which makes inferences about the person's state of mind, the experience which underlies his failure to make a decision. An inconclusive person finds it difficult to arrive at conclusions, to experience completion, to be satisfied that a problem has been resolved or a train of events completed. Among the many situations to which this applies are those where a formal choice or decision is required. The individual's inconclusiveness will hinder his ability to make a decision. But even when a decision is forced upon him, its production may not dispel his uneasy lack of conviction. His inconclusiveness is not totally dissipated. His decision was not decisive, in the sense that he does not feel satisfied that the issue in question has been resolved and that the matter is closed. He continues to feel uncertain. He may fear that he has made an error of judgement or logic and may be smitten with an urge to reconsider the situation or to redo whatever actions or logcial steps preceded his decision.

This may account for *procrastination*. Here, the decision has been made, but its implementation is put off. The individual is aware of the appropriate outcome at an intellectual level but seems reluctant to put it into effect.

PROCRASTINATION

Most normal people are familiar with the temptation to put off making awkward decisions or to delay doing something that is demanding or inconvenient. For the obsessional, such putting-off may become a central characteristic and the source of considerable anxiety and self-recrimination. His procrastination differs from that experienced by normal people in several ways.

First of all, it differs in *duration*. The obsessional puts off for much longer periods of time, and the longer he puts off the more difficult he finds it to reach a decision or initiate action.

Second, the attendant experience differs in *degree*—he feels far more helpless and less capable of acting. For most of us, procrastination may be accompanied by a twinge of guilt, but this is counterbalanced by the comfortable awareness of having evaded duty or activity for the time being.

Third, obsessional procrastination applies across a much wider *range* of situations. Everyday procrastination occurs in relation to wearisome chores—such as mowing the lawn—or to decisions of moderate importance—such as deciding upon what terms to renew a mortgage. The first group involves a determinable amount of undesired activity. If a negligible amount of activity is involved or if the activity is quite inescapable, we do not usually engage in procrastination. Similarly, if the outcomes of *not* acting are negligible, our failure to decide or to act cannot be termed "procrastination" because we are not putting anything off—we simply have no intention of doing anything. Thus, hanging up our coats upon entering our homes is not usually a matter involving procrastination. We hang up our coats either because we are tidy-minded and do that by habit, or because our spouses are tidy-minded and insist upon it being done. But the question is not of central significance for us, nor does it involve any major pragmatic inconvenience. If we are not tidy-minded and our spouses are absent, we may cheerfully dump our coats on the floor and never give them another thought. The obsessional, on the other hand, may procrastinate in relation both to the important decisions and acts in his life *and* to the most trivial. Where the latter are concerned he is *aware* that he is procrastinating and berates himself for his failure to resolve the situation. Often, this is because he experiences problems of decision in situations which others would not regard as involving decisions at the experiential level. For instance, most of us do not ask ourselves as we enter our homes: "I am unbuttoning my coat and am about to take it off. Should I hang it up? And, if so, where?" That is exactly what the obsessional may do, and in so doing present himself with *conscious* choice and action dilemmas. Furthermore, his quandaries may spawn others. Are there not already too many coats in the closet? Should he not remove all the garments currently hanging there and arrange them in a more economical manner, before deciding whether to hang up his coat there? Once he has removed the garments from the closet, would it not be wise to decide which of them should be sent to the cleaner? And, as the closet will be empty, would this not be a good time to clean and disinfect it? And why not seize the opportunity to repaint its interior? There are several half-filled cans of paint in the cellar. Which ... ? And so on. Thus, his initial problem relative to the trivial question of hanging up his coat— something which, for most of us, would not constitute a question—multiplies into a network of questions of varying degrees of importance.

Finally, in accordance with our original definitions of obsessionality, obsessional procrastination is not *ego-syntonic*. Whatever casuistry or logical nit-picking is employed by the obsessional, he is uneasily aware of the pointlessness of all this reflection. He reproaches himself for his failure to make a choice and to act upon it. For most of us, hanging up our coats or failing to do so is not a matter of concern; we do not consciously reflect upon the topic. We "do what comes naturally." The obsessional has difficulty in deciding upon an action which would be "natural" for him, and may consequently suffer anguish in the context of some quite mundane and insignificant event.

DOUBTS

By now, the perspicacious reader will doubtless have observed that our emphasis upon the feeling of uncertainty and the lack of conviction has shifted the focus of discussion from indecision to doubt. As indicated by the definitions at the beginning of this chapter, indecision refers to a failure to decide. Doubt refers to the feeling of uncertainty. It could be said that indecision is the inability to execute a mental act, whereas doubt is a state of mind. There would also seem to be a temporal difference between the two. Doubts reflect a lack of conviction as to the validity or justifiability of an attitude, belief, solution, action, or item of information. The attitudes, beliefs, etc., are the outcomes of decisions at some level or another. Thus, it would appear that doubts must be experienced *subsequent* to decisions. In summarizing obsessionals' problems as "decisions about decisions," the present writer is suggesting a sequential three-stage process involving a qualitative change. The sequence would be: (a) Indecision → (b) Decision → (c) Doubt. This stands in sharp contrast to the loose equivalence inferred by many writers. Any such distinction is rare in the literature, although Salzman (1980) suggests the same order of events: "When a decision can no longer be postponed, an element of doubt can then be introduced, so that one need not be entirely responsible for the consequences of the decision" (p. 40).

The position here, of course, is exactly that which obtains with compulsive checking. After considerable indecisiveness, the victim decides to check. He does so. Then he is subject to doubt as to whether the check was in fact effective. Again, he struggles with indecision, but eventually yields and decides to check again. … And so the vicious spiral continues.

Clearly, indecision and doubt are intimately interrelated. Not only are doubts experienced in reference to decisions, but at stages prior to final outcomes doubts may impede the act of decision-making. Doubts about the validity of a lower-level decision may retard or confuse the assessment and adjudication required (on the "rational" model of decision-making) to reach a decision at the next stage, and so. A spiralling effect progressively impairs each subsequent stage of decision-making. This will not necessarily affect the quality of the decision when this is eventually achieved. But it will certainly slow down the process significantly. And, in the sense that it impedes consideration of creative alternatives, it handicaps higher-level cognition. As Rado (1974) puts it, spells of doubting constitute "thought activities that tend to defeat the purpose of thinking."

As observed in earlier chapters, doubting produces distressing phenomenological concomitants. The doubter is unable to experience resolution and conviction, being plagued by second thoughts and uneasiness. Subjectively, completion and closure have not been achieved; doubts are the most direct manifestation of Janet's *sentiments d'incomplétude*.

17
Obsessional Ruminations

January 25, 1808.

Sir,

I write to you to seek relief in a case of disease of the most inveterate, though not uncommon, nature. It is a nervous affection of the most obstinate kind. ... My mind is liable to be excited by trifling and unsubstantial causes; disposed to cleave to unpleasant usages, to dwell on dreadful consequences from really trifling circumstances, to be appalled with vain apprehensions, and to cherish disgusts and disagreeable associations; indeed, to labour under a *fixidity* of ideas which causes my misery. I was attacked in the winter 1800 and 1801, and since that time have suffered an immensity of distress, with long intervals, however, of capacity for enjoyment. Moral causes are the sources of my afflictions. The barriers of reason are cobwebs to oppose to the intrusion of this host of enemies. ...

I can assure you that no cause of distress vexes my mind in which my conscience or my honour is implicated, or which would be even noticed by others. If I could indulge in religious duties and contemplations, to which my heart, my judgement, and natural disposition would lead me, it would, I really believe, cure me; but previous to my first attack, near eight years ago, in a previous state of debility and nervous affection, which pressed hard on my spirits, I wished to read on religious subjects, until all at once impious and profane ideas struck my mind: my soul recoiled, was shocked; I tried to banish them; nothing would do; not a moment were those ideas absent; at least they seized so fast, that I lost many nights and days sleep; and I was brought near the grave. ... How, Sir, can this dreadful state of mind be cured? Can I be made to possess less feeling, and more resolution to resist moral influences on the mind; to bear vexatious or distressing incidents; and to break this association, this *fixidity* of ideas?

Benjamin Rush, *Medical Inquiries and Observations upon the Diseases of the Mind,* 1812.

Obsessional ruminations are usually reported as *symptoms* of obsessional disorder or neurosis—in fact, along with discrete obsessional thoughts, checking, and rituals, they have been regarded by all writers as the classical symptoms of the disorder. Obsessional thinking has also attracted wide attention, but it is not always clear whether writers describing its subtleties are referring to it as characteristic of the obsessional disorder, the compulsive personality, or both. One of the purposes of the present chapter is to attempt to resolve the relation (if any) between ruminations and obsessional thinking, *and* the relations among them, the disorder, and the personality.

Obsessional ruminations may be defined as prolonged, preoccupying, pointless, and non-productive bouts of brooding. They afflict the majority of persons suffering from obsessional disorder, at least in its severe forms. As mentioned above, they are referred to by all psychiatric workers and are mentioned in all authoritative textbook accounts. But there have been surprisingly few detailed descriptions of the phenomena, and discussion has been mainly limited to speculations as to their significance from the psychoanalytic point of view. The same strictures apply to psychological approaches. The most authoritative recent surveys of obsessional disorders from the psychological viewpoint are in Beech (1974) and Rachman and Hodgson (1980). Both books make passing reference to ruminations; but neither describes them in detail or attempts any theoretical analysis.

Most dictionary definitions of "rumination" equate it with "contemplation." But there is another meaning of the first word, that of the mindless chewing of the cud engaged in by ruminant animals. This is a physiological requirement of the digestive processes of such beasts and does not connote any concurrent cognitive activity. The ruminations of obsessional people are certainly associated with cognition, for they possess determinable contents. On the other hand, as we shall see, these contents are always impossible to resolve and seem almost perversely selected because they are insoluble. In other words, the cognitive activities involved are circular and logically pointless.

The ability to ponder, to reflect upon problems, is one of the hallmarks of man's cognitive superiority over the lower animals. Our capacity for contemplation has long been regarded as one of the signs of our spirituality, indeed a requirement of the religious life. Contemplation is an essential ingredient in all the world's great religions, as it is for philosophical undertakings. In everyday life, few of us ponder upon abstruse matters of profound significance; we seldom contemplate the infinite wonders of the universe, its ultimate purpose, and our place within it. For the most part, we leave such questions to professional philosophers or divines. There are moments, of course, when ordinary people ask themselves what life is all about or bemoan its injustices, its tedious predictability, or its distressing unpredictability. But generally our topics for contemplation are less abstruse and more related to ourselves or our dear ones. At the same time, when in good health, we do not usually ponder upon routine or trivial matters. We are not prepared to devote too much time to the consideration of how many brush strokes are required each time we clean our teeth or to contemplation of the shape of our toenails. Obsessional ruminations can include both extremes. The range of topics can be summarized for convenience and illustrated by examples selected from many in our series.

Some topics are manifestly *trivial* and *mundane*. (This is not to deny, of course, that they may symbolize conflicts and disturbances of great significance to the individual ruminator.) But, although mundane, they are abstract, hypothetical, or at least insoluble. They pose questions or dilemmas which do not lend themselves to answers or resolutions:

> Mrs. E., a middle-aged housewife of average intelligence, engaged in protracted ruminations about household chores. Had she polished the kitchen floor? If so, had she polished it *sufficiently*? How could one know if a floor was polished sufficiently? Could it be polished on the surface, but not underneath?

> Mr. J., a 42-year-old property repairer of below-average intelligence, was a compulsive collector of such discarded rubbish as milk-bottle tops and broken glass. He would ruminate at home as to whether he might have missed such items in the street.

At the other extreme, in terms of superficial content interest, some topics appear to be of a profound and philosophical nature. However, they turn out to be just as pointless and insoluble as those cited above. They may be abstruse and metaphysical, involving meticulous consideration of detail and debate, but fundamentally they are sterile:

> Mrs. H., a 39-year-old married machine operator of high-average intelligence, ruminated about the nature of God and her own wickedness. Was He all-forgiving? Could He forgive her for her wickedness? If so, what was the point of the Ten Commandments? Could He forgive a person who was wicked enough to ask such questions?

> Mr. M., a 22-year-old post-graduate of superior intelligence, was forced to abandon his studies because of his profound indecision and ruminations. These all revolved around the hypothetical question ''What would have been the outlook for the State of Israel had the Red Sea not parted?'' During the previous two years he had faithfully recorded his ruminations. To date, he had filled fourteen large notebooks, two of which the present writer was privileged to examine. Mr. Y. had transcribed, in interminable detail, what might be described as a quite unstructured and unceasing stream of consciousness. It was replete with speculative questions, none of which was (or could be) answered. The work was tortuously labyrinthine, but ultimately circular and pointless. Yet it recruited an awe-inspiring range of erudition, including Middle Eastern history, physical and social geography, agronomics, economics, politics, and theology.

Another group of topics are those which focus upon the ruminator's personal history. They include the reviewing of memories and self-interrogations, somewhat like those engaged in by Mr. J., cited above. Very often they involve self-criticism and self-reproach:

> Mr. Z., a 21-year-old university student of superior intelligence, suffered from phobic fears of possible violence to himself. Upon returning from the Students Union, for example, he would ruminate for a couple of hours, mentally retracing every step of the short walk. Was it possible that the people at the bus stop had been a street gang? Could a hoodlum have been lurking behind the building? Might a mugger have leaped out from behind that tree?

> Mrs. X., a 55-year-old housewife of average intelligence, was compulsively preoccupied with guilt regarding an isolated episode of unfaithfulness to her husband, which had taken place ten years previously. She would ruminate for hours about every detail of this short liaison, up-braiding herself for her wickedness in relation to each recollection.

Finally, there are topics which are similar to those in the previous two categories, differing only in their degree of unlikelihood, their dramatic flavour, and general bizarrerie of content:

> Mr. D., an 18-year-old schoolboy of good intelligence, suffered from unceasing ruminations. The most intrusive revolved around the possibility that he had killed two middle-aged neighbours by cutting out their livers. He ruminated continually about whether this could have occurred, reviewing his recollections of every sighting of the "victims," pondering about his every action when in their vicinity, rehearsing the continual checking he found necessary to assure himself that they were alive and well.

> Mrs. F., a 28-year-old married typist of average intelligence, ruminated continually about the plight of drug addicts and the possibility of plagues and social disasters consequent upon universal drug abuse. For nine years the ruminations had continued in the form of increasing speculations and morbid queries. By now they were reinforced by regular checking aimed at allaying her doubts and fears. In this the checking (which included enquiries of hospitals, newspapers, and emergency services) invariably failed. The tragic news, she would tell herself, might have come in just after she had put the telephone down. ... Thus, her ruminative doubts and fears were not amenable to resolution, and the associated checking could not provide closure or satisfaction.

In summary, there is a wide variety of content expressed in obsessional ruminations. Topics range from the most prosaic and trivial, through to metaphysical speculations of apparent profundity on the one hand and bizarre, idiosyncratic problems on the other. As would be expected, topics reflect (a) individual experiences, and (b) individual intellect and education. It is of interest that even among the examples cited above, there was a wide range of intelligence, ranging from Mr. J.'s IQ of 72 up to Mr. M.'s IQ of 136 (as measured by the Wechsler Adult Intelligence Scale). Clearly, ruminations are not restricted to persons of superior intellect, as has occasionally been suggested. Again, levels of education and cultural interests varied widely and are reflected both in the "choice" of topics and in the elaboration of their treatment. Mr. M.'s speculations could not have been sustained without rich cultural resources and book-learning, whereas the prosaic topics of Mrs. E. and Mr. J. reflected their restricted knowledge and cultural interests.

When we turn to the *form* of ruminations, however, our examples can be shown to have much in common.

(1) They are all intrusive and preoccupying, thus sharing a compulsive flavour. In each case the rumination appears unbidden and then dominates consciousness for protracted periods, excluding both more pleasant and more productive thoughts as well as reality-orientated activity.
(2) They may be regarded as elaborations of discrete obsessional thoughts and are inextricably interwoven with obsessional doubts, fears, and self-reproaches.
(3) They are all tentative, usually being expressed as self-queries of the "What if ... ?" variety.
(4) They are all quite inconclusive, the propositions being abstract and hypothetical, and the questions insoluble. Not only are these not amenable to direct resolution, but they possess no intrinsic features which might indicate any boundaries beyond which it would be pointless to pursue them. One unresolved question simply leads to its repetition or to further questions, and there is no point at which the self-interlocutor can satisfy himself that he has run through the entire range of possible answers. No "stop rule" is available, and rumination generates yet more rumination.
(5) Their reasoning is tortuous and hair-splitting, but ultimately circular.
(6) They are all concerned with picayune detail, even when the topic is wide-ranging or universal.

The reader will immediately observe that the last four of these formal features of obsessional rumination all reflect the general characteristics of compulsive personality disorder presented in Chapter 5. They represent, in fact, a distillation of those *traits*. The first feature above is the fundamental criterion of obsessional *symptoms*, while the second shows the inter-connectedness of those symptoms.

Obviously, the most parsimonious conceptualization of these observations is that the symptom termed "rumination" is simply a pathological intensification of the style of cognitive activity associated with compulsive personality disorder. Rumination, it is suggested, is a microcosm of anankastic thought.

18
The Cognitive Characteristics of Obsessional Disorder

Like ruminations, obsessional thinking has always attracted attention. Its rich and paradoxical features have intrigued and puzzled almost all authoritative psychiatric writers since the classical works of Gadelius (1896) and Janet (1903). Yet again, exactly as with ruminations, there has been no recent theoretical study of note. As Rapaport (1951) complained, there seems to be no systematic treatment of obsessional thinking available. And such well-known psychiatric accounts as those of Fenichel (1945) and von Gebsattel (1958) eschew factual statements, favouring intuitive assertions, often brilliantly expressed but inspired only by their particular dogmas, and savouring of apostolic vision.

The rational analysis of cognitive processes and patterns of thinking is obviously a central concern for the profession of psychology. So it is little less than astounding that very few psychologists have shown any interest in obsessional cognition. Such scattered studies as then existed have been reviewed by Skoog (1964) and most readably discussed from a Kellyan standpoint by Fransella (1974).

Features of obsessional cognition figure among the characteristics of anankastic disorder listed in Chapter 5. Indeed, it needs scarcely be pointed out that most of those characteristics are to do with ways of thinking or perceiving. This is surely a fact of some importance and provides a basis for the integrative theory to be presented in a later chapter. It has become conventional to regard compulsive personality disorder, like obsessional neurosis, as being basically a problem of affect which happens to have some interesting cognitive features or side-effects. But if the majority of the characteristics which are used to define anankastic disorder are cognitive in nature, it seems unreasonable to classify them as merely secondary side-effects. We shall return to this central point in the "theory" chapter. Meanwhile, a reminder of the most prominent cognitive characteristics in question is indicated. They included accuracy, intolerance of ambiguity, concentration, details, doubts, inconclusiveness, over-categorization, pedantry, perseveration, persistence, precision, rigidity, scrupulosity, and thoroughness. In Chapter 11 we essayed a semantic study of the terms used to characterize compulsive personality disorder, demonstrating that all of them could be seen as having reference to the structuring and categorizing of experience. We have briefly examined the nature of obsessional categorization, emphasizing its stringency, the rigidity of its maintenance, and the inflexibility of class boundaries. However, our comments so far have derived from clinical observations. Let us now look at these features more closely, drawing upon such little experiemental evidence as is available.

OVERALL COGNITIVE EFFICIENCY

As we observed in Chapter 7, the conventional wisdom is that obsessionals are of superior intelligence. This has been generally accepted ever since the time of Gadelius (1896), Janet (1903), and Kraepelin (1904). Fenichel (1945) asserted that their over-valuation of intellect often makes obsessionals "develop their intellect very highly." Rado (1974) refers to the obsessional's "superior intelligence," and lists "intelligent foresight" as one of the five cardinal predisposing factors on which obsessive behaviour is based. Such authoritative opinions have been based, of course, upon clinical impressions. But, as we saw earlier, such limited psychometric evidence as has been reported tends to confirm the conventional wisdom. Indeed, the general consistency encouraged Rachman and Hodgson (1980) to conclude: "Despite the small samples, these findings seem to settle the matter; except in the negative sense of excluding some possibilities, confirmation of the slightly superior intelligence of obsessional patients, as a group, appears to have no further theoretical or practical significance. This provides us with a rare opportunity to conclude that further research is *not* necessary" (p. 35).

Would that this were so; it would certainly be a relief to find that at least one of the puzzles associated with obsessionality had been satisfactorily resolved. However, the present writer shares Black's (1974) reservations and feels that the matter deserves closer attention.

The general claim that obsessional people tend to be of superior intelligence seems to have sprung from two implicit but distinct assumptions or points of view—(a) the view that all obsessionals are of above average intellect, obsessionality being a disorder which happens to afflict more intelligent people: This seems to be the view implied by most textbook writers since Kraepelin (1904) and was nicely expressed by Pollitt's (1960) summary that obsessionals "are more likely to be found amongst more gifted, more intelligent and more energetic folk"; and (b) the view that dull people could not have the cognitive capacity to experience obsessional psychopathology. This was held by Jaspers (1923) and supported by Greenacre (1923), who reported that only five of her eighty-six patients could be regarded as dull.

It will be noted that in statistical terms these two standpoints differ in their view of the *distribution* of obsessionals' intellectual abilities. The first one implicitly assumes a normal distribution of IQs in the obsessional group, but around a mean which is higher than that of the general population. The second one describes a distribution which is positively skewed because it is truncated at the lower end. A variety of alternative distributions springs to mind; of these, one in particular seems plausible although apparently not advocated to date—(c) the view that any given group of obsessionals would have a normal distribution of IQs, but that there exists a sub-group of unusually high intelligence. In other words, some small proportion of the group is drawn from a different population.

Before the spectre of any infinite regress is raised, let it be hastily emphasized that what is being suggested here is not some subtle genetic anomaly, nor even the operation of nosological imprecisions. What is being suggested is the addition of members of what are literally different populations, members who are selected in a biased manner and whose intrusion therefore distorts the original sample.

Few studies of clinical populations make clear what sampling technique the investigators presume themselves to be employing. Although seldom made explicit, the usual patient "series" study implies an *area* sampling approach. But this is only valid if the clinic or hospital in question does in fact draw its patients from a given "catchment area." This is probably the case with most rural and small-town units, but the position is more complicated in city areas, where several clinics may be "in competition" with each other. Especially is this so if referring clinicians have built up personal or professional "status" relationships with particular consultants or investigators.

Because of the relative rarity of obsessional disorders, survey researchers have usually had recourse to the records of "special" clinics, hospitals, or centres. Such units are often associated with university teaching hospitals, are research-oriented, and are ones which have shown a particular interest in and have developed expertise in the handling of obsessional problems. They thus attract larger numbers of obsessional patients than the average treatment unit; but their patient series reflect neither random nor area sampling. They are directly contingent upon the *referral practices* of contributing clinics and individual clinicians. The latter are unlikely to refer "run of the mill" cases or those which readily yield to treatment. At the same time, they are likely to be favourably disposed towards intelligent and articulate patients, regarding them as most deserving of specialized investigation and treatment.

The present writer (Reed, 1966) examined the IQs of 62 obsessive–compulsive patients of a "status" clinic (the Professorial Unit of the Manchester Royal Infirmary). All had been individually tested by him, using the Wechsler Adult Intelligence Scale. The mean IQ of the group was 106.88. The standard deviation of the IQs was 16.65 (S.E. 2.11). The group mean IQ was thus significantly higher than that of the normal standardization population, a finding which is in line with those of other studies.

The range of the obsessionals' IQs was from 72 to 136. The high mean was due to an unusual distribution, this being pronouncedly skewed, with no fewer than 17 cases having IQs of 120 or above. And of these 17, only 5 lived in the clinic's "catchment area." The others had all been specially referred to the clinic from other parts of the U.K., because of the clinic's standing and its known interest in obsessional disorders.

The series was now re-examined, excluding all cases of "special" referral. Forty-two cases remained (21 were men and 21 women; as a matter of interest, no significant differences were found between the sexes). The mean IQ of this area sample was 101.09 (s.d. 15.56; s.e. 2.33) which is very close to that of the general population, while the distribution was substantially normal.

It was found possible to match 30 of the obsessionals with non-obsessional psychiatric controls (other personality disorders and neuroses). Almost perfect matching was accomplished by: (a) Sex, (b) Age, (c) Number of years of full-time education, (d) Occupation, and (e) Social class of origin. The difference in IQ between the two groups was not statistically significant, and such difference as did exist was in favour of the non-obsessional controls.

In short, it is suggested that the traditional judgement that obsessional patients as a group are of superior intelligence may simply reflect faulty sampling. This may well be due to the practices of clinicians in referring patients to the specialized centres in which many surveys have been conducted.

CATEGORY WIDTH

"Category width" was discussed as a cognitive variable in normal psychology by Pettigrew (1958). It referred to the range of components regarded by the individual as appropriately composing a concept or subsumed within a category. One aspect of this had been introduced in the study of abnormal cognition twenty years earlier by Cameron's (1938, 1944) concept of "over-inclusion," a characteristic of schizophrenic thinking. Cameron defined this as the inability to "restrict, eliminate and focus," and it is usually assumed to refer to a general loosening of conceptual boundaries, resulting in unduly broad categories. The idea excited considerable interest and experimental examination (reviewed by, e.g., Payne, 1960). It dropped from favour, not because the hypothesis itself came into doubt but because tests of over-inclusion were found not to correlate with each other, while battery scores failed to indicate diagnoses (Hawks, 1964).

The present writer (Reed, 1969a) studied twenty-five patients suffering from obsessional (compulsive) personality disorder, twenty-five matched psychiatric controls, and twenty-five matched normal controls. Triads were matched for age, sex, educational level, and occupation. The subjects were presented individually with a specially constructed test of the "Essentials" type, which could be scored conventionally by using standardized norms but lent itself to comparisons of individual classificatory approaches. The test included fourteen items, each consisting of a noun followed by five other words and the word "None." The subject was required to underline only those words which were *essential* to the "target" concept, or the word "None" if none of the other alternatives was judged to be essential. For example, the target word "knife" was followed by "Metal, blade, sharp, handle, fork. None." The word "sin" was followed by "Punishment, guilt, death, corruption, sadness. None."

When scores were determined by conventional marking, there was no significant difference among the scores of the three groups. However the answers were examined to determine whether errors were attributable to over-definition (too few of the alternatives accepted) or under-definition (too many of the alternatives accepted). Both in terms of predominant error-type and simply of number of words underlined, highly significant ($p<0.001$) differences among the groups now emerged. In each case, the difference was attributable to the results of the anankastic group; no significant differences were found between the control groups. The anankasts were *under*-inclusive (accepting fewer alternatives as essential to concepts) by comparison with their controls.

In a subsequent study (Reed, 1969b), the same tendency was detected using a different sort of test. This was a free sorting task using non-verbal material (the Vigotsky blocks). Subjects were ten anankastic patients, ten matched psychiatric controls, and ten matched normal controls. All ten anankasts also suffered from classical obsessional/compulsive symptoms. Each subject was tested individually, being asked to: (a) sort the blocks into groups or "families" according to common features and then (b) sort them into the smallest number of groups possible. On the first trial there was a highly significant ($p<0.002$) difference between the performances of the anankasts and the normals. The difference between the anankasts and the psychiatric controls was in the expected direction but just failed to reach an acceptable level of significance. On the second trial there were significant differences between the anankasts and both their normal controls and their psychiatric controls. In both trials the anankasts tended to be over-strict in their determination of class boundaries, thus allocating fewer members to each class and therefore requiring more classes. This offers further support for the idea of "under-inclusion" and may be taken as evidence for the obsessional's tendency to *over-structure* by over-classifying.

Foa and Steketee (1979) suggested that the obsessional's excessive concern with detail will lead to *over*-inclusion. However, Turner *et al.* (1983) have subsequently published evidence supportive of the present writer's contention. They studied the responses of twelve obsessional patients to a task devised by Neufeld (1976). This requires subjects to rate the degree of similarity between all possible pairs drawn from twelve emotional adjectives. Eight of the twelve subjects based their judgements on only a single dimension, categorizing emotion into a dichotomous system of all-none, good-bad, or strong-weak. They were thus clearly under-inclusive in their evaluations during this judgement task.

CONCEPTUAL LINKAGE

The semantic differential technique yields, in a quantifiable form, information about how a person construes his world through comparative study of his concepts. But it does not afford information about the *structural organization* of the concepts in question. Makhlouf-Norris derived a method for studying just this, using the Role Construct Repertory Grid technique with the Self Identification Method (Kelly, 1955). Results were reported in a series of interesting studies (Makhlouf-Norris *et al.*, 1970; Makhlouf-Norris and Jones, 1971; Makhlouf-Norris and Jones, 1971; Makhlouf-Norris and Norris, 1972). Subjects studied were eleven patients with obsessional neurosis and eleven matched normal controls.

Each subject was asked to name twenty people (elements) according to a list of prescribed roles which included three self-concepts (actual, ideal, and social selves), close family figures, friends, and authority figures. Sixteen triads, each containing the actual self, were then presented in turn; the subject was asked to say in what way two of the people were alike and thus different from the third. When this characteristic had been named, he was asked to name its opposite. The subject was then required to rate each of the twenty named people (on a scale of 1 to 7) on the sixteen bi-polar constructs. For each individual a 16 × 16 correlation matrix was then drawn up.

The topographical organization of constructs could be inferred from the pattern of correlations (each matrix being simplified by including only correlations significant at the 0.05 level). "Primary clusters," "secondary clusters," or constructs could now be identified, as well as "linkage" constructs which significantly correlated with constructs in two or more clusters and "isolate" constructs which did not correlate significantly with others. The conceptual structures of the normal controls turned out to be "articulated," with two or more independent clusters connected by a "linkage" cluster. The obsessionals' conceptual structures, on the other hand, were typically "monolithic" or "segmented." They consisted of one dominant cluster with secondaries ("monolithic") or several primary and secondary clusters ("segmented"). Both types were non-articulated, lacking linkage constructs.

Fransella (1974) attributes certain of Makhlouf-Norris's findings to the contents of the grid she used. In the original Grid Test, the elements are photographs of strangers and standard constructs are supplied. Fransella argues that the more personally meaningful the grid, the tighter the correlations between the constructs. She suggests that the obsessional will differ from other neurotics in the degree of reduction in the size of the correlations accompanying decreased meaningfulness. Fransella's own hypothesis is that the obsessional's construing system is tight as far as constructs to do with himself or his symptoms are concerned, but looser beyond that range. She discusses this in terms of Kelly's (1955) Fragmentation Corollary which states that the individual may employ sub-systems which are inferentially incompatible with each other. Kelly had argued that the obsessional's construct system is "impermeable." As conditions change, the number of incompatible sub-systems become so great that he finds difficulty in producing super-ordinate constructs which are permeable enough to maintain overall consistency.

More recently Millar (1980) has reported a significant failure to replicate Makhlouf-Norris's findings. He compared the responses of thirty obsessive–compulsive patients on a standard repertory grid with those of normal controls. The cognitive structures of the two groups did not differ; those of the obsessionals were *not* more monolithic than the controls'. But the *content* differed substantially. The obsessionals characteristically displayed a very negative view of themselves as isolated and unworthy. To some extent, these findings are at least reconcilable with Fransella's views.

SPECIFICITY OF CATEGORICAL LIMITS

Rosenberg (1953) compared the performance of twenty "compulsive neurotics" with that of thirty-eight normal controls on visual tests of closure and symmetry. The first consisted of a series of eleven incomplete circles with gaps increasing progressively in size from 0° to 10°, the positions of the gaps on the circle circumferences being randomized. Each circle was represented tachistoscopically, and the subject was asked to draw what he had seen as accurately as possible. The symmetry test consisted of eleven asymmetrical figures, presented briefly on slides. After each presentation the subject was shown a card containing the original figure and five variants, from which the subject was required to indicate the one he believed he had just seen. Results indicated that the compulsive subjects erred more systematically in the direction of symmetry than did the normals. There was no significant difference between the groups on the closure test, and such difference as existed was not in the expected direction.

The Rosenberg study suffered from three methodological defects:

(1) Most importantly, although the members of the experimental group were all psychiatric patients, they had not been diagnosed as obsessive–compulsives. They were selected, in fact, according to their profiles on the MMPI.

(2) No attempt was made to match the two groups, the members of the control group being unselected undergraduate volunteers.

(3) There was no non-obsessional psychiatric control group.

The negative finding in respect of closure was confirmed by the present writer (Reed, 1966) who used exactly the same procedure as Rosenberg but used as subjects ten anankasts with obsessional symptoms and ten psychiatric controls, matched for age, sex, and IQ.

"INTOLERANCE OF AMBIGUITY" IN PERCEPTUAL TASKS

The much-discussed concept of "intolerance of ambiguity" was introduced by Frenkel-Brunswik (1949), who suggested that it characterizes (or is, perhaps, equivalent to) rigidity. She claimed that the "inability to tolerate ambiguity" is manifested with intra-individual consistency in the perceptual, emotional, and social spheres. In perception it is manifested by a "preference for familiarity, symmetry, definiteness and regularity" (Frenkel-Brunswik, 1949). Frenkel-Brunswik played a central part in the "New Look" movement, insisting upon a "personality-centred" approach to the study of perception. Her main line of research concerned the "authoritarian personality," characterized by rigidity, intolerance, and prejudice. Although she made several references to the applicability of her concept to obsessionality, she apparently never made any direct study of this relationship.

An empirical study of the intolerance of ambiguity by neurotic patients was reported by Hamilton (1957a, 1957b) who studied the performance of twenty obsessionals, twenty hysterics, twenty-two anxiety states, and forty normal controls. A battery of potentially "ambiguous" tests were used, including three tests of discrimination (weight, length, and brightness); block-sorting; three series of ambiguous drawings; an "ambiguity scale" of statements to be adjudged "True" or "False"; reversible perspectives—the Rubin figure and the Necker cube. Significant differences were found between the neurotics and the normal controls in all tests except block-sorting. Significant differences between the obsessionals and the anxiety states were found on seven tests, but comparisons between obsessionals and hysterics yielded only three significant differences (and those only at the 0.05 level of probability). Both hysterics and obsessionals avoided the "can't decide" category in the block-sorting test. But whereas the hysterics classified by excessive use of a few, mutually exclusive categories, the obsessionals used a large number of small categories, which is in line with the present writer's findings (Reed, 1969b). Overall, Hamilton's results show: (a) intra-individual consistency in the avoidance or non-avoidance of ambiguity, (b) more avoidance of ambiguity by neurotics than normals, and (c) more avoidance by both obsessionals and hysterics than by anxiety states. However, there are problems involved in interpreting Hamilton's report. He does not make clear to the reader how test scores were derived. And, apart from the "can't decide" category in one test, the reader is not told how test scores would indicate tolerance or intolerance of ambiguity.

REASONING

Serban (1978) proposed that, in certain areas of experience, the neurotic individual uses different laws of reasoning from the normal. This faulty reasoning is applied to situations perceived to present immediate threat. There is a failure to differentiate between anxiety-producing situations and those posing real, objective threats. Obsessional thinking is cited as an obvious example of this faulty reasoning. Unhappily, Serban does not develop his argument, referring only to the "magical" thinking implied by the arbitrary selection of the number of repetitions required to terminate a compulsive act.

The present writer (Reed, 1977b) has argued that anankastic over-structuring might well prove advantageous in "closed" tasks requiring *deductive* reasoning. The obsessional will face most difficulty in open-ended tasks requiring an intuitive approach and/or *inductive* reasoning. I maintained that this style of cognitive functioning should be discernible in neutral and prosaic tasks as well as those which are affectively loaded and of personal significance. In other words, I suggested that the characteristic in question was a formal one, not necessarily associated with such factors as perceived threat or intra-psychic conflict.

To demonstrate my argument, I compared the performances on two arithmetic tests of thirty anankasts with those of thirty patients suffering from other types of personality disorder but matched for age, sex, educational level, occupation, and social class. One of the tests was a conventional, highly structured arithmetic problem test, demanding a deductive approach. The other was a specially constructed number series test, relatively open-ended and requiring a predominantly inductive approach. On the first test, the anankasts were superior to the controls ($p < 0.05$), but on the second test, the position was reversed, with the control group scores being clearly superior ($p < 0.01$).

SPOKEN LANGUAGE

There seems to have been no modern linguistic analysis of the speech of obsessionals, but Balken and Masserman (1940) studied some formal characteristics of the verbal utterances of five obsessional neurotics compared with those of five hysterics and five anxiety states. Verbal responses ("phantasies") to twenty cards of a TAT type were recorded and analysed in terms of eighty-five criteria. These included, for example, average number of words, relative number of active, passive, and intransitive verbs, and the ratio of expressions of certainty to expressions of uncertainty.

Results are expressed in an unusual manner and without recourse to inferential statistics. However, it appears clear that the obsessionals: (a) had used more words than other subjects; (b) scored high qualification-certainty quotients; (c) scored very low certainty-uncertainty quotients; and (d) used inordinately more expressions of means ("this is how," etc.) and derivation ("as a result").

The n's in this study were small; diagnostic criteria were suspect; there were no normal controls; and data analysis was primitive. Nevertheless, the findings are interesting and thought-provoking.

PATTERNS OF MEANING

The semantic differential (Osgood, *et al.*, 1957) provides a technique for the estimation of meaning and attitudes by the statistical analysis of responses to what is basically a controlled association test. A most sophisticated study by Marks (1965, 1966) compared the patterns of meaning elicited from matched groups of twenty obsessionals, twenty anti-social psychopaths, and thirty orthopaedic (non-psychiatric) controls. Subjects were required to rate their associations to a number of concepts, using identical sets of bi-polar adjectival scales for this purpose. Nineteen concepts were selected, including three personal concepts ("myself," "my father," "my mother"), and five from each of three clinically important areas of emotionality (anger–hostility, fear–anxiety, and affection–love), plus one control concept ("ugly"). Results were submitted to principal-components factor analyses. Reliability, validity, and clinical relevance were studied in detail, and the value of the technique in the study of psychiatric patients was clearly demonstrated.

Yet, despite Marks's impeccable methodology and the clarity and elegance of his presentation, his actual findings in regard to obsessional disorder are disappointingly slim. All three groups scored similarly on the control concept. With the concept "myself" both the obsessionals and the psychopaths significantly devalued themselves compared to the controls, whereas with "my father" and "my mother" the obsessionals scored like the controls. The most important finding to emerge was that on the anger–hostility concepts the obsessionals did not differ significantly from the controls. This contradicts the assertion which has often been made (e.g., by Fenichel, 1945; and Rado, 1974) that obsessional symptoms are a defence against the individual's own aggression, and that the obsessional's control and inhibition reflect fear of his hostile feelings.

MEMORY

One of the most clearly attested areas of paradox and contradiction in obsessionality is that of memory. On the one hand, obsessional individuals are usually reported to display recall which is uncannily accurate and detailed. In fact, they seem to be characterized by the ability to recall specifics beyond a level which would be regarded as optimal for normal living. As with obsessional thinking in general, they are reported to recall details which other people would regard as superfluous or insignificant. For this reason, obsessionals have been termed "hypermnesic" by writers such as Barucci (1954) and Petrilowitsch (1960).

On the other hand, obsessionals' doubts, indecision, and inconclusiveness suggest that their mnemonic processes are in some way grossly impaired. Indeed, many of the classical symptoms of obsessional disorder revolve around features which may be interpreted as indicative of pathological failures of memory. Ruminations are often related to the individual's fear that he *may* have committed some indecent or horrifying act. And compulsive checking, as we have seen, apparently reflects an inability to recall whether some routine action has in fact been carried out.

The problem has been tackled empirically by the present writer (Reed, 1977a), who began by pointing out that it was misleading to regard memory globally as a unitary ability or attribute. Remembering, as Bartlett (1932) emphasized, is a dynamic, constructive activity which involves the organization of a number of mnemonic processes operating at several levels. Clinicians' assessments of their obsessional patients' "superior memory" suggest some overall mnemonic efficiency. But such assessments are usually based simply on the meticulous precision of the patients' verbal reports. Generally speaking, no objective evidence is available whereby the validity of such reports can be gauged. "The validity of a recollection cannot be substantiated by its circumstantiality, nor by the solemnity of its presentation" (Reed, 1977a).

I compared the performance of thirty anankasts with thirty matched controls suffering from other types of personality disorder. The anankasts were significantly superior on the Digit Span test, the classical measure of immediate memory. But there was no significant difference between the groups on long-term recall as measured by the WAIS "Information" sub-test.

It was predicted that the anankast's difficulties in structuring and categorization will be manifested in relatively prolonged consideration of data which are not readily categorizable. In other words he will repeat or rehearse ambiguous experiences. Subjects consisted of ten anankasts and ten matched controls suffering from other types of personality disorder. Each subject listened to four anecdotal problems. Two of these (A and B) were versions of classical mental puzzles; the other two (C and D) were plausible but insoluble inventions. Subjects were encouraged to attempt to solve A and B, but in each case were interrupted after three minutes, the problem re-read, and attention turned to the next one. C and D were also read, but it was explained that they were insoluble. Two weeks later, subjects were asked to recall as much as they could of each problem. There was no significant difference between the groups on recall of problems A and B, but a significantly superior recall by the anankasts of problems C and D. A significantly higher number of anankasts than controls recalled as much or more of C and D as of A and B.

PERSONALIZATION AND REDINTEGRATION

The personalized flavour of reminiscence must reflect, it may be argued, both the level and the scope of schematization of the original experience (Bartlett, 1932; discussed by Reed, 1972, 1979). The present writer (Reed, 1977a) pointed out that if the anankast encounters problems in the structuring and integration of experience, this would imply some attenuation of schematization, including the personal stamp. Redintegration would be incomplete. I therefore predicted that the obsessional will experience reminiscence with a diminution or unevenness of personalization.

I was unable to devise any experimental method of assessing levels of redintegration in this context (which is scarcely surprising in view of the entirely subjective nature of personalization). Thus, I had recourse to the elicitation of phenomenological reports. Subjects were the ten matched pairs mentioned above. They were asked to: (a) describe some event from their last holiday; then (b) try to describe the experience of recollection itself; (c) recall their previous day's performance of some routine, daily activity; and (d) describe how they recalled it.

The eight controls who were able to formulate answers to (b) all used imagery in various modalities. The nine anankasts who were able to tackle the question did so at considerable length. They reported only visual imagery, although this was rich and immediate. The difference was that it was reported as though from the viewpoint of a non-participant observer, whereas the controls' imagery was described as experienced initially by themselves. In response to (c) all subjects selected a prosaic activity such as dressing or preparing for bed. But in the cases of five of the anankasts, their selected activities turned out to be ones subject to excessive checking. Both groups responded to (d) by identifying habit patterns and then utilizing a logical process of elimination. As before, the anankasts used visual imagery only. In every case, they were uncertain and uneasy, not so much about what was recalled as about the *quality of the recollection itself.*

Data which seem to support the present writer's findings have been reported by Sher *et al.* (1983). Checkers were identified from among a large group of college students on the basis of questionnaire responses. Their performances were compared with those of non-checkers on several tasks and their subsequent recollection of these. The checkers were found to have poorer memories for their prior activities than the non-checkers. More importantly, in the present context, they were found to underestimate their abilities to distinguish between their memories of real as opposed to imagined events.

The attenuated redintegration implied by both these studies may well play a part not only in compulsive checking, but in obsessional doubts, uncertainties, inconclusiveness, and ruminations.

At the same time, faulty redintegration parallels, in the sphere of remembering, the experience of depersonalization. Although depersonalization is non-specific and may appear in the context of any mental disorder, its association with obsessional disorders has often been remarked upon (e.g., Shorvon, 1946; Anderson, 1964; Slater and Roth, 1969). It would appear to be relatively rare in people suffering from gross obsessive–compulsive symptoms but most evident in people of compulsive personality suffering from depression (Sedman and Reed, 1963). It is thus at least possible that faulty redintegration and depersonalization are masked by severe obsessional symptoms but augmented by a depressive mood.

RISK-TAKING

As we have noted, obsessional individuals are reported to be cautious, fussy, and bound to fixed structures and precedents. In short, they would not be regarded as liable to take risks, if these could be avoided. Empirical evidence for this assumption, however, is almost non-existent.

Steiner (1972) expressed dissatisfaction with experimental measures of risk-taking, which have usually involved laboratory games where there is little actually at risk. He devised a questionnaire which asked subjects how they might be likely to behave in real-life situations. Twenty items covered the areas of driving, money, danger, conscientiousness, social risk, and drink/drugs. The questionnaire was administered to 503 subjects, including psychiatric patients, non-psychiatric patients, and medical registrars. As might be expected males proved to be higher risk-takers than females, and risk-taking correlated negatively with age but not at all with estimated intelligence. A group of fifteen obsessional patients proved to be significantly more cautious than any other group. (The highest risk-takers proved to be the doctors, followed by the sociopaths.)

Drawing upon Lazarus' (1966) idea of "threat appraisal," Carr (1974) proposed that "the compulsive neurotic has an abnormally high subjective estimate of the probability of occurrence of the unfavourable outcome." He will thus be more cautious in his assessment of the degree of threat involved in any situation.

There seems to have been no further experimental examination of this approach. This is probably because of the well-known difficulties of assessing risk-taking and the fact that low correlations have been found among tests thereof (see, e.g., Kogan and Wallach, 1964).

CREATIVITY

It is now accepted that creativity is associated with an ability to try new approaches and synthesize apparently incongruent features, with flexibility, and with a penchant for unlikely, novel associations (Guilford, 1959; Barron, 1969; Koestler, 1964). This would suggest a cognitive style diametrically opposed to that of the obsessional or anankastic person which, as we have seen, is characterized by inflexibility, rigidity, a liking for fixed order and pre-set rules, pedantry, and concern with finicky detail. It would seem extremely unlikely that the obsessional person would even embark upon creative endeavours, and impossible that such an attempt would achieve success.

Yet biographical and internal evidence does not support these reasonable assumptions; numerous top-flight creative artists seem to have manifested obsessional symptoms and traits. These include distinguished composers (e.g., Rossini and Stravinsky), diarists (e.g., Amiel), poets and essayists (e.g., Bunyan, Swift, and Dr. Johnson), playwrights (e.g., Ibsen), and novelists (e.g., Dickens and Proust).

We are thus faced with an intriguing paradox, but one which had received no empirical, psychological examination prior to 1981, when an elegant report by Binik, Fainsilber, and Spevack was published. Fifteen obsessional and sixteen phobic patients, with thirty-nine non-psychiatric controls, were studied. Subjects were tested on five tests of creativity selected for their known validity and reliability and because they were reported to vary independently of IQ. Multivariate analyses of covariance and variance indicated no significant differences in creativity among the groups. As the writers point out, these negative results may reflect diagnostic imprecision or defects in the tests of creativity. (As for the latter, it is a fact that the validity of even the best-known creativity tests has only been demonstrated indirectly. We have no way of knowing how Rossini, Ibsen, and Dickens might have fared on such tests.) But this appears to have been a carefully conducted study, using the best measures available. It would appear that obsessionality (as it is usually measured) does not correlate negatively with creativity (as *that* is usually measured). The puzzle remains. Either some variable contributes to creativity which can override those which are measured in the tests, or some variable exists in the make-up of obsessionals which can counteract or re-combine the traits which appear to be non-conducive to creativity.

CONCLUSIONS

Empirical findings regarding obsessional cognition are few and patchy. However, several summary statements can be made, albeit tentatively:

(a) Obsessionals tend to employ unduly strict categorical or conceptual limits.
(b) This limits the acceptance of members, examples, or attributes as appropriate to any given class ("under-inclusion").
(c) In turn, this over-definition entails the employment of many small classes rather than fewer large ones with flexible class-limits.
(d) The strictness of conceptual limits is associated with an absence of linkage between concepts or constructs.
(e) Similar tendencies to the above seem to apply to perceptual processing as well as to conceptual activity.

(f) Obsessionals perform better in structured, "closed" tasks requiring deductive reasoning than in open-ended tasks where an intuitive approach and inductive reasoning are indicated.

(g) The "superior memory" attributed to obsessionals is probably merely a reflection of their style of giving accounts—they respond to questions seriously and proffer inordinate detail.

(h) Their superiority on the Digit Span test is probably a function of the serious attention they apply to tasks.

(i) They tend to "rehearse" material which is ambiguous, insoluble, or otherwise un-categorizable.

(j) They seem to be uncertain, not about what they recall, but about the quality of their recalling. This suggests some impairment in redintegration.

(k) They are less prepared than other people to take risks.

(l) Despite their conceptual inflexibility, their performance is no worse than that of others on standard tests of creativity.

(m) Their circumstantiality, compulsivity, and uncertainty seem to be reflected in certain formal characteristics of speech.

The picture that emerges is in striking accord with the attributes reported by clinicians to be characteristic of the compulsive personality disorder, even though most of these findings were drawn from studies of patients with obsessional neurosis. It seems reasonable to suggest that the same cognitive style is shared by individuals suffering from obsessional symptoms and those with anankastic traits.

Some paradoxes or contradictions remain:

(1) Obsessionals are notably inconclusive. Yet they are reported to be intolerant of ambiguity.

(2) Obsessionals bemoan the irrationality of their concerns, ruminations, and preoccupations. Yet they are reported to be nit-pickingly precise and logical to a fault.

(3) Their fears, doubts, and prejudices become over-generalized. Yet they are reported to be under-inclusive.

(4) They are notoriously inflexible and un-shifting. Yet they are reported to be uncertain and vacillating.

It is suggested that these apparent discrepancies simply reflect different levels of observation and analysis. If schemata and constructs are organized hierarchically, then the obsessional pattern of cognitive structures may be one which is marked by over-specificity and rigidity at low levels in the hierarchy, but organizational looseness higher up.

19
Psychological Methods of Remediation of Obsessional Disorders

As recently as thirty years ago, both theoretical and therapeutic approaches to obsessional–compulsive disorder appeared to be quiescent, not to say moribund. In the pastures of theory, the old bull of Freudian orthodoxy reigned supreme. Existentialism had not fulfilled its earlier challenge, despite considerable ground-pawing, while several romantic dalliances between heifers of the post-Freudian herd and various sacred cows of learning theory had brought forth only sickly or short-lived progeny. Therapeutic developments were also at a standstill. The various styles of psychoanalysis had for long been recognized as relatively ineffective in dealing with obsessional disorders. The only alternatives seemed to be ''supportive'' counselling or, in severe cases, leucotomy. The first of these simply accepted the prepotency of the disorder and contented itself with consoling the sufferer. The second usually resulted in the continuance of the symptoms but a diminution of the accompanying anguish. As opposed to psychiatry and neurosurgery, psychology had made no particular contribution to the development of therapeutic techniques.

THE ADVENT OF BEHAVIOUR THERAPY

A dramatic turning-point occurred in the late 1950s, ushered in by Eysenck's (1959) call to arms and Wolpe's (1958) ground-breaking book. At first, the tidal wave of behaviour therapy scarcely touched obsessional disorder. By the mid-1960s, apart from Wolpe's own cases which were discussed in an earlier chapter, only eight reports had been published of behaviour therapy being applied to patients suffering from obsessive–compulsive states. As might be expected, the majority of these early studies were concerned with attempts to modify compulsive *behaviour*, such as hand-washing and associated rituals. The following criticism can fairly be levelled against these pioneering studies:

(a) The diagnoses of the patients described was often in doubt.
(b) Patients were often concurrently receiving other forms of treatment or had been leucotomized.
(c) There was a notable absence of controls.
(c) In only one case was a follow-up reported.

In 1963, the first issue of *Behaviour Research and Therapy* appeared, signalling the establishment of a new clinical/academic industry. The journal was edited by Dr. S. Rachman of the Institute of Psychiatry (Maudsley Hospital, London, England) who, with his associates, has been the most fruitful contributor to the study of behaviour therapy with obsessionals. Another group has been that of Temple University, Philadelphia, U.S.A., led by Dr. Edna Foa. They have published in a wider variety of journals, but perhaps most commonly in the *Journal of Behavior Therapy and Experimental Psychiatry*. This began in 1970, a year which saw a sudden increase of reports of behavioural approaches to obsessional disorder. The trend increased throughout the 1970s; in 1979 more than thirty relevant reports were published in English-language journals.

A wide variety of BT techniques have been applied to obsessional disorders (see Beech and Vaughan, 1978). But for several years, the one of choice was Wolpe's (1958) classical method of *reciprocal inhibition* or systematic desensitization, which has consistently proved of value in the treatment of monosymptomatic phobias. Unfortunately, it turned out to be not very effective when applied to obsessional disorders, and it rapidly fell from favour. Had it worked, it would doubtless have been retained, despite the theoretical shortcomings discussed in an earlier chapter.

As we have seen, the technique involves constructing a hierarchy of stimuli reported by the patient to evoke increasing anxiety, and then working through this graded series either imaginally or *in vivo*, with the patient in a non-anxious state induced by relaxation with tranquillizing drugs or hypnosis. Walton (1960) used this standard technique with a patient who found it necessary to kick stones and paper out of the way whenever he walked. He did this, he reported, for fear that some passer-by might trip and injure himself. The hierarchy was composed of walks along routes with differing amounts of litter, starting with a clean, hospital corridor. The patient, duly relaxed with chlorpromazine, was required to follow the therapist along the selected paths without kicking any stones or picking up any paper. Eventually, he was able to walk, without distress, along a road of half-bricks, which was still under construction. He remained free of the stone-kicking compulsion, but seven months later had to be re-admitted to hospital with renewed compulsive hand-washing and slowness.

Similarly, one of Walton and Mather's (1964) cases had suffered for ten years from compulsive hand-washing associated with fears of contamination. Seven hierarchies were devised, each to do with "contaminating" objects (e.g., handles and doorknobs) and "contaminating" events (e.g., washing one's hands without first cleaning the washbasin). Each hierarchy involved a series of activities to be performed *in vivo*. Some improvement took place over two months, but then the patient found it impossible to proceed to further hierarchies.

The vast majority of reports of desensitization of obsessionals were published between 1960 and 1971. Beech and Vaughan (1978) found considerable difficulty in attempting to compare and evaluate a representative sample of twenty-one cases, but report that among these only eleven improved significantly—an overall success rate of 52%.

The fundamental weaknesses of Wolpe's position were referred to in Chapter 9, and need not be repeated here. But one crucial point about the applicability of reciprocal inhibition or systematic desensitization to obsessional disorders should be mentioned. As we have seen, both the theory and the practice of reciprocal inhibition require the identification of a principal fear-provoking stimulus. This must be defined with some precision, and its features enumerated. The hierarchy is constructed by devising a gradient of similar stimuli which is assumed to be of diminishing anxiety-provoking effect, because these features are systematically reduced in intensity and number. In the case of monosymptomatic phobias only moderate ingenuity is required to achieve a plausible gradient. For example, the patient suffering from a phobic fear of cats may report that she suffers most terror when in close proximity to large, grey Siamese cats. Manipulable features can therefore include distance of the feared object, its size, colour, and ''Siamese''-ness, coupled with its degree of activity and perceived aggression. Thus, the gradient might begin with a cartoon illustration of a cuddly, blue, Persian kitten presented at a ''safe'' distance. The illustration is brought closer on subsequent occasions until eventually the patient can actually hold it without disturbance. The sequence is then repeated with a stuffed toy, then with a live kitten. Meanwhile, colour and appearance can be changed to approach the grey, Siamese qualities of the final stimulus.

The main problem about applying this technique to obsessional problems is that only rarely can a primary stimulus be identified. The obsessional individual may, indeed, suffer from phobic fears. But his obsessions themselves, as we have seen, do not usually involve fears of specific objects or situations. They are, by definition, intrusive and unwanted thoughts, impulses, etc. He may also be wracked by doubts, uncertainties, an inability to experience closure, and so on. None of these is amenable to consideration as a ''stimulus.'' The problem is more pervasive and often difficult to specify; it involves an experience or state of mind rather than a reaction to a determinable stimulus. Obsessional fears are often expressed, but these are seldom connected with environmental objects or situations. Most commonly, they refer to implausible or even impossible events, which the sufferer has never experienced and is exceedingly unlikely ever to experience. The phobic individual may fear heights, crowded places, cats, snakes, or spiders. These all have objective correlates which actually exist in the real world and of which the phobic has had personal experience. Obsessional fears are often not of this kind. They are usually of the "What if ... ?" variety, and might better be described as vague apprehensions or doubts. For example, Mrs. F.'s fears were of social cataclysms caused by illicit drug-taking. Mrs. H. feared the wrath of God: Mr. D. feared that he might have slaughtered two strangers; Mr. I. feared that he had been possessed by the spirit of a dead workmate; Mrs. C. was apprehensive that she might feel the urge to kill her children. None of these fears centres upon an external, objective stimulus which can be modified or manipulated. Sometimes, it is true, the obsessional may report a fear of some apparently determinable contingency. But this usually seems to be an attempted explanation or rationalization of some compulsive activity. Thus, Mr. E., Mrs. G., and Mrs. R. all invoked fears of some nameless and unidentifiable contamination as the "reason" for their compulsive hand-washing. But again, they had never experienced such contamination, nor had they any idea of how it might be recognized.

In short, the obsessional searches for content to carry the expression of his experience. But it could be argued that what he is afraid of is not the content vehicle but the obsessional experience itself.

Thus, the behaviour therapist who insists upon applying standard reciprocal inhibition to obsessional disorders may be forced to invoke "stimuli" and devise hierarchies which are of only indirect applicability to the basic problems. For example, in the Walton (1960) case cited above, the hierarchy was to do with the amount of stones and litter on different paths. But the patient had not expressed fear of stones and litter as such. His fear was that some passer-by might trip over them.

As the term implies, desensitization was designed to alleviate the anxiety associated with a feared stimulus or situation. Where compulsive rituals were concerned, it was presumed that lowering the anxiety would lead to the diminution and eventual extinction of the undesired behaviour. A quite different approach is to discourage or prevent the behaviour from occurring, even if this involves the exacerbation of the anxiety. Cessation of the behaviour should demonstrate that the feared, catastrophic consequences will not automatically follow. The technique of desensitization is based on the assumption that the function of the behaviour is to reduce anxiety; thus, if the anxiety is dissipated, the purpose of the behaviour is removed. Direct prevention of the behaviour, on the other hand, should not modify the anxiety at all, which offers difficulties for the basic anxiety-reduction model. In fact, the prevention method seems to be based in "reality-testing," an approach which, it will be noted, infers a rational, *cognitive* explanation. It is trickier to explain in terms of animal learning theories. Indeed, as Beech and Vaughan (1978) have pointed out, no adequate theoretical explanation has yet been developed.

Techniques utilizing this sort of approach have enjoyed a variety of titles— "apotrepic therapy," "implosion therapy," "flooding," "response prevention," and "modelling." But they all share two features in common: (a) The patient is encouraged or required to submit himself to the feared situation. When possible, this is done *in vivo*. But when it is not objectively replicable, the situation must be experienced in the patient's imagination; (b) The patient is discouraged or prevented from engaging in his compulsive rituals which, of course, are regarded as "avoidance behaviour." By not being allowed to avoid something, it is assumed that he is being forced to meet the "something" head-on. It will be noted that such procedures differ significantly from classical "reciprocal inhibition" in at least two respects: (i) In diametric opposition to the nub of Wolpe's technique, a graded approach to the feared situation or object is deliberately eschewed. The patient is, as it were, "thrown in at the deep end" to sink or swim; and (ii) The feared situation or conditioned stimulus is no longer an objective, real-world feature. It is accepted to be inside the patient's head, a non-observable phenomenon. This surely flies in the face of the tenets of classical behaviourism.

"*Apotrepic therapy*" is a term subsequently coined to describe a set of procedures used initially by Meyer (1966) in the successful treatment of two patients with compulsive rituals. The patients were admitted to hospital where they came under continual supervision by nurses to prevent them from engaging in their rituals. A wide variety of measures were introduced, including patient participation and occasional physical restraint (with the patients' consent) to achieve this. The technique was subsequently applied to a series of fifty cases (Meyer *et al.*, 1974). Of these, ten were reported to be at least "much improved" at the end of treatment, while of twelve followed up after intervals of between six months and six years, eight were at least "much improved."

The procedure known as "*modelling*" was developed from that of Meyer, but was strongly influenced by the work of Bandura (1969). Whereas Meyer and his group emphasized the central importance of response prevention, Rachman *et al.* (1970) simply requested their patients to refrain from their compulsive behaviours. They then acted as models for the patients to follow in facing feared objects and situations. "*Flooding*" was then introduced by Rachman *et al.* (1971). This sprang from earlier work with phobics by Stampfl (1967) and Hogan and Kirchner (1967) using "*implosion therapy*." The emphasis here is upon the maximization of anxiety which, it may be assumed, leads to habituation of the autonomic response. It seems to have been presumed that a diminution of anxiety would automatically involve the disappearance of the "avoidance behaviour" of compulsive rituals, in accordance with Mowrer's two-factor theory.

Perhaps the majority of more recent reports of behaviour therapy with obsessionals have been comparisons between or combinations of modelling and flooding, *in vivo* imaginal presentation (e.g., Foa, Steketee, Turner, and Fischer, 1980), and exposure *versus* response prevention (e.g., Foa, Steketee, and Milby, 1980). One or both techniques have also been studied in association with hypnosis (Scrignar, 1981), attention-focusing (Grayson *et al.*, 1982), clomipramine (Mawson *et al.*, 1982); self-monitoring (Turner and Van Hasselt, 1979), and imipramine (Foa *et al.*, 1979). Good summaries have been provided by Beech and Vaughan (1978), Rachman and Hodgson (1980), and Rachman (1982). Results are sometimes difficult to interpret and almost impossible to compare. But they have been at least promising; a ball-park estimate is that between two-thirds and three-quarters of the patients involved have shown improvement as far as compulsive ritual behaviour is concerned. On the other hand, the evidence suggests that the mental state of patients—anxiety, depressive mood, intrusive thoughts— shows little concurrent improvement, though it is modifiable by anti-depressants.

Whereas the early pioneering studies had usually been little more than case reports, those published more recently have shown a notable improvement in methodological sophistication, including controls, cross-over designs, and blind assessments of change. But, like the early studies, to this day reports have tended to focus upon attempted modification of compulsive *behaviour*.

Obsessional experiences are, by definition, the crucial characteristics of the disorder. As noted earlier, any associated *behaviour* can only be regarded as secondary to the experience. Indeed, behaviour can only be termed "compulsive" if it is associated with experiences characterized by the formal criteria discussed in Chapter 1. Some early behaviour therapists must have known this. Indeed, Wolpe, the "founding father," is a practising psychiatrist of considerable clinical sophistication. But clearly not all of them did, as witness various reports of behaviour therapy practised upon "obsessional" patients who were not diagnosable as obsessional at all. A notable example is the report by Taylor (1963) which is cited and respectfully discussed by Eysenck and Rachman (1965).

Nevertheless, the idea of tackling the obsessional experience directly was not totally ignored. Presumably, it did not find favour at first for two reasons: (a) it did not involve observable behaviour; and (b) it was difficult to envisage appropriate methodologies.

There has been a dearth of psychological techniques devised to modify obsessional thoughts which presumably accounts for the paucity of reports of attempts to alleviate them. But Wolpe's (1958) book had introduced a technique designed to tackle obsessional thoughts head on. This was *"thought-stopping,"* a procedure breath-taking in its directness and simplicity. The patient is required to indicate whenever an unwanted thought intrudes. Thereupon, the therapist shouts, "Stop!" Crude, but jolly. ... Modifications have subsequently been introduced. Some therapists have beaten their desk-tops with rulers as they shouted. Wolpe (1973) himself suggested accompanying the shouted command by the administration of an electric shock. Other workers have preceded and succeeded each thought-stopping attempt by relaxation exercises. But the introduction of these last two features—electric shocks and systematic relaxation— may imply little more than the invocation of two of the magic talismans of behaviour therapy.

At a common-sense level, thought-stopping as a procedure is straightforward, comprehensible, and appealing. The patient suffers from an unwanted train of thought. The technique involves startling the patient, distracting him, and thus breaking up the train of thought in question. Later, control can be devolved upon the patient himself. *He* can shout, bang the table, snap the rubber band, or what have you.

From the psychological, theoretical point of view, however, the rationale for the technique is not at all clear, or, at least, has not so far been convincingly expounded. Wolpe had not attempted a theoretical rationale in his original book. In his 1973 work he offers an explanation based upon the traditional learning theory concept of anxiety-reduction. Termination of the unwanted thought, he argues, will reduce the associated anxiety. But the shouting, banging, and electric shocking will surely evoke *heightened* autonomic responses, of exactly the kind usually associated with anxiety. Indeed, this has been demonstrated in the psychophysiological responses recorded by Stern *et al.* (1973) and Boulougouris *et al.* (1977). According to the classical conditioning model, therefore, thought-stopping can scarcely be regarded as a "rewarding" procedure. The intrusive, obsessional thought should become the signal or conditioned stimulus for a conditioned response of a painful kind. In other words, if the holding of an obsessional thought is anxiety-provoking, then thought-stopping is a procedure for *augmenting* the anxiety.

In fact, a second theoretical possibility, still using a learning paradigm, is that thought-stoping is an aversive procedure. The patient, it might be argued, will cease to harbour obsessional thoughts because he will be punished for so doing. But it is hard to make a case for this line of argument because, by definition, the patient did not wish to harbour the thought in the first place. Punishment can only confirm his feeling that the thought is undesirable. Furthermore, as Beech and Vaughan (1978) have pointed out, this approach meets difficulties in regard to generalization. The normal practice has been to transfer the stop signal to the patient's own control, to facilitate generalization from the clinic or consulting room into everyday life. On the "punishment" paradigm, the patient becomes his own punisher. After all, he is the only one who knows when an unwanted thought is intruding into his consciousness, and he is able to administer the punishment immediately. But patients are usually instructed to emit the "stop" signal sub-vocally and without associated banging and shocking. The "startle" effect is thus eliminated, and it is difficult to see how the situation can any longer be construed as one of punishment. Indeed, Blue (1978) has described two cases in which the snap of the rubber band became a cue for further rumination.

Other theoretical approaches to thought-stopping are discussed by Beech and Vaughan (1978); none is particularly convincing. This may well be because in this context we have become accustomed to look to learning theories of various kinds as appropriate sources of psychological explanation. Perhaps in this instance they are *not* the best sources.

In practice, thought-stopping has not been very promising, despite a few reports of successes with individual patients (e.g., Stern, 1970; Yamagami, 1971). However, it does not as yet seem to have been fully exploited. Stern *et al.*'s (1973) sophisticated study resulted in improvement in only four out of eleven ruminative patients, but only two clinical sessions were given to the patients (whose ruminations had persisted for between four and thirty-five years). In fact, considering the severity and duration of disturbance in the group, the marked improvement in four cases seems a most laudable outcome. Similarly, Hackman and McLean (1975) used a cross-over design to compare the effects of thought-stoping and flooding in a group of ten patients. But this allowed only four sessions of each treatment.

The main purpose of discussing thought-stopping here was to indicate that, by the early 1970s, behaviour therapists realized that obsessional problems are primarily ones of experience and that therapeutic intervention must address that experience as well as any associated behaviour.

It should be noted that the great majority of these reports, like their predecessors of the 1960s, refer to compulsive *behaviour*—usually of two kinds, cleaning and checking. Rachman (1982) suggests that these represent the most common types of obsessional disorder. But this does not appear to be the case. In the present series, it will be recalled, no fewer than 96% complained of obsessional *experiences*, as compared with 72% who displayed compulsive behaviour; 24% complained only of their experiences, whereas 4% showed compulsive behaviour in the absence of concurrent obsessional experiences. (And as a matter of interest, checking and washing accounted for only 34% of the compulsions.)

In other words, it has been demonstrated that modern behaviour therapy can be effective, but so far only with obsessional patients whose *behaviour* is pathological. What of the majority—those suffering from obsessional thoughts, images, and impulses, from ruminations, fears, doubts, and uncertainties?

The answer to this is that there have been remarkably few attempts made to remediate or modify obsessional experiences and thought processes and the few reported have not been notably effective.

Nevertheless, behaviour therapists have not been unaware of the central importance of cognitive variables in obsessionality. At the same time it is quite clear that behaviour therapy, itself, has become less and less behavioural. In fact, doubts have been expressed for many years as to how much behaviouristic concepts apply in even Wolpe's classical work. In an article entitled "Is Behaviour Therapy Behaviouristic?", Locke (1971) points out that the basic premises of behaviourism are determinism, epiphenomenalism, and the rejection of introspection as a scientific method. He then goes on to show that, despite the clear behaviouristic premises of Wolpe's formal, theoretical system, his procedures are dependent upon the patient's introspective reports, his conscious attitudes and beliefs, his reasoning and imagination, and his conscious self-control. In short, Locke demonstrates quite unequivocally that Wolpe's techniques flatly contradict each of the basic premises of behaviourism.

The same criticisms apply, sometimes with even greater force, to every one of the "behaviour" therapy techniques applied to obsessional disorders. Without exception, they rely upon subjective reports and introspection; the most potent of them call for conscious self-control and the use of imagination; and the majority imply modification of conscious attitudes and belief systems. So whatever behaviour therapists may aver, they are certainly not engaging in therapy of a behaviouristic nature. But what their techniques have in common is a reliance upon learning theories derived from animal studies. Not all psychological writers, however, have agreed that such learning models are the most appropriate ones to apply in the study of psychopathology or the practice of psychotherapy. Twenty years ago, Breger and McGaugh (1965) presented a scholarly and closely reasoned criticism both of the particular "principles of learning" embraced by behaviour therapists and of their applicability to clinical problems. Having noted that behaviour-therapy techniques in fact subsume a variety of activities, including many traditional interviewing and therapeutic techniques, they urged that results should not be accepted at their face value. Finally, they propounded their own view of learning as the "process by which information about the environment is acquired, stored, and categorized"—i.e., an information-processing or cognitive model.

Since Breger and McGaugh a number of other writers have expressed similar doubts about the suitability of the traditional animal-learning postulates for explaining human behaviour and experience. They have included Locke (1971), London (1972), McKeachie (1974), Bandura (1974), Mahoney (1974), and Brewer (1974). Writers who have expressed such doubts with specific reference to the treatment of obsessional disorders have included Beech and Liddell (1974), Carr (1974), Mohlenkamp (1977), Marks (1977, 1979), Beech and Vaughan (1978), and Nemiah (1980).

At the same time, the importance of cognitive factors in the study of obsessional disorders is being increasingly recognized even by avowed behaviour analysts such as, for example, Rachman and Hodgson (1980) and Rivière et al. (1980).

COGNITIVE THERAPIES

And meanwhile, the mid-1970s saw the dramatic emergence of what its adherents term "cognitive-behaviour therapy." The title is of course, a blatant contradiction in terms which no amount of semantic obfuscation can conceal. It may be regarded as a figure of speech, an oxymoron in which the conjunction of opposites serves at least to remind us of its origins. For apart from the founding fathers of the movement, its enthusiasts tend to be drawn from the ranks of behaviour therapists and betray a touching loyalty to the constituents of the classical BT creed—objectivity, reliability, appropriate controls, demonstrated statistical significance, cross-over designs, blind trials. ... There are several mortal sins, of which perhaps the most heinous is to commit subjectivity. Thus, it is absolutely forbidden to ask a client whether his spirits are low today. The approved procedure is to give him a pencil and a questionnaire, upon which he must rate on a five-point scale the statement: "My spirits are low today." It need scarcely be pointed out that such worthy tenets and good works are not specific to BT. They are part of the standard fare of experimental psychology, from which behaviour therapists borrowed them thirty years ago to demonstrate the respectability and serious-mindedness of their new movement. Now the CBT proponents use exactly the same means to evince *their* respectability to the mainstream behaviour therapists. Of this, the mainstreamers are not yet at all convinced. Ironically, BT, the cheeky young upstart of the 1950s, is now the established and conservative middle-aged parent, primly dubious about the adolescent enthusiasm of its progeny. Wolpe (1976) himself branded the newcomers as "malcontents," and skepticism has been well formulated by such critics as Wilson (1978) and Ledwidge (1978). Both these writers are suspicious of the claims made for CBT, seeing it merely as an adjunct to conventional BT, an adjunct which on its own is not so efficacious as the latter. Whether soundly based or not, such complaints will probably prove to be forlorn struggles with the inevitable. For as we have seen, BT was itself becoming increasingly cognitive, a point made both by supporters like Ledwidge (1978) and by critics like Locke (1971). And a double irony is that the most mainstream of behaviour therapists are now asserting that they were really cognitivists all along. Cognitions, we are led to understand, are in fact examples of behaviour! To emphasize their behavioural nature, thoughts must now be termed "self-statements," a piece of semantic legerdemain of awesome ingenuity. The academic debates regarding contemporary behaviourism and the relationship between behaviour therapy and cognitive approaches have been impassioned. They are reviewed in a lively and sophisticated manner by Ledwidge (1978).

What exactly is the theoretical basis of CBT? This is not an easy question to answer, partly because so many overlapping techniques have contributed to the movement, and partly because there has been a lack of clarity at the conceptual level. In one sense, despite its vigour, the "movement" is little more than a collation of therapeutic strategies. A sophisticated and consistent theoretical basis has not yet been developed. However, several thematic assumptions are held or implied by the various contributory approaches, and these have been elegantly summarized by Kendall and Bemis (1983, 1984). Very briefly, the basic principles emphasize that human learning is cognitively mediated, that we respond primarily to cognitive representations of environmental stimuli rather than to the stimuli themselves, and that thoughts, feelings, and behaviours are causally interrelated. The understanding and modification of psychopathology requires that such cognitive activities as beliefs, attitudes, and expectancies be taken into account. Like the conventional behaviour therapist, the cognitive-behavioural therapist can derive testable predictions and use objective measures, while working with the client to identify and remediate maladaptive cognitions.

There would be no point in attempting here even the briefest of overviews of the many techniques subsumed under the CBT banner. Many excellent accounts have been published, and the reader is recommended to consult, e.g., Mahoney (1974), Beck (1976), Meichenbaum (1977), Foreyt and Rathjen (1978), Kendall and Hollen (1979), Wilson and Franks (1982), or Kendall and Bemis (1983, 1984). But three main approaches deserve mention.

Rational–Emotive Therapy (RET) is the longest-established, best-publicized, and most widely known of the cognitive approaches, having been developed by Ellis (1962) prior to the introduction of BT itself. Basically, Ellis argues that we do not perceive the world objectively but through a screen of distorted ideas. Psychological disturbances are a direct result of these irrational beliefs. The therapist's task is to prevail upon clients to replace maladaptive ideas with rational, positive thinking. We can achieve this through challenge, exhortation, and debate.

The conceptual basis of RET is minimal, because Ellis's opus is mainly presented in a series of popular How-To manuals. Presumably deliberately, these eschew theory and use an exuberant and colloquial style more reminiscent of the revivalist tent than the clinic or laboratory.

Cognitive Therapy, of a similar chronological seniority to RET, was developed by Beck (1963), the other founding father of the CBT movement. Beck's ideas are expressed in more conventional terms than those of Ellis and have more theoretical sophistication. Psychological disorder results from faulty information-processing which is characterized by such logical errors as arbitrary inference and over-generalization. Types of psychological disorder are related to particular content. The therapist's task is to teach clients to recognize and monitor "automatic thoughts," to modify their negative cognitions and higher-order dysfunctional beliefs, etc. Specific techniques include self-monitoring, reality-testing, reattribution, and "prospective hypothesis-testing."

There have been many derivatives, elaborations, or developments from the classical duo. Of these, the most significant seems to be *Self-Instructional Training* (Meichenbaum, 1977), a behavioural-cognitive strategy derived from RET, but capitalizing upon the work of Luria (1961) on verbal self-regulation. The therapist's task is to help the client to verbalize aloud task-relevant observations and self-instructions, to comply with these instructions, and finally to deliver them covertly.

Obviously, obsessionality presents an open invitation for study from the CBT standpoint, at both the theoretical and therapeutic levels. As we have seen, both the personality disorder and the neurotic disorder display predominantly cognitive features; sufferers possess insight and tend to be intelligent and articulate; and the symptomatic psychopathology is distinctive, and its determination is relatively straightforward. In short, obsessionality and cognitive intervention seem to be made for each other. So, it is mystifying to discover that, whereas traditional behaviour therapists have tackled compulsive behaviour energetically, neither the founding fathers of CBT nor their most influential followers seem to have paid any attention to obsessional experiences.

An intensive search of the literature to date reveals only one theoretical discussion and one empirical study of obsessional disorder written from an avowedly CBT standpoint. The first of these is a thoughtful and well-informed article by McFall and Wollersheim (1979) who present a tentative model of obsessive–compulsive neurosis, modestly described as ''a first approximation that is of a preliminary and incomplete nature.'' Drawing upon the formulations of Lazarus (1966), the authors argue that obsessionals manifest ''primary appraisal deficits'' in over-estimating both the probability and the cost of occurrence of unfavourable events, as argued by Carr (1974). This primary appraisal of threat is followed by ''secondary appraisal deficits''; the obsessional under-estimates his abilities to cope appropriately with the threat. Therapeutic interventions should focus upon modification of the appraisal processes, and McFall and Wollersheim suggest a mélange of techniques drawn from several CBT approaches. (Unfortunately, the case cited as an example of successful treatment does not sound like an obsessive–compulsive at all, but rather a typical disorder of impulse control.)

The empirical report mentioned above is a comparison by Emmelkamp et al. (1980) of the effects of exposure in vivo alone and exposure preceded by self-instructional training. This study cannot be taken to offer substantial support for CBT because the results indicate that patients treated with exposure alone fared as well as those who also engaged in self-instruction. Fifteen obsessive–compulsive patients were treated, and outcomes were assessed by changes in anxiety and avoidance scales, anxious-mood and depression ratings, a self-rating depression scale, and the Leyton Obsessional Inventory. Significant improvements were found on all these measures, but CBT did not enhance the effectiveness of gradual exposure in vivo. The study is well designed and clearly reported, but two reservations must be expressed. First, no details are given of the nature of the obsessions experienced by the subjects. Thus, the same doubts must be felt as were expressed above in regard to the application of reciprocal inhibition and systematic desensitization to obsessional disorder. What we are told here is: ''An inventory was drawn up for each patient of the stimuli which might trigger passive and active (e.g., compulsive rituals) avoidance behaviour.'' The second reservation refers not to the type of behaviour therapy employed, but to the type of CBT selected. A standard form of self-instructional training was employed, patients being trained ''to emit more productive self-statements'' during the first half-hour of each session. After a short period of relaxation, they were then asked to mentally rehearse self-instructional means of handling anxiety, imagining situations described by the therapist. But this, of course, is what obsessionals are already doing. As Kendall (1982) acutely observes in his comments about this study: "One possibility is that the nature of the pathology is too similar to the intervention strategy—obsessive–compulsive clients are already engaging in excessive self-talk, rumination, and self-doubting, and a treatment that feeds into this pathological system may not be desired" (p. 150).

Why have both theorists and experimenters of the CBT persuasion paid such scant regard to the challenges posed by obsessional disorders? One possible answer is simply that CBT *has* been applied to obsessional cases but found to be ineffective. Whether that is so or not, the present writer would maintain that at least the best-known CBT techniques are manifestly inappropriate for use with obsessionals.

The basic thrust of Ellis's RET and such derivatives as Goldfried *et al.*'s (1974) "Systematic Rational Restructuring" is the teaching of clients to recognize that their beliefs, ideas, etc., are irrational and to accept that irrational cognitions can cause distress to their holders. But as we saw in Chapter 1, *by definition* obsessionals already recognize that their obsessions are irrational. That is presumably why they are resisted, and why their perpetuation is so distressing.

Similarly, whereas many of Beck's CT techniques are appealing, most of them are clearly not applicable to obsessional disorder. They focus upon the recognition and elevation to awareness of "automatic thoughts" and emphasize "distancing." *By definition*, these concepts do not apply to the obsessional, whose principal symptoms, after all, are "automatic thoughts" which have not only emerged into full consciousness, but dominate it. And, again by definition, his insight into the irrationality of the thought presupposes "distancing." The obvious aim of treatment of an obsessional symptom would be the opposite of Beck's technique—i.e., it should be the *de*-emphasis of the thought and the *reduction* of attention paid to it.

Again, while several features of Meichenbaum's self-instruction training sound promising for the treatment of obsessionals, it will be recalled that its basis was the development of verbally mediated self-control, and most testimonials to its efficacy have been reports of its use in the treatment of hyperactive or impulsive children. Obsessionals are accepted to be rigid and *over*-controlled, lacking in spontaneity and therefore notably *under*-impulsive. In the same way, while the armatorium of techniques which have been employed in association with Meichenbaum and Cameron's (1972) "Stress Inoculation Training" includes several of relevance, the main focus of the strategy is the improvement of coping with pain, anxiety, and stress. Defences are developed by exposure to graded stressful situations and, as with systematic desensitization, it is difficult to see how this could be applied to the obsessional experience.

FUTURE DEVELOPMENTS

It is the present writer's belief that some type of cognitive approach is indicated for the alleviation of obsessional disorder. However, it seems clear that the major

CBT techniques introduced to date are limited in their application. They focus upon the *contents* of cognitions, rather than their *forms*—*what* is believed, rather than *how*. This, of course, is very understandable; the most obvious feature of neurotics as well as psychotics is that they have some very odd ideas. Intuitively, the most direct approach to the remediation of their problems is to change or dismiss those ideas (beliefs, fears, attitudes, assumptions, images, etc.). In everyday life, this is usually done by rational argument, by the presentation of alternatives, by the tracing of faulty steps in logic, by the correcting of faulty premises, and so on. If rational argument fails, then in everyday life we resort to persuasion, suggestion, indoctrination, hectoring, or outright coercion. But anybody who has attempted to shift a delusion or even an over-valued idea by recourse to such techniques will be painfully aware of their shortcomings in dealing with psychopathological phenomena. It would seem that it is not the content of the delusion which is pathological, but the way in which it was reached and the manner in which it is maintained. Again it is not uncommon for a delusional belief to be factually quite valid. The point is that the individual is not cognizant of the relevant evidence. Thus, the present writer has known several patients who were consumed by delusions of jealousy, being totally and unshakeably convinced of their spouses' flagrant infidelity without a shred of supporting evidence. They devoted themselves to the search for proof and the plotting of revenge. Ironically, their spouses were in fact indulging in extra-marital affairs, though not with the persons suspected by the patients. Again, it should be pointed out that it is quite possible for the content of a delusion to be prosaic and unexceptional. What defines it as a delusion is the way in which it is held—its incorrigibility, degree of ego-involvement, and preoccupying propensity. The oddity or falsity of a belief is gauged by standards which are culturally determined, and what is regarded as a "normal" idea in one culture may be taken to be decidedly "abnormal" in another. In other words, the *content* of a pathological cognition varies across cultures and over time; what is consistent is its *form* (see Reed, 1972, for a fuller discussion).

Thus, it may be suggested that where a belief, opinion, attitude, etc., has been acquired by "normal" processes of information-assessment and reasoning, then it can presumably be modified or rejcted by the same processes. The belief is faulty because the individual has been misinformed, has assessed valid evidence incorrectly, or has been guilty of a logical error. Remedying the premises, information and reasoning should correct the belief itself. (This may explain why so many RET achievements have involved the use of student volunteers or mild complaints taken to be "analogues" of psychopathology.) But where the belief has *not* been derived from normal cognitive processes it is unlikely to be amenable to their influences. The processes themselves must come under scrutiny, because *they* are what must be changed. To take a simplistic parallel—if radio reception is distorted, we examine our receiver rather than the newscaster's announcements.

Now it is of interest that although contemporary cognitive therapists focus upon content, the major cognitive theorists have always been concerned with structures and, to a lesser degree, processes—i.e., with form. Significantly, there is little evidence in the CT literature that cognitive therapists other than Meichenbaum (1977) have been notably influenced by, or even concerned with, the work of mainstream cognitive theorists such as Piaget. It may be that this is attributable to a laudable pragmatism—''Let's get on with the job, rather than waste time theorizing.'' In the long term, this would be regrettable, especially since the CBT movement seems to have drawn unto itself some of the profession's liveliest intellects. Vigour, enthusiasm, and charisma can carry a movement only so far.

20
Obsessional–Compulsive Disorder: Conventional Approaches and a Different Look

The purpose of this chapter is to present a fresh way of looking at the disorder or disorders which have been the subject of this book. A cognitive/structuralist basis will be suggested as a potentially fruitful theoretical approach. Mainly because of the influence of Freud, with his emphasis on the study of content and its symbolic nature, no other line of attack seems to have been ventured since the regrettably ignored work of Janet (1903).

The position proposed will best be appreciated after consideration of the views espoused by the three major contemporary "schools." These will be presented by thumb-nail overviews, which are admittedly grossly over-simplified. However, the reader can refer to earlier chapters for expositions of the views in more detail. The three "schools" to be considered are:

(1) The Freudians and post-Freudians, termed here, for convenience, "*psychoanalysts.*"
(2) The proponents of German "mainstream" psychiatry, coupled with existential psychiatrists and termed here, again merely for convenience, "*phenomenologists.*"
(3) The behaviour therapists and (animal) learning theorists from whose work behaviour therapy has derived. These have for the most part been psychologists working in the tradition of behaviourism. For this reason, and once more, merely for convenience, they will be termed here "*behaviourists.*"

(a) *The experience of compulsion.* As the terms "compulsion" and "obsession" suggest, it has been assumed that the sufferer is driven or besieged. By what, and from whence? In earlier times it was believed that he was under assault from without—by evil spirits or Satan.

(1) Psychoanalysts agree that the sufferer is besieged—but from within. He is threatened by the emergence of taboo material from his unconscious.

(2) Phenomenologists postulate that an unanalysable upthrust of psychic force is responsible for the experience of compulsion.

(3) Behaviourists are not interested in compulsivity *per se*, because it is a subjective experience.

(b) What accounts for the *compulsive repetitiveness* of obsessional patients?

(1) Psychoanalysts interpret repetition as the acting out of repressed experiences. The distressing experience may be undone by being repeated in a different way.

(2) Phenomenologists view repetition as a striving for magical control in the search for order and form in a malignant and chaotic world.

(3) Behaviourists see repetition as the absence of extinction in the conditioning sense. They have tried to explain it in terms of avoidance learning.

(c) Obsessional phenomena are defined in terms of their *form*. Theoretically, the formal criteria can apply to *any* contents whatsoever.

(1) Psychoanalysts are concerned not with form, but with contents and what they are taken to symbolize, how they should be interpreted, etc.

(2) Phenomenologists are concerned with the flavour of experience. But "mainstream" authorities have emphasized form.

(3) Behaviourists reject the importance of subjective experience and consciousness, so ignore the form/content distinction. But they do focus on *specifics* (= contents) of compulsive behaviour.

(d) By definition, the phenomena are *phenomenological*. Any observable behaviour, also by definition, is simply the outcome of the inner experience.

(1) Psychoanalysts are certainly concerned with subjective experience—but with its contents and their historical development, rather than with the flavour of the experience itself.

(2) Phenomenological description is, of course, the basis of the phenomenologists' approach.

(3) As noted, behaviourists are not concerned with subjective experience, but with behaviour and its reinforcement.

(e) The place of *anxiety*.

(1) For psychoanalysts, this is central. Obsessional experiences and acts are the outcome of anxiety and guilt accompanying the attempted emergence of unconscious material. Obsessional phenomena are interpreted as "defence mechanisms" against psychic, emotion-laden threat.

(2) Phenomenologists have also stressed the role of emotions, such as hate, dread, and disgust.

(3) Anxiety is crucial also for behaviourists, but for quite different reasons. Reinforcement for the pathological behaviour is taken to be the *reduction of anxiety*.

(f) The place of *cognition*—ways of thinking, categorizing, conceptualizing, problem-solving, perceiving, etc.

(1) Psychoanalysts describe cognitive characteristics (particularly in relation to the "anal character"), but have not found these to be central to their approach.
(2) Phenomenologists, too, have described modes of anankastic thinking, but generally without considering their formal characteristics and theoretical implications.
(3) Behaviourists have not been interested.

(g) What is the connection between *obsessional compulsive disorder* (neurosis) and the *compulsive (anankastic) personality disorder*?

(1) Psychoanalysts see the two as distinct, because anal traits represent successful defence against the emergence of the forbidden material.
(2) Phenomenologists either do not distinguish between the two or regard the personality as providing a "fruitful soil" for the symptoms.
(3) Behaviourists reject the very concept of a compulsive personality—or indeed, *any* type of personality. For them, "personality" merely reflects, in any given individual, the totality of his schedules of reinforcement.

The present theory takes a different approach from any of the accepted "schools." It was derived from a rational examination of known facts, making no aetiological assumptions and accepting no "school" credos. It is original (at least, as far as published work is concerned) and will doubtless encounter skepticism, surprise, or hostility. But it is backed by considerable clinical experience and fits the facts and the demands of logic as well as or better than other approaches. And in several features it is at least reconcilable with the views of such classical authorities as Janet and Westphal, the Gestalt school of perception, and such modern writers as Kelly and Beck. Furthermore, it may be argued, it is more directly applicable to the problems of obsessional experience than the behavioural approach while, unlike the psychoanalytical approach, it is amenable to experimental examination.

In brief, the present argument runs as follows. (For expository convenience, we shall retain the headings used above.)

(a) It denies the almost metaphysical assumption that the sufferer is *besieged* or under assault by something. The point is simply that he *feels* as though he is. Again, as described in a previous chapter, sufferers do not emphasize the power of the besieging "force," thought, etc. What they stress is their own "weakness of will" in being unable to resist it, to prevent its occurrence, to switch to other thoughts, etc. The present argument is that there is some impairment of the negative feedback processes which facilitate equilibrium by providing for adaptation, switching and balance in the stream of consciousness.

(b) In the same way, it suggests that compulsive repetition reflects a defect of inhibition. The repeater is unable to establish terminal limits for certain actions and finds it difficult to achieve the experience of completion, satiation, closure, or satisfaction.

(c) The present argument acknowledges that, *by definition*, obsessional problems are *formal*. As with other psychopathological phenomena, such as delusions and hallucinations, the content details are idiosyncratic, reflecting each individual's life history, cultural concerns, and taboos. The deluded person may be convinced that he is Alexander the Great, Napoleon, or Adolf Hitler. These are different contents, but the underlying form is the same—the individual is convinced that he is someone other than he is. The hallucinator may "see" his dead wife or "hear" the voice of God or the chirrup of a sparrow, but the form is the same— he is "perceiving" something with no objective correlates. Similarly, the obsessional's predominating thought, etc., may be that he is contaminated, that he has killed his grandmother, or that he is an embarrassment to society. But it is the *form* of the experience which makes it obsessional—it dominates his consciousness, he regards it as ego-alien and irrational, and he struggles to resist it.

(d) Again, it acknowledges, that, *by definition*, obsessional phenomena are *phenomenological*. They are matters of subjective experience and occur inside one's head; how one acts is a secondary issue. Indeed, one may be prevented from acting at all without the compulsive experience being in the slightest alleviated. At the same time, it is the flavour or quality of the experience which is central, not the channel through which it is expressed.

(e) In opposition to the conventional "school" approaches, the present argument denies that *anxiety* has a primary causal role in obsessional disorder. On the contrary, interviews and observations of patients strongly suggested that it is the *result* of the obsessional–compulsive experience. It increases on each occasion as the sufferer finds himself in the grip of his obsession and recognizes his helplessness. On the other hand, the sufferer's *mood state* plays an important part in determining how he copes with compulsive experiences.

(f) It argues that examination of the relevant symptoms and traits indicates that the problems are basically *cognitive* in nature. A cognitive theory has been developed which will now be presented. The conventional "schools" will find such an approach hard to swallow. But it should be remembered that both "dynamic" and "social-learning" approaches to schizophrenia ruled the roost for many years, only to be discredited and replaced by approaches based upon biochemistry and "cognitive deficits."

(g) *Traits and Symptoms*. The present argument is that the relevant personality traits reflect a pattern or style of cognitive functioning which is susceptible to the development of obssessional/compulsive symptoms. The experience of compulsivity is simply an extreme example of the central problem. But accentuation of the central problem does not necessarily lead to obsessional neurosis; in fact, depressive disorders are more likely to intervene.

OBSESSIONALITY—THE CENTRAL PROBLEM

What *is* the central problem? In an earlier chapter we engaged in a semantic exercise to induce some order among the variegated traits reported to be typical of the compulsive individual. When stripped of their connotative implications, it became clear that the thirty-three traits could be reduced to seven clusters or categories:

(1) Inability to tolerate the absence of structure
(2) The structuring of performance
(3) The determination of terminal limits
(4) The structuring of cognition
(5) The structuring of social codes
(6) Compliance with prescriptions and rules
(7) The maintenance of prescribed structures

It will be noted that these are all to do with failure in spontaneous categorizing and integration. This leads to the artificial over-structuring of input, of fields of awareness, of tasks and situations. The central, formal phenomenon may thus be seen as a striving towards boundary fixing or the setting of limits in the cognitive/perceptual modalities.

In other words, it is postulated that the obsessional finds difficulty in the spontaneous structuring of experience and attempts to compensate for this by imposing artificial, rigidly defined boundaries, category limits, and time markers. The rigidity and specificity of definition themselves lead to further uncertainty as to the "appropriate" allocation of category items, schematization, completion times, etc.

Operational predictions can readily be derived from this statement, and experimental evidence has been adduced which offers support for the hypothesis.

Where *symptoms* are concerned, the classical ones can be shown to be susceptible to analysis in light of the above:

The central experience of *compulsivity* itself can be conceptualized as a failure to terminate or shift from a sequence of thought. The difficulty can be seen as a *defect in inhibition or switching*, not necessarily related to the strength, power, or prepotence of the thought in question.

Repetitions and continuation, it is suggested, are further examples of this impairment of inhibitory process. It is not a question of something making the sufferer go on, but the absence of something to indicate when he should stop (achieve satiation, experience closure, etc.).

Checking and ruminations may be seen as reflecting a failure in "terminating response," coupled with uncertainty in categorical-limit attribution ("Is it finished?"). This applies to inner reasoning ("Has everything been considered?"), to mnemonic brooding ("Are my recollections sufficient and correct?"), and to the consideration of activities ("Did I do it properly?"). The questions are insoluble, because such qualifiers as "finished," "sufficiently," "satisfactorily," and "properly" cannot be defined in any ultimate and fixed manner.

Ritualization is one pathological example of the imposition of artificial structure geared to the arbitrary definition of such imponderables.

Obsessional *doubts and indecisiveness* reflect difficulty in determining structural boundaries and limits, with a consequent failure to experience surety and closure.

What are the implications of this approach in practice—how can the approach be applied to remediation or therapy? This will be discussed in the final section.

THERAPEUTIC IMPLICATIONS

The cognitive approach proposed above is not merely an academic exercise. On the contrary, it has immediate pragmatic implications, especially in the field of therapeutic intervention. Let us precede consideration of positive suggestions by noting some popular therapeutic measures, which, in the light of the present theory, are either *contra*-indicated or at least time-wasting. This may shed some light on why obsessional disorder is conventionally regarded as an intractable problem which is notoriously difficult to treat and relatively immune to standard, psychotherapeutic approaches.

(i) Very often, the first step taken in attempts to help obsessional patients is to administer tranquillizing drugs. The purpose, presumably, is to alleviate anxiety and tension which, as we have seen, are conventionally assumed to have a causal relationship with the disorder. Tranquillizers will have a transient effect in alleviating acute distress. But, in the present theory, they will be of no help in the long run and may, in fact, do more harm than good. If the drug in question is basically a muscle relaxant, then no harm will be done. But if it is a cortical depressant, then its effect will be to exacerbate the basic difficulty. But in any case, in the present argument, the alleviation of anxiety will have no direct effect on the central problem.

(ii) The insight manifested by obsessionals, coupled with their apparent intelligence and verbal ability, offers a temptation to the psychotherapist to approach the patient's complaints at their face value. He may engage in rational disputation and encourage the patient to "be sensible," to "get a hold of himself," etc. Freud himself observed that exhortation is ineffectual in cases of obsessional neurosis, and the present theory would suggest that it can do nothing other than to exacerbate the sufferer's sense of helplessness and weakness of will.

(iii) Sedation and rest are often recommended. The present theory suggests that these can only make matters worse. Not only does rest not facilitate cognitive structuring, but it actively encourages the patient to engage in pointless ratiocination and rumination, while offering ample opportunity for self-recrimination.

(iv) The vast majority of psychotherapeutic approaches rely upon the detailed examination of the contents of consciousness and attempt to "interpret" these. On the present theory, such activity can be of little help and may well be actively harmful. It encourages the patient to engage in the hair-splitting, self-questionning, and circular arguments which are at the heart of his disturbance. *He is being asked to practise the very cognitive activities which are causing him distress.*

(v) The same argument applies against the emphasis upon the elicitation of personal reminiscence, developmental crises, etc. Such emphasis, engaged in at regular intervals throughout the course of "treatment," merely serves to widen the zone of doubts about mnemonic accuracy, to encourage further self-recrimination, and to augment the range of categorical and boundary difficulties.

(vi) Neither "sensitivity training" nor "assertiveness training" seem to be even remotely relevant to obsessional disorder. Obsessional patients are usually pathologically *over*-sensitive, in the sense of being morbidly concerned with their own perceived inadequacies. Related to this, the compulsive personality is notoriously "spiky," tending to be opinionated and *over*-assertive.

(vii) We have discussed at length how the obsessional disorder is one of subjective experience. Compulsive *behaviour* is secondary to the experience and may be conceptualized as either yielding to obsessional urges or controlling them. Behaviour therapy, in the conventional sense, is unlikely to be of much direct help in alleviating obsessional experience or in modifying the obsessional style of thinking.

What of the positive implications of the present theory? It does not so much suggest a single, "magic" therapy as an overall approach. But this does include a selection of therapeutic strategies. All of these have been used at times, but in the context of quite different theoretical assumptions.

The overall approach indicated by the present theory includes the de-limiting of areas of doubt and indecision and the encouragement of those characterized by relative conceptual clarity. In other words, the patient should be encouraged to focus his activities upon relatively clear-cut activities, to routinize his life without unnecessarily limiting it, to operate within a fairly orderly environment, and to actively avoid metaphysical preoccupations and philosophic hair-splitting.

(i)   Where physical medication is concerned, cortical inhibitors should be replaced by cortical *stimulants*. Inhibitors by definition result in the blurring and loosening of cognitive activities. To assist in the structuring of input, categorical limits, etc., *heightened* cortical activity is indicated. At the same time, as we have seen, obsessional patients are usually distressed by their feelings of weakness and failure. Cortical stimulation involves feelings of increased drive and determination so that, at least subjectively, the subject feels more in command of himself. For this reason, it is suggested, anti-depressants may be of direct value.

(ii)   For the same reasons, both physical fitness and general mental activity should be encouraged, rather than rest, holidays, etc. In any case, obsessional people usually enjoy work and welcome pressure, so long as this does not involve continual decision-making, flexibility, and intuitive responses.

(iii)   For the same reasons, occupational/career counselling should be offered. Some persons of obsessional personality suffer stress simply because their jobs are too open-ended. They may have ample intelligence as well as the requisite professional skills, but they are better suited to occupations demanding a close eye for detail, predictability, and clear parameters.

(iv)   It is generally accepted that rapport is important for any effective clinical relationship. This is particularly important in the case of obsessionals (whether obsessive–compulsive neurotics or individuals with compulsive personality disorders), because they are reserved and suspicious, even in the retailing of their problems. And until they have developed trust in the therapist, they may be averse to accepting his or her advice and suggestions.

(v)   Role-modelling can be used to advantage in encouraging patients to dispense with some of their doubts and fears, to be more decisive, and in general to be more flexible and accepting of unclear situations and objectives. But, to be effective, trust and respect for the clinician must have been established.

(vi)   Considerable relief may be afforded to the obsessional if he feels able to delegate some decisions to the therapist. He will only do this if he has developed appropriate trust and respect for the latter, who must show seriousness and responsibility in "handing down judgements." At the same time, the therapist must act in accord with his role, by treating each decisively and promptly, refusing to debate the issue in question, or to engage in reconsideration. It is preferable, of course, for the decisions to be sound, but the therapist must remember that from the therapeutic standpoint it is the perceived manner of handling problems that is of most importance. It is not his personal possession of ultimate wisdom that he should be attempting to demonstrate, but a style of decision-making. This should be a compound of detached weighing of the relevant factors, rapidity and assurance in making choices, the dismissal of elaborations and second thoughts, and a manifest awareness that the world will not stop if the decision is faulty.

(vii)   Earlier in this book, the role of *mood states* was discussed. In brief, it can be argued that while a patient's mood may not be an important independent variable, variations in mood certainly correlate with degree of suffering. A depressed mood is associated with diminished self-esteem and the will to fight; a lightening of mood involves improved self-confidence, a renewed drive to cope with difficulties, and relative optimism about future developments. At the very least, therefore, any technique which helps to elevate the patient's mood (without confusing his thought processes) should be utilized.

(viii)   It has been maintained that compulsive *behaviour* is secondary to compulsive experience. But where a patient is handicapped by compulsive rituals, their alleviation will raise his morale and his mood, proving to him that all is not lost and renewing his will to beat his problems. To date, the results of behaviour therapy, as we have seen, do not inspire total confidence, and it is probable that the approach's underlying assumptions are faulty. Nevertheless, some of its specific techniques offer promise as at least adjunctive methods. Systematic desensitization may well be effective in dealing with associated phobias, particularly if these are monosymptomatic. Flooding and modelling have proved to be effective. Such techniques as satiation and thought-stopping, while conceptually simplistic, may yet prove to be valuable.

So far, what has been outlined in regard to therapy has been general groundwork. It could be said to be necessary but not sufficient to successfully treat severe cases, especially those characterized by crippling symptoms. It may, however, be amply sufficient to help milder cases, especially when long-term, infrequent supportive or "hand-holding" therapy is possible. Much will then depend upon the patient's lifestyle, his type of occupation, career demands, the stability of his entourage, amount and type of stress, etc. In severe cases, a more systematic and intensive approach is obviously indicated. To be consistent with the theory, some version of cognitive therapy will be the one of choice, but as was observed in the last chapter, the CT techniques in current use do not entirely lend themselves to remedial work with obsessional patients. The general objective of the treatment of obsessional *symptoms* should be the re-deployment of attention and the restoration of harmony and balance among cognitive elements.

The above comments apply to treatment of the symptoma of obsessional neurosis. Beck does not refer to treatment of the compulsive personality disorder, but one of his major techniques would be highly relevant there:

(ix) "Changing the Rules": In this technique, the therapist teases out the patient's attitudes, concepts, premises, etc., used to regulate his own life and applied to the behaviour of others. In obsessionals, these "rules" are often framed in absolute terms and become maladaptive, causing distress to their proponent. They are used as the basis of assessing the probability of danger, threat, and social evaluations. The therapeutic technique consists of working with the patient to re-evaluate each "rule" in an attempt to make it more realistic, more narrow in application and, in the present case most importantly, more flexible.

Other cognitive exercises include the following:

(x)   "Devil's Advocate": A handicapping generalization, attitude, or precept is identified. A form of debate is initiated, where the patient is encouraged to argue for the appropriateness of his belief. When his catalogue of its virtues and rationality has been exhausted, he is required to reverse roles and produce arguments *against* it, the therapist undertaking its defence.

(xi) "Families": Sorting tasks are presented, the material including word lists, shapes, objects, etc. The stress is placed upon speed of performance, rather than accuracy. To avoid irritation and frustration, the task is self-paced and self-administered, the patient being given sets of material to work through between clinical sessions. He must log his own performance times and note down his reactions. The emphasis upon speed is aimed at de-emphasizing the "correctness" of answers and to obviate prolonged consideration, indecisiveness, etc.

(xii) "In-laws": An extension of (xi), it is intended to encourage flexibility and the ability or willingness to switch concepts and categories. There are two phases. In the first, the patient is presented with long lists or collections of items, and his task is to devise as many practicable classes ("families") as possible— i.e., to think up different categorical dimensions or criteria. In the second phase, he is required to sort items first on one criterion, then on the others. Tasks must be repeated between sessions, the logged times not only demonstrating improvement in "switching" ability but yielding diagnostic information as to where "blockages" occur.

(xiii) "Check and Switch": Patients are required to check off, for example, the *t*'s in a page of print (e.g., from a newspaper). Obsessionals are usually very accurate in this sort of task, but over-thorough and therefore very slow. As before, this is done on a "take-home" basis, and the aim must be to speed up their performance. After improvement has been achieved, switching is introduced. After checking a given letter, they must go on to check each of several other letters.

(xiv) "Changing Trains": The patient is given typewritten lists of topics. Initially, these are all of a neutral nature. Later, the therapist will introduce more and more topics of a disturbing nature, according to the patient's progress. Armed with a stopwatch, the patient allows himself, for example, ten seconds to think about each topic before going on to the next, noting down (timing) any difficulties he has in changing (switching) from one train of thought to another.

The "games" above are offered simply as examples of apposite remedial exercises, and the field is wide open for ingenious contributions from therapists and experimenters. The main thrust of such mental exercises, of course, is to encourage sufferers to abandon their obsessional style of cognitive functioning. In line with what has been maintained throughout this book, the emphasis should be on form rather than on content. What causes the obsessional individual incovenience or distress, it is asserted, is not *what* he or she thinks, but *how*.

For obsessionals to break out of their ingrained patterns of thought, they must be helped to work towards dual objectives: (a) a ready acceptance, without hesitations or second thoughts, of predetermined structures (targets, criteria, categorical limits, etc.), and (b) a facility for switching from one structure to another. At first sight, these two aims may appear to be irreconcilable, involving, as they do, both compliance and relinquishment. However, the two are orthogonal, one being to do with static filtering and application, the other with temporal sequences. The modifications of cognitive style to be aimed for will include the clarification and stabilization of categories and criteria, but will encourage facility in rapid and flexible switching between categories, in reassessing targets, and in changing lines of thought.

References

Abraham, K. (1923). Contributions to the theory of the anal character. *International Journal of Psycho-Analysis*, *4*, 400–18.

Adams, P. L. (1973). *Obsessive Children: A Sociopsychiatric Study*. New York: Bruner/Mazel.

Akhtar, S. (1978). Obsessional neurosis, marriage, sex and fertility: Some transcultural comparisons. *International Journal of Social Psychiatry*, *24*, 164–66.

Akhtar, S., Wig, N. N., Varma, V. K., Pershad, D., and Verma, S. K. (1975). A phenomenological analysis of symptoms in obsessive–compulsive neurosis. *British Journal of Psychiatry*, *127*, 342–48.

American Psychiatric Association (1980). *DSM* III. *Diagnostic and Statistical Manual of Mental Disorders*. 3rd ed. Washington, D.C.: American Psychiatric Association.

Ananth, J. (1983). Clomipramine in obsessive–compulsive disorder: A review. *Psychosomatics*, *24*, 723–27.

Anderson, E. W. (1964). *Psychiatry*. London: Baillière, Tindall and Cox.

Apter, M. J. (1970). *The Computer Simulation of Behaviour*. London: Hutchinson.

Arbib, M. A. (1972). *The Metaphorical Brain*. New York: Wiley.

Balken, E. R., and Masserman, J. H. (1940). The language of phantasy: III. The language of the phantasies of patients with conversion hysteria, anxiety state, and obsessive–compulsive neuroses. *Journal of Psychology*, *10*, 75–86.

Bandura, A. (1969). *Principles of Behavior Modification*. New York: Holt, Rinehart and Winston.

Bandura, A. (1974). Behavior theory and models of man. *American Psychologist*, *29*, 859–69.

Barron, F. (1969). *Creative Person and Creative Process*. Eastbourne: Holt, Saunders.

Bartlett, F. C. (1932). *Remembering: A Study in Experimental and Social Psychology*. Cambridge, Cambridge: University Press.

Bartlett, F. C. (1958). *Thinking*. London: Allen & Unwin.

Barucci, M. (1954). Analisi e classificazzione dei fenomeni di cosidetta ipermnesia. *Rivista di patologia nervosa e mentale*, *75*, 663–75.

Beck, A. T. (1963). Thinking and depression. *Archives of General Psychiatry*, *9*, 324–33.

Beck, A. T. (1976). *Cognitive Therapy and the Emotional Disorders*. New York: International Universities Press.

Beech, H. R. (1971). Ritualistic activity in obsessional patients. *Journal of Psychosomatic Research*, *15*, 417–22.

Beech, H. R., ed. (1974). *Obsessional States*. London: Methuen.

Beech, H. R., and Liddell, A. (1974). Decision-making, mood states and ritualistic behaviour among obsessional patients. In H.R. Beech, ed. *Obsessional States*. London: Methuen.

Beech, H. R., and Vaughan, M. (1978). *Behavioral Treatment of Obsessional States*. New York: Wiley.

Binik, Y. M., Fainsilber, L., and Spevack, M. (1981). Obsessionality and creativity. *Canadian Journal of Behavioural Sciences*, *13*, 25–32.

Birnie, W. A., and Littmann, S. K. (1978). Obsessionality and schizophrenia. *Journal of the Canadian Psychiatric Association*, *23*, 77–81.

Black, A. (1974). The natural history of obsessional neurosis. In H.R. Beech, ed. *Obsessional States*. London: Methuen.

Blue, R. (1978). Ineffectiveness of an aversion therapy technique in treatment of obsessional thinking. *Psychological Reports*, *43*, 181–82.

Boren, J. J., Sidman, M., and Herrnstein, R. J. (1959). Avoidance, escape and extinction as a function of shock intensity. *Journal of Comparative and Physiological Psychology*, *52*, 420–25.

Boulougouris, J. C., Rabavilas, A. D., and Stefanis, C. (1977). Psychophysiological responses in obsessive–compulsive patients. *Behaviour Research and Therapy*, *15*, 221–30.

Bratfos, O. (1970). Transition of neuroses and other minor disorders in psychoses. *Acta Psychiatrica Scandinavica*, *46*, 35–49.

Breger, L., and McGaugh, J. L. (1965). Critique and reformulation of "learning-theory" approaches to psychotherapy and neurosis. *Psychological Bulletin*, *63*, 338–58.

Brewer, W. (1974). There is no convincing evidence for operant or classical conditioning in adult humans. In W. Weimer and D. Palermo, eds. *Cognition and the Symbolic Processes*. New York: Halsted.

Brown, F. W. (1942). Heredity in the psychoneuroses. *Proceedings of the Royal Society of Medicine*, *35*, 785–90.

Cameron, N. (1938). Reasoning, regression and communication in schizophrenics. *Psychology Monographs*, *50*, no. 221, 1–33.

Cameron, N. (1944). Experimental analysis of schizophrenic thinking. In J.S. Kasanin, ed. *Language and Thought in Schizophrenia*. Berkeley and Los Angeles: University of California Press.

Campbell, R. J. (1981). *Psychiatric Dictionary*. 5th ed. New York, Oxford: Oxford University Press.

Capstick, N. (1975). Clomipramine in the treatment of the true obsessional state: A report on four patients. *Psychosomatics*, *16*, 21–25.

Carr, A. (1974). Compulsive neurosis: A review of the literature. *Psychological Bulletin*, *81*, 311–18.

Comrey, A. L. (1965). Scales for measuring compulsion, hostility, neuroticism, and shyness. *Psychological Reports*, *16*, 697–700.

Cooper, J. (1970). The Leyton Obsessional Inventory. *Psychological Medicine*, *1*, 48–64.

Cooper, J., and Kelleher, M. (1972). The Leyton Obsessional Inventory: A principal components analysis on normal subjects. *Psychological Medicine*, *3*, 204–08.

Curran, D., and Guttmann, E. (1949). *Psychological Medicine*. Edinburgh: Livingstone.

Dollard, J., and Miller, V. G. (1950). *Personality and Psychotherapy*. New York: McGraw-Hill.

Ellis, A. (1962). *Reason and Emotion in Psychotherapy*. New York: Stuart.

Ellis, A., and Grieger, R. (1978). *Handbook of Rational-Emotive Therapy*. New York: Springer.

Emmelkamp, P. M. G., van der Helm, M., van Zanten, B. L., and Plochg, I. (1980). Treatment of obsessive-compulsive patients: The contribution of self-instructional training to the effectiveness of exposure. *Behaviour Research and Therapy*, *18*, 61–66.

Emslie, Judith R. (1984) Obsessive Compulsive Disorder: The Clomipramine revolution. Unpublished manuscript, York University, Canada.

Esquirol, J. E. D. (1827). *Memoire sur la monomanie homicide*. Paris: J. B. Baillière.

Esquirol, J. E. D. (1838). *Des maladies mentales*. Paris: Baillière.

Eysenck, H. J. (1947). *Dimensions of Personality*. London: Routledge, Kegan Paul.

Eysenck, H. J. (1952). *The Scientific Study of Personality*. London: Routledge, Kegan Paul.

Eysenck, H. J. (1953). *The Structure of Human Personality*. London: Methuen.

Eysenck, H. J. (1959a). Learning theory and behaviour therapy. *Journal of Mental Science*, *105*, 61–75.

Eysenck, H. J. (1959b) *The Maudsley Personality Inventory*. London: U.L.P.

Eysenck, H. J., and Eysenck, S. B. G. (1963). *The Eysenck Personality Inventory*. London: U.L.P.

Eysenck, H. J., and Rachman, S. (1965). *The Causes and Cures of Neurosis*. London: Routledge and Kegan Paul.

Fenichel, O. (1945). *The Psychoanalytic Theory of Neurosis*. New York: Norton.

Ferenczi, S. (1926). *Further Contributions to the Theory and Technique of Psychoanalysis*. London: Institute of Psychoanalysis and Hogarth.

Fischer, S. (1950). *Principles of General Psychopathology*. New York: Philosophical Library.

Fish, F. (1964). *An Outline of Psychiatry*. Bristol: John Wright.

Fisher, S., and Greenberg, R. P. (1977). *The Scientific Credibility of Freud's Theories and Therapy*. New York: Basic Books.

Foa, E. B., and Emmelkamp, P. M. G., eds. (1983). *Failures in Behavior Therapy*. New York: Wiley.

Foa, E. B., and Goldstein, A. (1978). Continuous exposure and strict response prevention in the treatment of obsessive–compulsive neurosis. *Behavior Therapy*, *17*, 169–76.

Foa, E. B., and Steketee, G. S. (1979). Obsessive–compulsives: Conceptual issues and treatment interventions. In M. Hersen, R. M. Eisler, and P. M. Miller, eds. *Progress in Behavior Modifications*. New York: Academic Press.

Foa, E. B., Steketee, G., and Groves, G. (1979). Use of behavioural therapy and imipramine: A case of obsessive–compulsive neurosis with severe depression. *Behavior Modification*, *3*, 419–30.

Foa, E. B., Steketee, G., and Milby, J. B. (1980). Differential effects of exposure and response prevention in obsessive–compulsive washers. *Journal of Clinical and Consulting Psychology*, *48*, 71–79.

Foa, E. B., Steketee, G., Grayson, J. B., and Doppelt, H. G. (1983). Treatment of obsessive–compulsives: When do we fail? In E. B. Foa and P. M. G. Emmelkamps, eds. *Failures in Behavior Therapy*. New York: Wiley.

Foa, E. B., Steketee, G., Turner, R. M., and Fischer, S. C. (1980). Effects of imaginal exposure to feared disasters in obsessive–compulsive checkers. *Behaviour Research and Therapy*, *18*, 449–55.

Foreyt, J. P., and Rathjen, D. P. (1978). *Cognitive Behavior Therapy*. New York: Plenum.

Foulds, G. A. (1951). Temperamental differences in maze performance. Part 1: Characteristic differences among psychoneurotics. *British Journal of Psychology*, *42*, 209–17.

Foulds, G. A. (1965). *Personality and Personal Illness*. London: Tavistock Publications.

Fransella, F. (1974). Thinking and the obsessional. In H. R. Beech, ed. *Obsessional States*. London: Methuen.

Freeman, W., and Watts, J. W. (1950). *Psychosurgery*. 2nd ed. London: Oxford University Press.

Frenkel-Brunswik, E. (1949). Intolerance of ambiguity as an emotional and perceptual personality variable. *Journal of Personality*, *18*, 108–43.

Freud, S. (1894). The neuro-psychoses of defence. *Standard edition of the complete psychological works of Sigmund Freud*. Trans. and ed. J. Strachey. *3*, 45–61. London: Hogarth Press and the Institute of Psychoanalysis.

Freud, S. (1895). Obsessions and phobias. *Standard Edition*, *3*, 74–82.

Freud, S. (1896a). Heredity and the neuroses. *Standard Edition*, *3*, 141–56.

Freud, S. (1896b). Further remarks on the neuro-psychoses of defence. II-The nature of mechanism of obsessional neurosis. *Standard Edition*, *3*, 168–74.

Freud, S. (1907). Obsessive actions and religious practices. *Standard Edition*, *9*, 117–27.

Freud, S. (1908). Character and anal erotism. *Standard Edition*, *9*, 169–75.

Freud, S. (1909). Notes upon a case of obsessional neurosis. II. Theoretical. *Standard Edition*, *10*, 221–49.

Freud, S. (1913). The disposition to obsessional neurosis. *Standard Edition*, *12*, 317–26.

Freud, S. (1914). Remembering, repeating and working-through. (Further recommendations on the technique of psycho-analysis II). *Standard Edition*, *12*, 147–56.

Freud, S. (1917a). On transformations of instinct as exemplified in anal erotism. *Standard Edition*, *13*, 127–33.

Freud, S. (1917b). Introductory lectures on psychoanalysis. *Standard Edition*, *16*, 258–72.

Freud, S. (1918). The history of an infantile neurosis. VI. The obsessional neurosis. *Standard Edition* *17*, 61-71.

Freud, S. (1920). Beyond the pleasure principle. *Standard Edition*, *18*, 7–64.

Freud, S. (1926). Inhibitions, symptoms and anxiety. V and VI. *Standard Edition*, *20*, 111–23.

Freud, S. (1939). Moses and monotheism. *Standard Edition*, *23*, 7–137.

Gadelius, B. (1896). *Om Tvangstankar*. Stockholm: Lund.

Gantt, W. H. (1941). *See* Pavlov, I. P.

Gittleson, N. L. (1966a). The effect of obsessions on depressive psychosis. *British Journal of Psychiatry*, *112*, 253–59.

Gittleson, N. L. (1966b). The phenomenology of obsessions on depressive psychosis. *British Journal of Psychiatry*, *112*, 261–64.

Gittleson, N. L. (1966c). The fate of obsessions in depressive psychosis. *British Journal of Psychiatry*, *112*, 705–08.

Gittleson, N. L. (1966d). Depressive psychosis in the obsessional neurotic. *British Journal of Psychiatry*, *112*, 883–87.

Gittleson, N. L. (1966e). The relationship between obsessions and suicidal attempts in depressive psychosis. *British Journal of Psychiatry*, *112*, 889–90.

Goldfried, M. R., Decenteceo, E. T., and Weinberg, L. (1974). Systematic rational restructuring as a self-control technique. *Behavior Therapy*, *5*, 247-54.

Gottheil, E., and Stone, G. C. (1968). Factor analytic study of orality and anality. *Journal of Mental Diseases*, *146*, 1–17.

Gray, J. A. (1971). *The Psychology of Fear and Stress*. New York: McGraw-Hill.

Grayson, J. B., Foa, E. B., and Steketee, G. (1982). Habituation during exposure treatment: Distraction vs. attention-focusing. *Behaviour Research and Therapy*, *20*, 323–28.

Greenacre, P. (1923). A study of the mechanisms of obsessive compulsive conditions. *American Journal of Psychiatry*, *79*, 527–38.

Greer, H. S., and Cawley, R. H. (1966). Some observations on the natural history of neurotic illness. *Mervyn Archdall Medicine Monographs*, *No. 3*, Australian Medical Association.

Grimshaw, L. (1965). The outcome of obsessional disorder: A follow-up study of 100 cases. *British Journal of Psychiatry*, *111*, 1051–56.

Guilford, J. P. (1959). Traits of creativity. In H. H. Anderson, ed. *Creativity and Its Cultivation*. New York: Harper.

Gutheil, E. (1949). Preface to his trans. of *Compulsion and Doubt* by W. Stekel. New York: Liveright.

Hackmann, A., and McLean, C. (1975). A comparison of flooding and thought-stopping treatment. *Behaviour Research and Therapy*, *13*, 263–69.

Hamilton, V. (1957a). Conflict avoidance in obsessionals and hysterics, and the validity of the concept of dysthymis. *Journal of Mental Sciences*, *103*, 666–76.

Hamilton, V. (1957b). Perceptual and personality dynamics in reactions to ambiguity. *British Journal of Psychology*, *48*, 200–15.

Hare, E. H., Price, J. S., and Slater, E. T. O. (1972). Fertility in obsessional neurosis. *British Journal of Psychiatry*, *121*, 197–205.

Haslam, M. T. (1965). The treatment of an obsessional patient by reciprocal inhibition. *Behaviour Research and Therapy*, *2*, 213–16.

Haugeland, J., ed. (1981). *Mind Design*. Cambridge, Mass.: MIT.

Hawks, D. N. (1964). The clinical usefulness of some tests of over-inclusive thinking in psychiatric patients. *British Journal of Social and Clinical Psychology*, *3*, 186–95.

Hays, P. (1972). Determination of the obsessional personality. *American Journal of Psychiatry*, *129*, 217–19.

Henderson, D., and Gillespie, R. D. (1950). *A Text-book of Psychiatry*. 7th ed. London: Oxford University Press.

Herrnstein, R. J. (1969). Method and theory in the study of avoidance. *Psychological Review*, *76*, 49–69.

Hildebrand, H. O. (1953). A factorial study of introversion–extroversion by means of objective tests. Unpublished Ph.D. thesis, University of London.

Hodgson, R. J., and Rachman, S. (1972). The effects of contamination and washing in obsessional patients. *Behaviour Research and Therapy*, *10*, 110–17.

Hogan, R. A., and Kirchner, J. H. (1967). Preliminary report of the extinction of learned fears via short-term implosive therapy. *Journal of Abnormal Psychology*, *72*, 106–09.

Hollingshead, A. B., and Redlich, F. C. (1958). *Social Class and Mental Illness*. New York: Wiley.

Hopkinson, G. (1964). The anankastic personality and depressive psychosis of late onset. *Psychiatrie, Neurologie, und Medizinische Psychologie (Basel)*, *148*, 93–100.

Horowitz, M. J. (1975). Intrusive and repetitive thoughts after experimental stress. *Archives of General Psychiatry*, *32*, 1457–63.

Horowitz, M. J., and Becker, S. (1971). Cognitive response to stress and experimental demand. *Journal of Abnormal Psychology*, *78*, 86–92.

Horowitz, M. J., Becker, S., Moskowitz, M., and Rashid, E. (1972). Intrusive thinking in psychiatric patients after stress. *Psychological Reports*, *31*, 235–38.

Ingram, I. M. (1961a). The obsessional personality and obsessional illness. *American Journal of Psychiatry*, *117*, 1016–19.

Ingram, I. M. (1961b). Obsessional personality and anal-erotic character. *Journal of Mental Science*, *107*, 1035–42.

Insel, T. R., and Murphy, D. L. (1981) The psychopharmacological treatment of obsessive–compulsive disorder: A review. *Journal of Clinical Psychopharmacology*, *1*, 304–11.

Janet, P. (1892, trans. 1901) *État mental des hystériques*. Paris: Rueff. Trans. by C. R. Corson. "The mental state of hystericals." New York: Putnam.

Janet, P. (1903). *Les Obsessions et la Psychasthénie*, Vol. I, 2nd ed. Paris: Alcan.

Janet, P. (1907). *The Major Symptoms of Hysteria*. New York: Macmillan.

Janet, P. (1909). *Les Névroses*. Paris: Flammarion.

Janet, P. (1919, trans. 1925). *Les Médications psychologiques*. Paris: Alcan. Trans. by E. and C. Paul. "Psychological Healing." London: Allen and Unwin. New York: Macmillan.

Jaspers, K. (1923, trans. 1963). *General Psychopathology*. Trans. by J. Hoenig and M. W. Hamilton. Chicago: University of Chicago Press.

Jenike, M. A. (1983). Obsessive–compulsive disorder. *Comprehensive Psychiatry*, *24*, 99–115.

Johnson, M., and Raye, C. (1981). Reality monitoring. *Psychological Bulletin*, *88*, 67–85.

Jones, E. (1918). The anal-erotic character traits. In *Papers on Psycho-analysis*. London: Baillière, Tindall and Cox.

Jones, H. G. (1958). Neurosis and experimental pscyhology. *Journal of Mental Science*, *104*, 55–62.

Jung, C. G. (1920). Psychological types. In *Collected Works of C.G. Jung*. London: Routledge & Kegan Paul.

Kanner, L. (1948). *Child Psychiatry*. Springfield, Ill.: Thomas.

Kazdin, A. E. (1978). *History of Behavior Modification: Experimental Foundations of Contemporary Research*. Baltimore: University Park.

Kelly, G. A. (1955). *The Psychology of Personal Constructs*, 2 vols. New York: Norton.

Kendall, P. C. (1982). Cognitive processes and procedures in behaviour therapy. In C. M. Franks, G. T. Wilson, P. C. Kendall, and K. D. Brownell, eds. *Annual Review of Behavior Therapy: Theory and Practice*. New York: Guildford.

Kendall, P. C., and Bemis, K. M. (1983). Thought and action in psychotherapy: The cognitive-behavioral approaches. In M. Hersen, A. E. Kazdin, and A. Bellack, eds. *Handbook of Clinical Psychology*. New York: Pergamon.

Kendall, P. C., and Bemis, K. M. (1984). Cognitive behavioral interventions: Principles and procedures. In N. A. Endler and J. McV. Hunt, eds. *Personality and the Behavioral Disorders*. Vol. 2. New York: Wiley.

Kendall, P. C., and Hollon, S. D., eds. (1979). *Cognitive-behavioral Interventions: Theory, Research and Procedures*. New York: Academic.

Kendell, R. E., and Discipio, W. J. (1970). Obsessional symptoms and obsessional personality traits in patients with depressive illness. *Psychological Medicine*, *1*, 65–72.

Kinkelin, M. (1954). Verlauf und Prognose des manisch-depressiven Irreseins. *Schweizer Archiv für Neurologie, Neurochirurgie und Psychiatrie*, *73*, 100–07.

Kline, P. (1967). Obsessional traits and emotional instability in a normal population. *British Journal of Medical Psychology*, *40*, 153–57.

Koestler, A. (1964) *The Act of Creation*, London: Hutchinson.

Kogan, N., and Wallach, M. A. (1964). *Risk Taking*. New York: Holt, Rinehart & Winston.

Kraepelin, E. (1904), *Textbook of Psychiatry*. 8th German ed. Trans. by R. M. Barcley. Edinburgh: Livingstone.

Krasner, L. (1982). Behavior Therapy: On roots, contexts, and growth. In G. T. Wilson and C. M. Franks, eds. *Contemporary Behavior Therapy*. New York: Guildford.

Kringlen, E. (1965). Obsessional neurotics. A long-term follow-up. *British Journal of Psychiatry*, *111*, 709–22.

Lange, J. (1927). Psychiatrie. In E. Kraepelin and J. Lange. *Allgemeine Psychiatrie*. 9th ed. Leipzig: Barth.

Lazare, A., Klerman, G. L., and Armor, D. J. (1966). Oral, obsessive and hysterical personality patterns. *Archives of General Psychiatry*, *14*, 624–30.

Lazare, A., Klerman, G. L., and Armor, D. J. (1970). Oral, obsessive and hysterical personality patterns: Replication of factor analysis in an independent sample. *Journal of Psychiatric Research*, *7*, 275–79.

Lazarus, R. S. (1966). *Psychological Stress and the Coping Process*. New York: McGraw-Hill.

Ledwidge, B. (1978). Cognitive behaviour modification: A step in the wrong direction? *Psychological Bulletin*, *85*, 353–75.

Lewis, A. J. (1934). Melancholia: A clinical survey of depressive states. *Journal of Mental Science*, *80*, 277–318.

Lewis, A. J. (1936). Problems of obsessional illness. *Proceedings of the Royal Society of Medicine*, *29*, 325–36.

Lewis, A. J. (1938). The diagnosis and treatment of obsessional states. *Practitioner*, *141*, 21–30.

Lewis, A. J. (1957). Obsessional illness. *Acta neuropsiquiatria Argentina*, *3*, 323–34.

Lewis, A. J. (1965). A note of personality and obsessional illness. *Psychiatria et Neurologia (Basel)*, *150*, 299–305.

Lewis, A. J. (1978). Obsessional disorder. In *Price's Textbook of the Practice of Medicine*. 16th ed. London: Oxford University Press.

Likierman, H., and Rachman, S. (1982). Obsessions: An experimental investigation of thought stopping and habituation training. *Behavioural Psychotherapy*, *10*, 324–38.

Lion, E. G. (1942). Anancastic depression: Obsessive–compulsive symptoms occurring during depressions. *Journal of Nervous and Mental Disease*, *95*, 730–38.

Lo, W. H. (1967). A follow-up study of obsessional neurotics in Hong Kong Chinese. *British Journal of Psychiatry*, *113*, 823–32.

Locke, E. A. (1971). Is "behavior therapy" behavioristic? (An analysis of Wolpe's psychotherapeutic methods.) *Psychological Bulletin*, *76*, 318–27.

London, P. (1972). The end of ideology in behavior modification. *American Psychologist*, *27*, 913–20.

Luria, A. (1961). *The Role of Speech in the Regulation of Normal and Abnormal Behaviors*. New York: Liveright.

Luxenburger, H. (1930). Hereditat u. Familientypus der Zwangsneurotiken. *Archiv fuer Psychiatrie und Nervenkrankheiten*, *91*, 590–601.

McFall, M. E., and Wollersheim, J. P. (1979). Obsessive–compulsive neurosis: A cognitive–behavioral formulation and approach to treatment. *Cognitive Therapy and Research*, *3*, 333–48.

McKeachie, W. (1974). The decline and fall of the laws of learning. *Educational Researcher*, *3*, 7–11.

Mackintosh, N. J. (1974). *The Psychology of Animal Learning*. London: Academic.

MacMillan, M. (1963). Pavlov's typology. *Journal of Nervous and Mental Disease*, *137*, 447–54.

Magnan, V. (1895). *Les Dégénérés*. Paris: Rueff.

Mahoney, M. J. (1974). *Cognition and Behavior Modification*. Cambridge, Mass.: Ballinger.

Makhlouf-Norris, F., and Jones, H. G. (1971). Conceptual distance indices as measures of alienation in obsessional neurosis. *Psychological Medicine*, *1*, 381–87.

Makhlouf-Norris, F., Jones H. G., and Norris, H. (1970). Articulation of conceptual structure in obsessional neurosis. *British Journal of Social and Clinical Psychology*, *9*, 264–74.

Makhlouf-Norris, F., and Norris, H. (1972). The obsessive compulsive syndrome as a neurotic device for the reduction of self-uncertainty. *British Journal of Psychiatry*, *121*, 277–88.

Marks, I. M. (1965). Patterns of meaning in psychiatric patients. *Maudsley Monographs*, *13*. London: Oxford University Press.

Marks, I. M. (1966). Semantic differential use in psychiatric patients. *British Journal of Psychiatry,* *112*, 945–51.

Marks, I. M. (1977). Phobias and obsessions: Clinical phenomena in search of a laboratory model. In J. D. Maser and M. E. P. Seligman, eds. *Psychopathology: Experimental Models.* San Francisco: Freeman.

Marks, I. M. (1979). Cure and care of neurosis. *Psychological Medicine,* *9*, 629–60.

Marks, I. M. (1983). Are there anticompulsive or antiphobic drugs? Review of the evidence. *British Journal of Psychiatry,* *139*, 338–47.

Marks, I. M., Crowe, M., Drewe, E., Young, J., and Dewhurst, W. G. (1969). Obsessive–compulsive neurosis in identical twins. *British Journal of Psychiatry,* *115*, 991–98.

Marshall, W. K. (1981). Behavioral treatment of phobic and obsessive–compulsive disorders. In L. Michelson, M. Hersen, and S. M. Turner, eds. *Future Perspectives in Behavior Therapy.* New York: Plenum.

Masserman, J. H. (1946). *Principles of Dynamic Psychiatry.* London: Saunders.

Mather, M. D. (1970). Obsessions and compulsions. In C. G. Costello, ed. *Symptoms of Psychopathology: A Handbook.* New York: Wiley.

Maudsley, H. (1895). *The Pathology of the Mind.* Revised ed. London: Macmillan.

Mavissakalian, M. (1983). Antidepressants in the treatment of agoraphobia and obsessive–compulsive disorder. *Comprehensive Psychiatry,* *24*, 278–84.

Mawson, D., Marks, I. M., and Ramm, L. (1982). Clomipramine and exposure for chronic obsessive–compulsive rituals: III. Two-year follow-up and further findings. *British Journal of Psychiatry,* *140*, 11–18.

Mayer-Gross, W., Slater, E., and Roth, M. (1954). *Clinical Psychiatry.* London: Cassell.

Meichenbaum, D. (1977). *Cognitive-Behavior Modification: An Integrative Approach.* New York: Plenum.

Meichenbaum, D., and Cameron, R. (1972). Stress inoculation: A skills training approach to anxiety management. Unpublished manuscript, University of Waterloo.

Metzner, R. (1963) Some experimental analogues of obsession. *Behaviour Research and Therapy,* *1*, 231–36.

Meyer, V. (1966) Modification of expectations in cases with obsessional rituals. *Behaviour Research and Therapy,* *4*, 273–80.

Meyer, V., and Levy, R. (1973). Modification of behaviour in obsessive–compulsive disorders. In H. E. Adams and I. Punikel, eds. *Issues and Trends in Behavior Therapy.* Springfield, Ill.: Thomas.

Meyer, V., Levy, R., and Schnurer, A. (1974). The behavioural treatment of obsessive–compulsive disorders. In H. R. Beech, ed. *Obsessional States.* London: Methuen.

Michaels, J. J., and Porter, R. T. (1949). Psychiatric and social implication of contrasts between psychopathic personality and obsessive–compulsive neurosis. *Journal of Nervous and Mental Disease,* *109*, 122–32.

Millar, D. G. (1980). A repertory grid study of obsessionality: Distinctive cognitive structure or distinctive cognitive content? *British Journal of Medical Psychology,* *53*, 59–66.

Milner, A. D. (1966). A decision theory approach to obsessional behaviour. Unpublished doctoral dissertation, University of London.

Milner, A. D.; Beech, H. R.; and Walker, V. J. (1971). Decision processes and obsessional behaviour. *British Journal of Social and Clinical Psychology,* *10*, 88–89.

Mohlenkamp, G. (1977). Discussion of a support theory for compulsions. *Zeitschrift für Klinische Psychologie,* *6*, 116–29.

Monroe, R. R. (1974). Obsessive behavior: B. Integration of psychoanalytic and other approaches. In S. Arieti, ed. *American Handbook of Psychiatry.* 2nd ed. (Vol. III). New York: Basic Books.

Morgan, M. J. (1968). Negative reinforcement. In L. Weiskrantz ed. *Analysis of Behavioural Change.* London: Harper & Row.

Mowrer, O. H. (1950). *Learning Theory and Personality Dynamics.* New York: Ronald.

Mowrer, O. H. (1960). *Learning Theory and Behaviour.* New York: Wiley.

Muncie, W. (1931). The rigid personality as a factor in psychoses. *Archives of Neurology and Psychiatry,* *26*, 359–70.

Nagera, H. (1976). *Obsessional Neuroses: Developmental Psychopathology.* New York: Jason Aronson.

Nemiah, J. C. (1980). Obsessive–compulsive disorder (Obsessive–compulsive neurosis). In H. I. Kaplan, I. Freedman, and B. J. Sadock, eds. *Comprehensive Textbook of Psychiatry,* 3rd ed. (Vol. II). Baltimore: Williams and Wilkins.

Neufeld, R. W. J. (1975). A multidimensional scaling analysis of schizophrenics' and normals' perceptions of verbal similarity. *Journal of Abnormal Psychology, 84,* 498–507.

Noreik, K. (1970). A follow-up examination of neuroses. *Acta Psychiatrica Scandinavica, 46,* 8–95.

Noyes, A. P. (1954). *Modern Clinical Psychiatry.* London and Philadelphia: Saunders.

Orme, J. E. (1965). The relationship of obsessional traits to general emotional instability. *British Journal of Medical Psychology, 38,* 269–71.

Osgood, C. E., Suci, G. J., and Tannenbaum, P. H. (1957). *The Measurement of Meaning.* Urbana, Ill.: University of Illinois.

Parkinson, L., and Rachman, S. (1981a). Part II. The nature of intrusive thoughts. *Advances in Behaviour Research and Therapy, 3,* 101–10.

Parkinson, L., and Rachman, S. (1981b). Part III. Intrusive thoughts: The effects of an uncontrived stress. *Advances in Behaviour Research and Therapy, 3,* 111–18.

Pavlov, I. P. (trans. 1941). *Conditioned Reflexes and Psychiatry.* Vol. II of "Lectures on conditioned reflexes." Trans. and ed. by W. H. Gantt. London: Lawrence and Wishart.

Paykel, E. S., and Prusoff, B. A. (1973). Relationships between personality dimensions: Neuroticism and extraversion against obsessive, hysterical and oral personality. *British Journal of Social and Clinical Psychology, 12,* 309–18.

Payne, R. (1960). Cognitive abnormalities. In H. J. Eysenck, ed. *Handbook of Abnormal Psychology.* London: Pitman.

Petrilowitsch, N. (1956). Über die charakterologischen Voraussetzunger der Phobien. *Schweizer Archiv für Neurologie und Psychologie, 76,* 223–37.

Petrilowitsch, N. (1960). *Abnorme Persönlichkeiten.* Basel: Karger.

Pettigrew, T. F. (1958). The measurement and correlates of cognitive width as a cognitive variable. *Journal of Personality, 26,* 532–44.

Pollak, J. M. (1979). Obsessive–compulsive personality: A review. *Psychological Bulletin, 86,* 225–41.

Pollitt, J. D. (1957). Natural history of obsessional states. *British Medical Journal, 1,* 194–98.

Pollitt, J. D. (1960). Natural history studies in mental illness: A discussion based on a pilot study of obsessional states. *Journal of Mental Science, 106,* 93–113.

Pritchard, J. C. (1835). *A Treatise on Insantiy.* London: Sherwood, Gilbert and Piper.

Rachlin, H. (1980). *Behaviorism in Everyday Life.* Englewood Cliffs, N.J.: Prentice-Hall.

Rachman, S. (1971). Obsessional ruminations. *Behaviour Research and Therapy, 9,* 229–35.

Rachman, S. (1974). Primary obsessional slowness. *Behaviour Research and Therapy, 11,* 463–71.

Rachman, S. (1976a). The passing of the two-stage theory of fear and avoidance. *Behaviour Research and Therapy, 14,* 125–31.

Rachman, S. (1976b). Obsessional–compulsive checking. *Behaviour Research and Therapy, 14,* 269–77.

Rachman, S. (1976c). The modification of obsessions: A new formulation. *Behaviour Research and Therapy, 14,* 437–43.

Rachman, S. (1981). Part I. Unwanted intrusive cognitions. *Advances in Behaviour Research and Therapy, 3,* 89–99.

Rachman, S. (1982). Obsessional–compulsive disorders. In A. S. Bellack, M. Hersen, and A. E. Kazdin, eds. *International Handbook of Behavior Modification and Therapy.* New York: Plenum.

Rachman, S., and de Silva, P. (1978). Abnormal and normal obsessions. *Behaviour Research and Therapy, 16,* 233–48.

Rachman, S., and Hodgson, R. J. (1980). *Obsessions and Compulsions.* Englewood Cliffs, N.J.: Prentice-Hall.

Rachman, S., Hodgson, R., and Marks, I. M. (1971) The treatment of chronic obsessive–compulsive neurosis. *Behaviour Research and Therapy, 9,* 237–47.

Rachman, S., Hodgson, R., and Marzillier, J. (1970) Treatment of an obsessional–compulsive disorder by modeling. *Behaviour Research and Therapy*, *8*, 385–392.

Rachman, S., Marks, I., and Hodgson, R. (1973). The treatment of chronic obsessive–compulsive neurosis by modeling and flooding *in vivo*. *Behaviour Research and Therapy*, *11*, 463–71.

Rado, S. (1974). Obsessive behavior; A. So-called obsessive-compulsive neurosis. In S. Arieti, ed. *American Handbook of Psychiatry*. Vol. III. 2nd ed. New York: Basic Books.

Rapaport, D. (1948). Diagnostic Psychological Testing, Vol. II. 2nd ed. *The Menninger Clinic Monograph Series*, *3*.

Rapaport, D. (1951). Commentary to Chapter 26: "The basic symptoms of schizophrenia" by E. Bleuler. In D. Rapaport, ed. *Organization and Pathology of Thought*. New York: Columbia University Press.

Ray, S. D. (1964). Obsessional states observed in New Delhi. *British Journal of Psychiatry*, *110*, 181–82.

Reed, G. F. (1966). Some cognitive characteristics of obsessional disorder. Unpublished doctoral dissertation, University of Manchester.

Reed, G. F. (1968). Some formal qualities of obsessional thinking. *Psychiatria Clinica*, *1*, 382–92.

Reed, G. F. (1969a). Obsessionality and self-appraisal questionnaires. *British Journal of Psychiatry*, *115*, 205–09.

Reed, G. F. (1969b). "Under-inclusion"—a characteristic of obsessional personality disorder: I. *British Journal of Psychiatry*, *115*, 781–85.

Reed, G. F. (1969c). "Under-inclusion"—a characteristic of obsessional personality disorder: II. *British Journal of Psychiatry*, *115*, 787–90.

Reed, G. F. (1972). *The Psychology of Anomalous Experience*. London: Hutchinson.

Reed, G. F. (1976). Indecisiveness in obsessional–compulsive disorder. *British Journal of Social and Clinical Psychology*, *15*, 443–45.

Reed, G. F. (1977a). Obsessional personality disorder and remembering. *British Journal of Psychiatry*, *130*, 177–83.

Reed, G. F. (1977b). Obsessional cognition: Performance on two numerical tasks. *British Journal of Psychiatry*, *130*, 184–85.

Reed, G. F. (1977c). The obsessional–compulsive experience: A phenomenological re-emphasis. *Philosophy and Phenomenological Research*, *37*, 381–84.

Reed, G. F. (1979). Everyday anomalies of recall and recognition. In J.F. Kihlstom and F.J. Evans, ed. *Functional Disorders of Memory*. Hillsdale: Lawrence Erlbaum Associates.

Reich, W. (1949). *Character Analysis*. New York: Orgone Institute.

Rivière, B., Julien, R.-A., Note, I. D., and Calvet, P. (1980). Traitment comportemental et cognitif des obsessions et compulsions. Methodologie et techniques. *Annales Medico-Psychologiques*, *138*, 347–52.

Röper, G., and Rachman, S. (1975). Obsessional–compulsive checking: Replication and development. *Behaviour Research and Therapy*, *14*, 25–32.

Röper, G., Rachman, S., and Hodgson, R. (1973). An experiment on obsessional checking. *Behaviour Research and Therapy*, *11*, 271–77.

Rosen, I. (1957). The clinical significance of obsessions in schizophrenia. *Journal of Mental Science*, *103*, 773–86.

Rosenberg, B. G. (1953). Compulsiveness as a determinant in selected cognitive-perceptual performances. *Journal of Personality*, *21*, 506–16.

Rosenberg, C. M. (1967). Personality and obsessional neurosis. *British Journal of Psychiatry*, *113*, 471–77.

Rosenberg, C. M. (1968). Complications of obsessional neurosis. *British Journal of Psychiatry*, *114*, 477–78.

Salter, A. (1949). *Conditioned Reflex Therapy*. New York: Creative Age.

Salzman, L. (1973). *The Obsessive Personality: Origins, Dynamics and Therapy*. 2nd ed. New York: Jason Aronson.

Salzman, L. (1980). *Treatment of the Obsessive Personality*. New York: Jason Aronson.

Sandler, J., and Hazari, A. (1960). The "obsessional": On the psychological classification of obsessional character traits and symptoms. *British Journal of Medical Psychology*, *33*, 113–22.

Schilder, P. (1935). The psychoanalysis of space. *International Journal of Psychoanalysis*, *16*, 387–99.

Schneider, K. (1925, trans. 1958). *Psychopathic Personalities*. Trans. J. W. Hamilton. London: Cassell.

Schneider, K. (1959). *Clinical Psychopathology*. Trans. J. W. Hamilton, New York: Grune and Stratton.

Scrignar, C. B. (1981). Rapid treatment of contamination phobia with hand-washing compulsion by flooding with hypnosis. *American Journal of Clinical Hypnosis*, *23*, 252–57.

Sedman, G., and Reed, G. F. (1963). Depersonalization phenomena in obsessional personalities and in depression. *British Journal of Psychiatry*, *109*, 376–79.

Seligman, M. E. P. (1975). *Helplessness: On Depression, Development and Death*. San Francisco: W. H. Freeman.

Seligman, M. E. P., and Johnston, J. (1973). A cognitive theory of avoidance learning. In J. McGuigan and B. Lumsden, eds. *Contemporary Approaches to Conditioning and Learning*. Washington: Wiley.

Serban, G. (1978). The cognitive origin of neurotic thinking. In G. Serban, ed. *Cognitive Defects in the Development of Mental Illness*. New York: Brunner/Mazel.

Sher, K. J., Frost, R. O., and Otto, R. (1983). Cognitive deficits in compulsive checkers: An exploratory study. *Behaviour Research and Therapy*, *21*, 357–63.

Shields, J. (1973). Heredity and psychological abnormality. In H. J. Eysenck, ed. *Handbook of Abnormal Psychology*. 2nd ed. London: Pitman.

Shorvon, H. J. (1946). The depersonalization syndrome. *Proceedings of the Royal Society of Medicine*, *39*, 779–87.

Simon, H. A. (1957). A behavioral model of rational choice. In H. A. Simon, ed. *Models of Man: Social and Rational*. New York: Wiley.

Skoog, G. (1959). The anancastic syndrome. *Acta Psychiatrica et Neurologica Scandinavica*, *34*, suppl. 134.

Skoog, G. (1964). The anancastic individual in psychological research. *Modern Problems of Psychiatry and Neurology*, *1*, 422–42.

Skoog, G. (1965). Onset of anancastic conditions: A clinical study. *Acta Psychiatrica Scandinavica*, *41*, suppl. 184.

Slade, P. (1974). Psychometric studies of obsessional illness and obsessional personality. In H. R. Beech, ed. *Obsessional States*. London: Methuen.

Slater, E. (1943). The neurotic constitution. *Journal of Neurology, Neurosurgery and Psychiatry*, *6*, 1.

Slater, E., and Roth, M. (1969). *Clinical Psychiatry*, 3rd ed. London: Baillière, Tindall & Cassell.

Slater, P. (1945). Scores of different types of neurotics on tests of intelligence. *British Journal of Psychology*, *35*, 40–42.

Sluckin, W. (1960). *Minds and Machines*, Revised ed. Harmondsworth: Penguin.

Snaith, R., McGuire, R., and Fox, K. (1971). Aspects of personality and depression. *Psychological Medicine*, *1*, 239–46.

Snowdon, J. (1979). Family-size and birth-order in obsessional neurosis. *Acta Psychiatrica Scandinavica*, *60*, 121–28.

Solomon, R. L., and Wynne, L. C. (1953). Traumatic avoidance learning: Acquisition in normal dogs. *Psychology Monographs*, *67* (4, whole No. 354).

Solyom, L., Zamanzadeh, D., Ledwidge, B., and Kenny, F. (1969). Aversion relief treatment of obsessive neurosis. In R. Rubin, *et al.*, eds. *Advances in Behavior Therapy*. New York: Academic Press.

Spence, K. W. (1956). *Behavior Theory and Conditioning*. New Haven: Yale Univ.

Stampfl, T. G. (1967). Implosive therapy. In S. G. Armitage, ed. *Behaviour Modification Techniques in the Treatment of Emotional Disorders*. Battle Creek: V. A. Publication.

Steiner, J. (1972). A questionnaire study of risk-taking in psychiatric patients. *British Journal of Medical Psychology*, *45*, 365–74.

Stekel, W. (1927), trans. 1949. *Compulsion and Doubt*. Trans. E. A. Gutheil. New York. Liveright.

Stengel, E. (1945). A study on some clinical aspects of the relationship between obsessional neurosis and psychotic reaction types. *Journal of Mental Science*, *91*, 166–87.

Stengel, E. (1948). Some clinical observations on the psychodynamic relationship between depression and obsessive compulsive symptoms. *Journal of Mental Science, 94*, 650–52.

Stern, R. S. (1970). Treatment of a case of obsessional neurosis using a thought-stopping technique. *British Journal of Psychiatry, 117*, 441–42.

Stern, R. S., and Cobb, J. P. (1978). Phenomenology of obsessive–compulsive neurosis. *British Journal of Psychiatry, 132*, 233–39.

Stern, R. S., Lipsedge, M., and Marks, I. M. (1973). Obsessive ruminations: A controlled trial of a thought-stopping technique. *Behaviour Research and Therapy, 11*, 659–62.

Sternberg, M. (1974). Physical treatments in obsessional disorders. In H. R. Beech, ed. *Obsessional States*. London: Methuen.

Stone, G. C., and Gottheil, E. (1975). Factor analysis of orality and anality in selected patient groups. *Journal of Nervous and Mental Disease, 160*, 311–23.

Straus, E. W. (1948). On obsession: A clinical and methodological study. *Nervous and Mental Disease Monographs, 73*.

Sykes, K., and Tredgold, R. F. (1964). Restricted orbital undercutting. A study of its effects on 350 patients over ten years, 1951-60. *British Journal of Psychiatry, 110*, 609–40.

Taylor, J. G. (1963). A behavioural interpretation of obsessive compulsive neurosis. *Behaviour Research and Therapy, 1*, 237–44.

Teasdale, J. (1974). Learning models of obsessional–compulsive disorder. In H. R. Beech, ed. *Obsessional States*. London: Methuen.

Templer, D. I. (1972). The obsessive–compulsive neurosis: Review of research findings. *Comprehensive Psychiatry, 13*, 375–83.

Turner, S. M.; and Van Hasselt, V. B. (1979). Multiple behavioral treatment in a sexually aggressive male. *Journal of Behavior Therapy and Experimental Psychiatry, 10*, 343–48.

Turner, R. M., Newman, F. L., and Foa, E. (1983). Assessing the impact of cognitive differences in the treatment of obsessive–compulsives. *Journal of Clinical Psychology, 39*, 933–38.

Vaughan, J. (1976). The relationship between obsessional personality, obsessions in depression and symptoms of depression. *British Journal of Psychiatry, 129*, 36–39.

Volans, P. J. (1976). Styles of decision-making and probability appraisal in selected obsessional and phobic patients. *British Journal of Social and Clinical Psychology, 15*, 305–17.

von Gebsattel, V. E. (1958). The world of the compulsive. In R. May, E. Angel, and H. F. Ellenberger, eds. *Existence: A New Dimension in Psychiatry and Psychology*. New York: Basic Books.

Walker, V. J. (1973). Explanation in obsession neurosis. *British Journal of Psychiatry, 123*, 675–80.

Walker, V. J., and Beech, H. R. (1969). Mood states and the ritualistic behaviour of obsessional patients. *British Journal of Psychiatry, 115*, 1261–68.

Walton, D. (1960). The relevance of learning theory to the treatment of an obsessive-compulsive state. In H. J. Eysenck, ed. *Behaviour Therapy and the Neuroses*, Oxford: Pergamon.

Walton, D., and Mather, M. D. (1964). The application of learning principles to the treatment of obsessive compulsive states in the acute and chronic phases of illness. In H. J. Eysenck, ed. *Experiments in Behaviour Therapy*. Oxford: Pergamon Press.

Warren. H. C. (1935). *Dictionary of Psychology*. London: Allen & Unwin.

Westphal, C. (1877). Über Zwangsvorstellungen. *Berliner Klinische Wochenschrift, 46*, 669–84.

Wiener, N. (1948). *Cybernetics*. New York: Wiley.

Wilner, N., and Horowitz, M. (1975). Intrusive and repetitive thoughts after a depressive experience. *Psychological Reports, 37*, 135–38.

Wilson, G. T. (1978). Cognitive behavior therapy: Paradigm shift or passing phase? In J. P. Forey and D. P. Rathjen, eds., *Cognitive Behavior Therapy: Research and Application*. New York: Plenum.

Wilson, G. T., and Franks, C. M., eds. (1982). *Contemporary Behavior Therapy: Conceptual and Empirical Foundations*. New York: Guilford.

Wolman, B. B., ed. (1973). *Dictionary of Behavioral Science*. New York: Van Nostrand Reinhold.

Wolpe, J. (1958). *Psychotherapy by Reciprocal Inhibition*. Stanford: Stanford University Press.

Wolpe, J. (1973). *The Practice of Behavior Therapy*. 2nd ed. New York: Pergamon.

Wolpe, J. (1976). Behavior therapy and its malcontents. II. Multimodal eclecticism, cognitive exclusivism and "exposure" empiricism. *Journal of Behavior Therapy and Experimental Psychiatry*, *7*, 109–16.

Woodruff, R., and Pitts, F. N. (1964). Monozygotic twins with obsessional neurosis. *American Journal of Psychiatry*, *120*, 1075–80.

Yamagami, T. (1971). The treatment of an obsession by thought-stopping. *Journal of Behavior Therapy and Experimental Psychiatry*, *2*, 133–35.

Yates, A. J. (1962). *Frustration and Conflict*. London: Methuen.

Yates, A. J. (1975). *Theory and Practice in Behavior Therapy*. New York: Wiley.

Yde, A. (1950). Den anankastiske Konstitution. *Ugeskrift foer Laeger*, *112*, 39–50.

Author Index

Subject Index

Pedantry, 51, 116
Perfectionism, 51, 115
Perseveration, 52, 115
Persistence, 52, 115
Personalization, of obsessionals, 197–198
Possible harm
  to others, 31–32;
  to self, 31–32
Precision, 52, 115
Procrastination, obsessional, 178–179
Propriety, 52–53, 116
Punctiliousness, 53, 116
Punctuality, 53, 116

R

Rational–emotive therapy, 211
Reasoning, in obsessional thinking, 194
Rectitude, 53
Redintegration, of obsessionals, 197–198
Reliability, 54, 115
Remediation of obsessional disorders,
    psychological methods of, 201–215
  behaviour therapy, 201–209;
  cognitive therapies, 209–215
Repititon compulsion, 158–162, 165–169, 217
Resistance
  as a criterion of obsession, 6–7;
  differences in, between depressives and
    obsessionals, 140–143
Rigidity, 54, 116
Risk-taking, of obsessionals, 198
Routine, 54, 116
Rules, subservience to, 54, 116
Ruminations, obsessional, 15–16, 181–185

S

Schneider, Kürt, studies of personality
    disorder, 86–90
Scrupulosity, 54–55, 114–115
Self-instructional training, 211
Shame of one's physique, 28–29
Shame of self,
  moral and characterological, 27–28;
  social adequacy and abilities, 27
Spoken language of obsessionals, 194–195;
  in association tests, 195

Suffering, as a criterion of an obsessional–
    compulsive experience, 7
Symmetry, 55, 116

T

Thinking, obsessional, 186–200, 218;
  category width and, 189–191;
  conceptual linkage and, 191–192;
  creativity and, 198–199;
  intolerance of ambiguity in, 193–194;
  memory and, 195–197;
  overall cognitive efficiency and,
      187–189;
  personalization and redintegration in,
      197–198;
  reasoning and, 194;
  risk taking and, 198;
  specificity of categorical limits and,
      192–193;
  spoken language and, 194–195
Thoroughness, 55, 115
Tics and stammers, 39
Tidiness and neatness, 55–56, 116
Trivial details, stress on, 47, 115

U

Urges and impulses, as a mode of obsession,
  17

V

Visual images, as a mode of obsession, 17

W

Washing and cleaning, as compulsive
    behaviour, 38
Wolpe, Joseph, behavioural/learning approach
    to obsessional disorder, 102–105,
    201–209

Z

Zwang, inconsistency in translation of, 8

PERSONALITY AND PSYCHOPATHOLOGY

A Series of Monographs, Texts, and Treatises

David T. Lykken, Editor

*Titles initiated during the series editorship of Brendan Maher.

PERSONALITY, PSYCHOPATHOLOGY, AND PSYCHOTHERAPY

A Series of Monographs, Texts, and Treatises

David T. Lykken and Philip C. Kendall, Editors